Lambert Laring

Proceedings, principally in the county of Kent

In connection with the Parliaments called in 1640

Lambert Laring

Proceedings, principally in the county of Kent
In connection with the Parliaments called in 1640

ISBN/EAN: 9783337153830

Printed in Europe, USA, Canada, Australia, Japan

Cover: Foto ©Andreas Hilbeck / pixelio.de

More available books at **www.hansebooks.com**

PROCEEDINGS,

PRINCIPALLY IN

THE COUNTY OF KENT,

IN CONNECTION WITH THE

PARLIAMENTS CALLED IN 1640,

AND ESPECIALLY WITH

THE COMMITTEE OF RELIGION

APPOINTED IN THAT YEAR.

EDITED

BY THE REV. LAMBERT B. LARKING, M.A.

FROM THE

COLLECTIONS OF SIR EDWARD DERING, BART., 1627-1644,

WITH

A PREFACE BY JOHN BRUCE, Esq. F.S.A.

PRINTED FOR THE CAMDEN SOCIETY.

M.DCCC.LXII.

PREFACE.

THE volume which is now offered to the Camden Society possesses many distinct and considerable claims to the attention of historical inquirers. That it contains valuable papers, before unpublished, which have reference to public affairs in the memorable year 1640, is alone sufficient to ensure it attention; but, when it is known that the majority of these papers relate to the proceedings of the House of Commons in reference to the ecclesiastical administration of Archbishop Laud, and that they illustrate the state of the Church of England, and the character of its ministers, principally in the county of Kent, at that period, a portion of our history which has been as yet very imperfectly set forth, we are sure that the volume will be perused with avidity.

There is another point of interest in this volume in connection with the place whence these papers have been procured. All of them have come from the manuscript collections at Surrenden, collections to which English historical literature already owes no inconsiderable debt. From the days of Sir Robert Cotton, who derived from Surrenden an original of Magna Charta; and those of Hearne, who published Sprot's Chronicle from the same historical storehouse; and those of Blomefield, who thence obtained many valuable documents for his History of Norfolk; down to our own days, in which the elegant volumes of the Archæologia Cantiana have been indebted to the same collection for some of the earliest and most interesting documents which they have made known, the successive owners of the Surrenden Papers have been ever ready to acknowledge the honourable obligations which attach to the possession of such ines-

b

timable stores. Among the gentlemen to whom these papers have belonged during a period of more than two hundred years, no one has ever advanced a claim to be entitled to lock up that portion of the history of England which they contain, or to prevent duly qualified inquirers from using the information upon public affairs, which, by the power of wealth or of other private circumstances, has chanced to come into his possession.

At the period to which the papers now published relate, the collection at Surrenden was in the process of formation by Sir Edward Dering, then the head of the family, and some acquaintance with Sir Edward's position and personal character is necessary to the understanding of the papers themselves. A full biography, with a detailed account of his collections, would be an excellent subject for the Archæological Society of Kent, and would form a grateful tribute to his memory; all that we can do is to put together such a sketch as may be formed from the materials at our command.

Sir Edward Dering was descended from an ancient and well-connected Kentish family. A pedigree registered in the College of Arms traces the Derings back, step by step, to the reign of Henry IV.;[a] but family tradition connects them with periods and persons of an almost mythical antiquity. Domesday Book and the Textus Roffensis are quoted in their behalf. A *miles* of their stock is alleged to have flourished as far back as the year 880, and Dering son of Sired, who is recorded in Domesday Book as a landholder in Kent in the time of Edward the Confessor, is reported to have shed his blood by the side of King Harold on the field of Hastings. His descendants were not less loyal to the Norman dynasty than the Dering of Domesday was to that of their predecessors. A

---

[a] A magnificent copy of this pedigree, emblazoned with great skill and taste, has been kindly lent to us for the purposes of this publication by the widow of the late Mr. Cholmeley Dering, at whose expense it was compiled.

Dering was slain, it is said, at the Battle of Lincoln in the year 1141, fighting manfully to release King Stephen; and others of the same name have been ever ready to display their prowess and fidelity on all honourable occasions. Leaving to others inquiries too remote for our present purpose, it will be sufficient to go back with the Derings to the reign of Elizabeth, when two brothers of this stock were conspicuous in their several stations. The one was a popular preacher in London, a man of distinguished eloquence and zeal, and successively Lady Margaret professor of Divinity at Cambridge, a preacher at Paul's Cross, the holder of the family living of Pluckley in Kent, and a prebendary of Salisbury. These promotions did not suffice to keep him out of trouble. He was plain-spoken to excess. Even the Queen did not escape his lash. In a sermon which he preached before her Majesty in 1569, he warned her lest she, who had been, *tanquam ovis*, as a sheep appointed to be slain (Psalm xliv. 22), should come to be chastised, *tanquam indomita juvenca*, as an untamed and unruly heifer. (Jerem. xxxi. 18.) Her Majesty deemed the allusion a little too forcible, and Dering was forbidden to preach any more before the Court. Some time afterwards he was prosecuted for Puritanism before the High Commissioners, and, after a long suit, was suspended from the exercise of all his clerical functions.

Whilst EDWARD DERING, the preacher, ran his distinguished, but somewhat troublous, course—strengthening the foundations of protestantism in the hearts of thousands who listened with rapture whenever he preached, and bought up with eagerness large editions of his published sermons—his elder brother RICHARD fulfilled the duties of the head of the house at Surrenden. His goods and lands increased under his careful management. He married into the Twysdens, a family of high consideration in their common county, and died in 1612, at the good old age of 82.

Richard Dering's eldest son, SIR ANTHONY (one of the 133 knights made by King James on his first arrival in London), married first Mary third daughter of Sir Henry Goring of Sussex, and afterwards Frances third daughter of Lord Chief Baron Bell. By his first wife he had no children; by his second he was the father of SIR EDWARD DERING, whose untoward fortunes we are about to relate.

He was born in the Tower of London on the 28th January, 1598, probably in the lodgings assigned to the Deputy-Lieutenant, an office held by his father.[a] Named after his relative the eminent preacher, who was the first Edward in the family, he inherited a considerable share of his great-uncle's peculiar gifts, an eloquence that was unquestionable and most persuasive, a natural tendency of his mind towards religious subjects of inquiry, a strong dislike of Rome, an aversion from ceremonialism, and an anti-prelatic feeling in reference to the titles, wealth, and worldly occupations of the hierarchy. Of his education we find little trace. His namesake was of Christ's College, Cambridge, and Sir Edward of Magdalen College in the same university. That there or elsewhere he obtained a proficiency in literature, both sacred and classical, may be safely inferred from his speeches and publications. Readiness in classical quotation was a talent by which, on at least one occasion, he was seriously misled. At the age of 20, if we interpret rightly the evidence of his portrait and his papers, he was a young man of a handsome presence, pleasing and ready in speech, singularly affectionate in disposition, ever ready to do kindly actions, conscious of his own good gifts, fond of applause, liberal, and not without ambition, although at first it scarcely seemed to develope itself in the direction of politics. We have not found that he ever entered of any Inn of Court, or was trained in any way for the management of public business. His means and allowances as an eldest son, although never large, were probably sufficient for his

---

[a] Notes and Queries, iii. 220, from a paper in the Surrenden collection.

maintenance, and on his first entry into life he devoted himself to the cares of an establishment, to his duties as a country gentleman, and to that which was his great delight—the study and collection of antiquarian remains, and the formation of a library of manuscripts. He was knighted by King James in Jan. 1618-19, going to New-market, probably from Cambridge, to procure that honour; and in the November following was married to Elizabeth, the eldest of the nine daughters of Sir Nicholas Tufton, subsequently created Lord Tufton and Earl of Thanet. The young lady's mother was a daughter of Thomas Cecil, the first Earl of Exeter, the eldest son of the great Lord Burghley. The Cecils were for a long time one of the most powerful families of the kingdom, and Sir Edward was thus brought into connection with many most influential persons, but we do not find that the relationship was in any special way beneficial to his worldly prospects. Both parties were very young, the marriage was probably entirely one of affection, and was soon dissolved by the death of the lady. She gave birth to a son, named Anthony after his paternal grandfather, but survived her marriage little more than two years. She died on the 24th Jan. 1622, in her twenty-first year.

Sir Edward's second adventure in matrimony was a more determinate attempt to obtain advancement in the world. The Ashburnhams of Sussex, although of an antiquity which even the Derings might envy, had themselves acquired little distinction; but Sir John Ashburnham, otherwise most unfortunate, had married a Beaumont, one of the same stock as the Countess of Buckingham, the mother of George Villiers, the royal favourite. Such an alliance opened a way to the employment of Sir John's children at Court, and was soon found to be more than a sufficient shelter against the absolute poverty in which at his death he was compelled to leave them. In two years from his decease, not bequeathing them, as the family

record informs us, " the least substance," such was the influence
exerted on their behalf, and such the cleverness of a mother "very
eminent for her great temper and prudence,"[a] that " there was
not any of them but was in condition rather to be helpful to others
than to want support themselves." Sir Edward secured the hand
of Anne the third daughter of this fortunate family, and soon got
into the rapid current of preferment. His letters now begin to
contain allusions to public events; his valuable mother-in-law is
treated with infinite respect; he takes his father's place in the
business of the county; he seeks to get into Parliament under the
Duke's wing; he is appointed a gentleman of the privy chamber,
and leaves his wife at Pluckley, although suffering with a bad
cough and advanced in pregnancy, in order to wait on the Duke
and take his turn in Court attendance. His position early in 1626,
as well as the great value of the friendship of the inestimable Lady
Ashburnham, are clearly indicated in the following letter:

ELIZABETH LADY ASHBURNHAM to SIR EDWARD DERING.

[Orig. Surrenden MS. About the middle of Jan. 1625-6.]

Most deare and my beloved Son, I was exceeding glad to heare from
you all; but very sorry that my sweet little Anthony[b] is sicke. I pray
God send him soone well againe. It was Fryday night last before I could
speake with my son John,[c] and then he tolde me it was past time to get
a burgess-ship, and that Rhemes and Harper (the court steward) and
others stood for the place of Hopton; but I finde that it staies till my
Lady[d] comes, and then I will do my best every way, as I finde occasion.
Yet I could not be so satisfied, because he had not, as I send [sent?] him
word, spoken to my Lord,[e] but I went my selfe to my Lord to present your

---

[a] Family Monument, quoted in Collins's Peerage, iv. 260.

[b] Sir Edward Dering's son by his first marriage.

[c] John Ashburnham, of the privy chamber, afterwards of the bedchamber; subsequently
well known in connection with the history of Charles I.

[d] The Countess of Buckingham.   [e] The Duke of Buckingham.

service, and let him know you were coming to waite on his Lordship, but
were caried, by the report of his going to Dover, thither to meat him;
excused the chri[s]tninge of the boye,[a] as well as I could, though I wish
I had given a £100 we had stayed. I also moved him for a burges place.
My Lord said, if he had knowne in time, you should have bin served as
soone as any, but all his letters went that morning before I came to towne,
and yet too late, for he is denied at Dover and Hyde,[b] and another place;
for which Sir John Ipsley[c] is much blamed, and other absurdities he hath
comitted, so that I imagine he will not continue long, though he have a
bolde toung to excuse him selfe. After this, being not satisfied, I mustered
the secretaries together, Packer, Nickolas, for the sinke portes, and the
other new one, and found that all the letters did goe a Tusday, who professed you should not have failed if I had sent but a Monday. Now there
is only one hope, which they will all watch to do you service in, that is,
if any be dubble returned, as perhaps some, not trusting only to my Lord,
make meanes in other places. My Lady Den:[d] and my Lord tolde me you
had made much of me, I was growne fatt, and I said I was fatter till I
fretted at our ill fortune to misse his favor for my boye, and they said
you must get another, which I said you promised me to do. Comend my
deere love to my kinde brother and my sister,[e] whom I love with all my
hart, if I had meanes to shew it. And, chiefly out of respect to my Lady,
I was with my Lady Fintch and M[rs] Goldwell, who are both very well,
being reported he should have my Lord Huberd's[f] place, but I thinke it
not so: she will wryte to my Lady Deering as soone as she can. Her
children also are well, but at Kinsington. They goe to lye in the Stran,
neere Exeter house. And there I mett Barou Travers,[g] who, as coye as
he was, is now towards marriage, tell my Lady, and that my Lady
Huberd is well, but in Norfolke. I was also with my Lord of Dorsett to
remember your service and thanks, who purposeth to send you shortly a
christning remembrance, with a deale of complement, and hath promised
me to speak effectually in favor of you to my Lord. I was also with my

---

[a] Edward, Sir Edward's son by his second marriage.

[b] Hythe.   [c] Hippisley.

[d] The Countess of Denbigh, Buckingham's sister.   [e] Sir Anthony and Lady Dering.

[f] Sir Henry Hobart, Lord Chief Justice of the Common Pleas.   [g] Trevor.

Lord Keeper, the new,[a] to get a burdgesship, but all too late.   God send
us good speed for your busines!   There shalbe no failing in poore me to
do you all the service and good I am able, who thinke I cannot bestow
my care and love upon one more worthy, saving my quarrell that you will
not leave the common title of Madam, in your particular love, to honor me
with the name of Mother, who is ever affectionately yours,

ELIZA: ASHBURNHAM.

There is a proclamation out against papistes,[b] and much other newes
that I have not now time to write.

But all these zealous strivings were ineffectual.   The fatal year
1628 witnessed not only the assassination of the royal favourite,[c] on

---

[a] Coventry, in place of Williams.   [b] 11 Jan. 1625-6.

[c] In a letter of Sir Edward Dering to his brother Robert, a merchant at that time at
Dantzic, dated 8 Sept. 1628, he thus describes the death of Buckingham.   The account
is not altogether accurate, but as the statement of a contemporary, who was in a position
to be well informed, it is worthy of being printed entire, besides that a part of it has a
bearing upon Sir Edward's own fortunes.   " Upon Bartholomew eve was fulfilled a pre-
diction by the Lady Eleanor Davyes,* made long since (as I remember I had itt almost att
last August, 1627) viz. that the Duke of Buckingham should not outlive August 1628 ;
which others also had calculated out of the numerall letters of his name, as thus, GeorgIVs
DVX BVCkInghaMEe.   MDCXVVVIII.   1628.   These thinges *I knew before*, which
make me *consider the event* the more ; nay himselfe was told of these and others *all*
many several times, which still out of the bravery of his sperett he ever slighted and con-
temned, *which sperett* if it did arise out of the innocency of *his heart*, did then deserve a
pretious memory.   I can not *tell*,† but I am sorry that he lived not to be more fully discovered, and I feare the wheeles of this state will goe never the smoother for his being
layd by.   My shallow capacity, or els my slender intelligence, could never yett derive unto
my understanding a knowledge, or into my mind a beleef, of the hundredth part of his
plotts upon the ruine of this state, which many men yett confidently sweare.   If I did think
so, I should be gladd of his good riddance as any ; although even at that instant I was a
looser by his death, for I was then upon treaty with the Leivetenant of Dover Castle

---

* The wild anagrammatic prophecies of Dame Eleanor Davies were very much regarded
at this time, although one would have thought that such a man as Sir Edward Dering
might have escaped the infection of such nonsense.   Her prophetical reputation was seriously
damaged in public estimation by an ingenious application or retort of her own weapon.   It
was discovered that " Never soe mad a ladie," could be derived as an anagram from her
own name.

† The words printed in italic are nearly worn away in the original.   I have supplied
them, I think correctly, from the slight remains, but it is right to mention the fact.

whom the value of the family connection with the Ashburnhams depended, but also the death of Lady Dering. In the only letter of hers which we have seen she complains, "I cannot send any good news of my couges [cough's] going away, yet I eat ioyes [juice] of lecarich [liquorice.]" The poor lady's spelling of hard words was a little peculiar, but the story she told was, and, alas! still is, a common one. The cough hurried her to the grave at the age of twenty-three.

The Villiers connection left an abiding trace on the family of Dering in a Baronetcy, which was granted to Sir Edward on the 1st February, 1626-7; one among innumerable evidences of the favourite's zeal for the interest of persons connected with him by even the remotest family tie. Lady Dering left two children, the son before alluded to, named after his father, and who ultimately succeeded to the family honours, and a daughter named

about resignation of his place unto me, which the Duke had consented unto, even vpon that very day that the news arrived att the Castle of his death, which was acted att Portsmouth about a day and a half before, by one Felton, a Leivetenant, something discontented with want of pay, and with not succeeding into his captain's place upon the death of his captaine. The place was the Duke's chamber, where watching opportunity (as the Duke was bowing in courtesy unto some commanders there present [_Margin._ Unto Colonel Fryer], and taking theire leaves of him), Felton, having a prepared knife under his hatt, stabbed the Duke into the left side through the lunges, and left the knife in the wound. The Duke presently said, ' Villain, thou hast stabbed me!' and drew out the knife himselfe, laying his hand on his sword, but not able to stirre or speake more. The noise of the distracted company drew thither from the next chamber his miserable Duchesse, who came to see his heart bloud gushe out att his mouth, for that way he bledd more then att his wound. In this meane time Felton went away, but presently returned to the place, and doth seeme to carry this act with the bosome of a quiett settled constancy. The King received the newes with passion and the Queen with teares. None of his offices are yet bestowed, nor shall be untill the solemne funerall be over, for the King sayth he shall carry all his offices to his _grave._ The Earles of Holland and Dorsett are almost never from the King. Felton gives no other account of his fact, but that _after_ the Parliament had by theire remonstrance unto the King declared how hurtfull to the Commonwealth the excessive power of the Duke was, he ever thought the Duke so greate a burden that he accounted the removing of him a good acte ; and yett professeth he would do itt were itt to do againe. The King sayth he will be a husband to his Duchesse, a father to his children, a master to his servants, and an executor to pay his debtes."

CAMD. SOC. c

Elizabeth, after her grandmother, the clever widow of Sir John Ashburnham. Amidst her care for the welfare of her friends, it is pleasant to know that this excellent lady did not neglect her own advancement. In 1627 she was married to Lord Chief Justice Richardson, and by the King's special favour was separately ennobled in the following year by the Scottish title of Baroness Cramond; a precedent followed, as every body will remember, in very recent times.

Having tried two matrimonial ventures at court, Sir Edward Dering's next attempt was in the city. In the parish of St. Olave, in the Old Jewry, there had died, some few months before the second Lady Dering, a mercer, of the name of Richard Bennett.[a] His connections were extremely respectable. Sir Thomas Bennett, Alderman and Mercer of London, who died in 1626, was his father. Sir Thomas was Lord Mayor in 1603, on the death of Queen Elizabeth, and was knighted by King James at his coronation. One of Richard Bennett's brothers was Sir Simon Bennett, of Beachampton, in the county of Bucks, created a Baronet in 1627, and one of his sisters was wife to Sir George Croke, the judge. The wealthy and well-connected mercer left a widow, named Elizabeth, and one child, a son, named Simon after the boy's baronet uncle. He had two other sons, both christened Thomas, after their grandfather the alderman, but neither of them survived their father. Mrs. Bennett was of the Staffordshire family of the Cradocks, a daughter of William Cradock, esq., of that county. Her father is mentioned as if resident at Hamburgh in 1628, perhaps as a mercantile agent.

By the custom of London and under the will of her husband, of which she was the sole executrix, Mrs. Bennett took two-thirds of

[a] Buried 29 April, 1628. Register of St. Olave's, Old Jewry. Kindly procured for me, with much other similar information by my friend James Crosby, Esq. F S.A.

her husband's property, besides all her jewels and chains of pearl and gold, her diamond and other rings, and her husband's coach, and the four grey coach mares and geldings, "with all things thereunto belonging." These adequate indications of Mrs. Bennett's comfortable position in the world drew around her a host of suitors. How many she had dismissed before November, 1628, does not appear, but at that time the gossiping world was amused by the names of three of her most conspicuous admirers, Finch, Crow, and Raven [a] The Finch was a prosperous lawyer, of good standing and reputation, Sir Heneage Finch, one of the family of that name seated at Eastwell in Kent. · He was Recorder of London, had been Speaker in the parliament of 1626, (a proof that he was a man of dignified person,) and, besides a residence in the city, possessed a handsome house at Kensington, the same which was purchased from his descendants and converted into a palace by William III., and the gardens of which have long been a source of health and of daily enjoyment to thousands. The Crow was Sir Sackville Crow, who in laying siege to this "Twenty thousand pounds widow" [b] was making a desperate cast to relieve himself from a serious *minus* in his public accounts, which shortly afterwards compelled him to retire from his office of Treasurer of the Navy. The Raven was a physician of that name. After having been long a suitor, it occurred to this foolish person that the invaluable widow might be won by a *coup-de-main*. Making his approaches through the widow's servants, he found means to silence her personal attendant, and, by her collusion, found his way into the lady's bedchamber after she had retired to rest and had fallen asleep. Not satisfied, like Iachimo, with merely making observations on the scene before him, the medical intruder awoke the widow, and began to demonstrate his ardent love. His reception was such as might have been anticipated by any one but the silly perpetrator of so scan-

[a] Court and Times of Charles I. i. 437.   [b] Ibid. i. 436.

dalous an outrage. The lady screamed " Thieves ! " and " Murder ! "
her men-servants rushed to the rescue, the Doctor was secured,
and was handed over to that great enemy of Dan Cupid, the parish
constable. On the day following he was taken before Mr. Recorder, who, nothing loath, performed the duty of consigning
his rival to the safe custody of a gaoler until the succeeding
sessions. In completion of the story of this unlucky suitor,
it may be as well to add, that, being ultimately indicted
for (of all things in the world) a burglary, he wildly contem-
plated pleading guilty, perhaps with an idea of making some
amends to the lady whose house he had so madly invaded. Judge
Richardson (Lady Ashburnham's second husband), who presided at
his trial, " jeered him out of his frantic humour." Under the
Judge's advice he withdrew his plea, or his intention, and was
condemned, not of burglary, but of " ill-demeanour." After imprisonment and payment of a fine, the poor discomfited and no doubt
repentant wretch was turned out to face the laughter of his patients,
and the scorn of the rest of the world.[a]

Dr. Raven's *escapade* took place on the night of Wednesday, the
19th November, 1628. On the day following Sir Edward Dering
entered the field. How much there was of premeditation in this
coincidence of dates who can say? The town must have been full
of talk of Dr. Raven's folly, and perhaps Sir Edward deemed the
moment when the widow felt a peculiar sense of her loneliness
more than ordinarily appropriate for his purpose.

Although unable to answer this particular question, we are
in a position to give a very minute narrative of the general
course of this incident in Sir Edward's life, for, as if to assist us in
these inquiries, he kept a most singular journal of his whole proceedings throughout this courtship. What was said or done during

<hr>
[a] See Rous's Diary, p 34 ; Munk's Roll of Physicians, i. 158.

every day and almost every hour that he devoted to the widow
Bennett, what gossip was retailed, what suspicion was afloat, or what
flattery was uttered, whatever was written or meditated, or even
dreamed, in connection with this affair, what money was expended
in bribing the widow's servants, and who interfered from the mere
love of mixing up in transactions which implied confidence and
secrecy, is all registered in this, perhaps one of the most marvellous
of records ever kept by a sane man. We shall henceforth for a time
be greatly indebted to it, and its exact character will soon become
apparent to the reader. It opens thus:—

" Nov. 20, Edmund, King," i.e. the day of St. Edmund the King
and Martyr, no doubt deemed propitious for such undertakings, " I
adventured, was denied. Sent up a letter, which was returned,
after she had read it."

Although denied admission, perhaps a little to the baronet's
surprise, the event recorded in the last few words gave hope to
an experienced person like Sir Edward. He determined at once to
invest the fortress, and opened the siege in due form by attack-
ing the lady's servants.

" [Nov.] 21. I inveigled G. Newman with 20s.

" [Nov.] 24. I did re-engage him, 20s.

I did also oil the cash-keeper, 20s.

" [Nov.] 26. I gave Edmund Aspull [the cash keeper] another
20s.

I was there, but denied sight.

" [Nov.] 27. I sent a second letter, which was kept.

I set Sir John Skeffington [a] upon Matthew Cradock.[b]

[a] Sir Edward's aunt Elizabeth Dering married William Skeffington of Fisherwick,
co. Stafford, Esq.

[b] A cousin of the lady, on whom she much relied for advice. He was a London merchant, largely engaged in some of the important adventures for colonization which
distinguished this period of our history.

" [Nov.] 27.   The cash keeper supped with me.

" [Nov.] 28.   I went to Mr. Cradock, but found him cold.

" [Nov.] 30.   I was at the Old Jewry Church, and saw her, both forenoon and afternoon."

The sight of the lady at her devotions, and the hope that she might not have been altogether untouched by a handsome presence, set off with all the care that tailors, barbers, and valets could bestow upon it, inspirited the ardent suitor, who records on Monday, " December 1, I sent a third letter, which was likewise kept."

The 2nd was devoted to another attack on Mr. Cradock, who was still " cold of kindness," and to further dealings with the oiled and inveigled servants.

On the 4th, Sir Edward called at the lady's residence three times, " but she was already abroad about Dr. Raven's business;"—it was the day of the silly Dr.'s trial.   On the day following Sir Edward went again at ten o'clock, and communicated his desires through Mr. George Loe, a very influential person with Mrs. Bennett. Loe brought back a very prudent answer,—" that Steward[a] was so testy that she durst not give admittance unto any until he and she were fully concluded for the wardship.

That she had a good opinion of me.

That he [i.e. Loe] heard nobly of me.

That he would inform me when Steward was off.

That he was engaged for another.

That I need not refrain from going to the church where she was, unless I thought it to disparage myself."

---

[a] This person had evidently a grant from the crown of the wardship of Mrs. Bennett's little boy, then four years old. He had also used the authority thus obtained, as a shelter to matrimonial proposals made to Mrs. Bennett herself. Her endeavour at this time was to make a bargain with Steward, by which, for a money payment to himself, he should assign to her the right to the care and custody of her own child.

On the 7th, Sir Edward again united the worship of Mrs. Bennett with that ordinarily offered at St. Olave's, and on coming out of the sacred building George Newman, the inveigled servant, came up to Sir Edward and whispered in his ear, " Good news! good news!" After dinner he called on the suitor, who had taken up his abode in the neighbourhood, within sight of the widow's mansion, and buoyed up his hope by an assurance that the widow " liked well his carriage, and that, if his land were not settled on his eldest son, there was good hope." For his good news, Sir Edward chronicles, " I gave him 20s." Elated and hopeful, Sir Edward in the course of the evening proceeded to call on the Recorder, who was not only of Sir Edward's own county, but was also related to him by affinity. Sir Edward stayed to supper, and Sir Heneage was communicative and confidential. He let Sir Edward understand that he altogether despaired of success on his own account, and indeed that he was wise enough to retire. He disclaimed all desire or purpose of proceeding any further, and made a merit of his willingness to assist Sir Edward. In the course of the evening the two suitors chatted over the widow and her affairs, and Sir Heneage related the whole story of his love, and his withdrawal.

Rumours current during the 8th and 9th December were thought to confirm the lady's previous good impressions in reference to Sir Edward, whilst, at the same time, affairs with Mr. Steward approached to a crisis. On the 10th Sir Edward was informed by the friendly cash-keeper that he had in his mistress's presence offered Steward the sum of 1,500l. in ready gold for a release of his right to the ward. He had refused; whereupon the indignant widow had sworn never to see or speak with him again, with her good will. This incident was deemed favourable by Sir Edward, and, on the following day, he again presented himself at her house. Newman announced his presence to his mistress, and brought back her answer, that she desired Sir Edward to excuse her, she was not willing to entertain discourse of that kind. Sir Edward records that he paused sadly, and remarked aloud that he was then "in a wilderness of uncertainty." Aspull, who was present, carried up the pretty phrase to his persecuted mistress, and brought back word that she would see Sir Edward.

The interview was prudently managed on both sides. There were no raptures. Sir Edward saluted her of course, but could get " no answer of certainty, nor yet indeed any denial. Her words were, that as yet she had no purpose of marriage." Sir Edward went into money details, he declared the full of his incumbrances, but unaccountably forgot to mention that he had a daughter. He was freely and kindly heard. She evidently was but little worked upon, and he begged her not to give him an answer until after a second meeting. She acquiesced, but postponed the naming of any day until her cousin Cradock, who was absent, had returned to town. " So I saluted her again," records the baronet, " and withdrew myself, as I saw she was desirous I should."

On the memory of this interview, and on reports from her servants of her comments on his conduct, he lived for several days. She was said to have remarked that he " did not come so boisterous as Steward and Temple," — the former being the grantee of the wardship, the latter, Sir Peter Temple of Stow, an ancestor of the Duke of Buckingham. Of Steward she observed, that, when she had obtained from him " the broad seal," which would confer upon her the wardship of her child, " he should be hanged ere she would have any more to do with him." Inspirited by these reports, Sir Edward waited on Sir George Croke to solicit his recommendation to the widow. The careful but somewhat illogical judge replied that he knew no ill of the baronet, and therefore could not but speak well of him. He asked Sir Edward if he had seen the lady? " I let him ask the question twice," remarks Sir Edward, " and then answered that, although I kept it strange to others yet, I must not deny to him but that I had seen her as yesterday."

Here there occurs an unfortunate hiatus in the original manuscript. A sheet which recorded the progress of Sir Edward's suit from the 12th December, 1628, to the 5th January, 1629, is missing. From another manuscript by Sir Edward, which contains a brief abstract of the events of this period, it appears that after another letter, and an unsatisfactory interview with one of the Cradocks, apparently not the one designated " Cousin Cradock," Sir Edward not being able to get any positive answer, aye or no, deemed it advisable to make it be believed that he was a person not to be trifled with, and therefore sent to the lady on the 1st January for the return of all his letters. His somewhat brusque New Year's Day's request was instantly complied with, and the widow and her friends concluded that the suit of the touchy baronet was at an end. But such was not at all Sir Edward's intention. On the 5th of January, when the larger manuscript recommences, we find him calling at Mrs. Bennett's in the most friendly manner to see a Mrs. Norton, a cousin of Mrs. Bennett, whom Sir Edward had known for seven years, and who had then come to live with the widow as a companion. If the tales brought to Sir Edward, and which he carefully chronicles, are to be exactly believed, Mrs. Norton and many of those about the widow pestered her at this time with continual praises of the Kentish baronet. Wiser than her annoyers, the lady took refuge in silence, and in a protestation which was duly conveyed to Sir Edward, by whom it was perhaps regarded as a compliment, that she would never marry. " The cash-keeper," whom Sir Edward still kept his fast friend, " told me," records the baronet, " that she was very sad, and that she sat two hours together upon the bed without speaking a word, and that she hath often done so of late, and Mrs. Norton in

the chamber, both silent." Such silence could not long be maintained, and on the day after it is recorded we learn that the widow
turned upon Mrs. Norton and "beshrewed her" for speaking so much
of Sir Edward Dering, alleging that she could not sleep all night
for dreaming of him.

At this Christmas time, indeed, many of the principal parties to
this narrative seem to have been very much given to dreaming.
Mrs. Bennett, who had not yet recovered from her terror of Dr.
Raven, dreamed that Mrs. Norton bringing to her, when in bed, a
mess of milk, Sir Edward came into the room behind her, whereat
she ran out of her bedroom into the parlour, "in her smock," and
so caught cold Sir Edward dreamed that the widow sent him a
cake — a twelfth cake of course, it being the 7th January, —
and, if we read this passage in the manuscript correctly, another
person one whose name has not before occurred in connection with Sir Edward's biography, Isaak Walton, the angler, the
biographer, and the worthy man-milliner of Fleet Street, he also
had his dream, that the lady came to Sir Edward on his sending
for her, but, offering to go again, something ensued which is
prudently shrouded under an " &c." None of these dreams were
very well worth recording, but it is certainly a point of additional
interest in the story to know that Isaak Walton shared the perplexities of his baronet-friend. Isaak's dream acted as a retainer
to him on Sir Edward's behalf. As an ambassador or a volunteer
—it does not very well appear which—he went on the following
day to George Newman, and spoke to him on the one all-interesting
topic. Newman doubted Isaak's credentials or his discretion, and
visited Sir Edward by way of reply. He described the widow as
overwhelmed with perplexity. She had made a bargain with
Steward, and afterwards discovered that the ingenious gentleman
had sold his right to the wardship to another before he transferred
it to her; a striking illustration of the difficulties of this relic of

the old feudal law, and a circumstance which occasioned the widow
a world of fresh trouble.

In the midst of such perplexities, it was not surprising that she
forbore to make any fresh sign to Sir Edward, but he was playing
his game too deeply to understand a course of conduct so simple
and so natural. He began to fear that she had not understood, or
had not been sufficiently impressed by, the noble self-appreciation
which had dictated his demand for the return of his letters. In his
fear he flew to his friend Mrs. Norton, in Mrs. Bennett's house, and
"sat at table with her almost an hour." He argued with her that
some one had done him ill offices, or that he had done himself some,
for the difference and denials before and since New Year's Day did
infer no less. Mrs. Norton did not absolutely deny so much, nor
confess which it was, "but was very earnest," he writes, "that there
was no hope for me." "I replied, I would stay the utmost, and see
her [*i e.* the widow] married before I would desert." She said,
"Her [*i.e.* the widow's] troubles would not suffer her to marry, and
that, if I resolved to continue on, yet I had best do nothing till
Mr. Cradock came to town. I told her, I resolved so before she said
so." This was on the 9th January, and the day's entry, after some
further tantalisation from Mr. Aspull, concludes thus:—" George
Newman says she hath two suits of silver plate, one in the country
and the other here, and that she hath beds of 100*l.* the bed!"—Oh,
the folly of demanding the return of those letters!

Sir Edward began to think so, and deemed a desperate effort
necessary to regain his lost position. The opportunity occurred on
the 12th January. The widow went to make a call at Sir George
Croke's. As her coach drew up to the door, Sir Edward stepped
forward, desired her to pardon an unasked service, assisted her to
alight, and gallantly conducted her into the Judge's house. At the
going into the parlour, he says, she stayed to let him go in before

her.   It was a mark of respect which he was not slow to take advantage of.   He ushered her into the apartment, and then advanced to salute the ladies who were there.   They placed chairs for their visitors, but Sir Edward intreated the favour of the widow for a few words. She yielded, he says, privately, the others standing by. " I renewed" he goes on, " my request, whereunto she answered that she would not marry."   After an interruption arising from the coming in of Sir George Croke, Sir Edward continues, that he returned to his widow " with entreating to stand in her good thoughts as formerly, upon expectation of Mr. Cradock's coming.   She told me that she had denied me, and I had denied myself.   I desired that my strong affection might excuse at least one error and indiscretion, &c. and added my entreaty to stand in the hope, &c.   She said she could make no other answer then, than now.   I desired still to have it then, though.   She said, yes, if I would take it from him.   I replied, ' Pray sweeten the answer with your own breath.'   She said, yet she should not change it.   So, in hope of another sight, then I kissed her, and took leave.   Then Sir George Croke drinking to me in a glass of muscado, I commended it to her, and came away. Sir George brought me to the door, saying he saw no likelihood, &c."

Two days after this bold attempt Sir Edward made an attack in another quarter.   George Newman, with Susan the widow's nurse-maid, and her little child, " going into the fields [Finsbury Fields] to walk," were met by Tayler, a friend of Sir Edward, perhaps the landlord of the house in which he was lodging.   Tayler won the child to be content to come with him, and the others not unwillingly followed.   " I, " notes Sir Edward, " entertained the child with cake, and gave him an amber box, and to them, wine.   Susan professed that she and all the house prayed for me, and told me the child called me ' father.'   I gave her 5s., and entreated her to desire her mistress not to be offended at this, which I was so glad of. She said she thought she would not."

In these singular notes Sir Edward records, with the greatest candour, the judgments of his friends passed upon himself and his widow. A Mr. Smith said, that if the widow knew what Sir Edward Dering was, she would not refuse him. Smith declared him to be such a man as the kingdom had not his fellow, and recorded his belief that God had a blessing in store for him. Lady Cleere told old Sir Anthony Dering that she wondered his son should undervalue himself so much as to think of this widow, and of one of such parentage. Lady Wroth, on the contrary, declared her to be a good and a wise gentlewoman. She evidently was a person of intellect, and knew how to defend herself. Sir Edward does not any where personally allude to any beauty that she possessed, although in one place he records that her companion Miss Norton, a lady possessed of all the customary companionable qualities, was reported to have made mention, in speaking to the widow herself, of what she would do if she had such an estate, and were so young and handsome as the widow. In some places a freedom, or even a coarseness of expression, is attributed to her, which savours more of the city than of the court, but probably the effect of even this was tempered by a buoyant good humour, and by a fondness for the use and application of proverbs, under which a good deal of her plain speaking was covered.   ·

At length the long expected " Cousin Cradock " arrived in town. " Isaak Walton undertook him," remarks Sir Edward, " at his first coming, and did his part well. Cradock said he would do his best, if I would be ruled by him, &c." But the widow stood upon her professed determination not to marry. Suitors came and went. Great ladies from court visited the mansion in St. Olave's, and set forth the merits of knights and gentlemen, but without effect. Lady

Skinner introduced herself to plead the cause of Mr. Butler, probably one of the Butlers of Bramfield, but the widow's description of him as " a black, blunt-nosed gentleman," ended his suit. Sir Peter Temple renewed his pretensions, but made little way, although he challenged an infinite superiority over Sir Edward Dering in birth, estate, and person. The Countess of Bridgewater introduced the battered old sailor Sir Henry Mainwaring, who was steeped in poverty to the very lips, and he and another ancient knight had an interview of an hour with the widow, but never came again. Lord Bruce put in a claim, but soon retired. More persevering, and of all the suitors the one whom Dering esteemed his most serious rival, was the new-made Viscount Lumley, who was strongly supported by the widow's brother-in-law, Loe.

After having wasted precious time, and by his ill-tempered indiscretion in sending for his letters allowed a host of new competitors to enter the field, Sir Edward was now driven to rest all his hopes on Isaak Walton and cousin Cradock. On Sunday the 25th January Isaak attempted the cousin again, and procured from him an appointment for an interview with Sir Edward at Isaak's house on the following day. They met, and Sir Edward registers that he ·' found him free of promise, and that the business is yet treatable; only, he saith, Mr. Loe doth much importune her for Viscount Lumley, whom he says she hath seen three times. I told him what conditions I could make, which he liked well, and said they were better than my Lord Lumley's, and that he [she?] would do well enough with those conditions, if she were not engaged He bade me pursue my way as formerly, and then, as called to advise, he would work for me the stronger and with less suspicion, and did promise that on Wednesday morning he would give knowledge to Isaak Walton of what might be done.'

Whilst plotting cousin Cradock was thus working, in shew or

reality, for Sir Edward, Lord Lumley was prosecuting his suit by the most assiduous attention to the widow. Five times in that week had his coach driven up to the Old Jewry church, where the bran-new Viscount alighted and thence made his way, the observed of all observers, to St. Olave's, and there on each occasion enjoyed a *tête-à-tête*, from all chance of which Sir Edward had excluded himself by his unlucky precipitancy. All this looked very threatening, but on Wednesday Isaak Walton changed the whole course of Sir Edward's anticipations. He was persuaded that the game was still afoot, that the soft nonsense of a *roué* Viscount might attract a city widow, and yet make but slight impression on her heart. At Isaak's interview with cousin Cradock on Wednesday morning he was shewn a peep behind the scenes. Cradock told him that he and that worthy nobleman the Lord North " did labour to draw her off from Lumley, and that, upon their persuasions, she was well content it should be broken, and desired them to be a means to break it." Oh, slippery widow, and oh, sly cousin Cradock! The news elated Sir Edward to the stars. He instantly posted off to St. Olave's, to call on his friend Mrs. Norton, and there found, not success, but ruin! He learned, to his infinite dismay, that the confidential communication of cousin Cradock to friend Isaak, although perfectly true as far as it went, was not the whole truth. Lumley was to be got rid of, true, but Sir Edward was not to be accepted. " Mrs. Bennett had a week since said that her affection was bestowed; that she had a singular good opinion of me," [*i.e.* Sir Edward,] " but she would not marry me. I told her " [*i.e.* Mrs. Norton] " this was the fullest answer that ever I had, yet not full enough, because it came not immediately, neither in time nor person, from herself; therefore, I did entreat her to tell Mrs. Bennett that I could have no other satisfaction than from her own mouth, which I would within a few days attend, and Mrs. Norton promised to do her best to obtain a parting sight."

Lumley was a kind of person whom it was more easy to determine to get rid of than actually to do so. On the first rumour of his impending fate, he brought down on his behalf the Earl of Dorset, Lord Chamberlain to the Queen, and a most influential person in the general government, especially in that important city branch of it, the Admiralty, and courtly civility and polite attention delayed for a time the *congé* that awaited him. In the mean time Sir Edward and his friend Isaak engaged their influential acquaintances to call upon the widow, and sing the praises of their candidate. The stayed parishioners of St. Olave's must have wondered at the unwonted concourse to the widow's residence, and she herself must have been teased and bewildered almost beyond endurance, to find herself exposed to the selfish addresses of a host of cunning flatterers, many of them utterly beggarly and worthless, who traded upon their power of communicating to her a title which, shared with them, could not have been any very considerable honour.

Mrs. Norton's declaration that the widow had made her choice was evidently not believed. Sir Edward's hopes were still buoyed up by the reports of those around him. Isaak Walton and Sir Edward's other friends, principally the widow's servants, were continually bringing him favourable news. Whenever the widow dropped a word in his commendation, there was some injudicious friend or feed retainer ready to carry to him the tale, with exaggeration. One person declared that she said of him that he wrote better than any other, spoke better than any other, and was better spoken of than any other; whilst Cousin Cradock, who paid little attention to what she said herself, and put great faith in his own subtilty, declared on a certain evening, that if Sir Edward would follow his directions he would be hanged if he had her not at last; and a certain Mr. Catesby took his oath that none but Sir Edward should have her.

On the 4th February Sir Edward seems to have been able to bear the uncertainty of his position no longer. He went to the house, and through the intervention of Mrs. Norton was admitted to an interview on condition that he did not renew his suit. When the widow entered the parlour, he told her that no man ever received a favour so precious and so fatal, and asked her if it must be the last time that ever he should see her. " She said, No, for I might casually see her hereafter many times. I intreated of her to grant me one suit, vizt, to love herself, which I said she now was put upon the trial of, vizt, to choose that man with whom she might live happiest. I told her I thanked her for forbidding me to renew my suit, unless she meant to grant it, for by that means, I not asking, she could not deny. She said, she wished me well, and should be glad of my [good] wishes. I answered, I take you at your word. She told me I had the child's good will, &c. I asked her, what I should give for the reason of her denial. She said, Say that you left me, and take the glory of it, &c. This and other discourse did fill an hour and a half. I told her the danger of trusting her friends, and bade her be sure to choose a better now she refused me. I said, I could not withdraw my affection, nor would not my respects, till I saw her give her hand to another," &c.

Slowly, even after this interview, did the curtain descend upon the hopes of Sir Edward Dering. Isaak Walton, as sincere as he was precise, worked for his friend with might and main, but his power does not seem to have extended very far beyond his Staffordshire friends the Cradocks. Besides Cousin Cradock, there was a Lawyer Cradock in the Temple, and the celebrated Merchant Cradock in the City. All these were so far influenced by Isaak as to become warm supporters of Sir Edward. But Lumley had a stronger hold than was anticipated. Even after what we have already seen he was a continual visitor, and persuaded the widow to accept a ring from him under circumstances which very nearly amounted to a marriage contract. Day by day the widow intended to get rid of him, but was

unable to utter the fatal word. At length Sir George Croke and
Viscount Campden spoke their minds so freely against the suitor that
Mrs. Norton was called upon to accomplish the task of his dismissal,
and on the 14th February his hopes were ended and his ring rede-
livered.

Whilst the fate of Lord Lumley hung in doubt, Sir Edward's
friends exerted themselves vigorously on his behalf. Mr. Chamberlain, a person of importance in the city, who seems in some cases
to have been confounded with the letter writer, extorted from the
widow a promise that she would see Sir Edward once more after
Lumley was dismissed. Mr. Purefoy interfered on his behalf with
cousin Cradock. The Dean of Canterbury, Dr. Isaac Bargrave, Sir
Edward's relative, came up to London on his solicitation, and pro
cured the celebrated city clergyman Dr. Featley to call upon the
widow and use his powerful influence for Sir Edward. Lady Cramond, Sir Edward's experienced mother-in-law, whose power in
such matters must have been immense, taking with her Kate Ashburnham, a sister of Sir Edward's late wife, went as a volunteer,
and pleaded his cause with all her power; whilst Sir Henry Wotton,
coming from Eton to pay his respects to his Majesty, proved how
much the knowledge of this famous siege occupied the common
talk, by wishing Sir Edward, whom he met in the Privy Chamber,
" a full sail, &c." Against all this solicitation the widow stoutly
maintained her position. Steward still tormented her. She had
increased her offer of a composition with him, or those who claimed
under him, from 1,500*l.* to 3,000*l.*, but 4000*l.* was now demanded.
So troublesome a litigation fully accounted for her inability to
attend to the claims of her suitors; but she intimated that she had
made her selection, that her mind was settled, but that she would
not marry until after Easter; and Mrs. Norton, who no doubt
knew her friend's real determination, and probably acted under her

direction, warned Sir Edward that, " if Lumley were off, she could not find any hope for him, but could not say why." Mrs. Norton knew the why, but could not state it. The Cradocks, and the rest of the people about the widow, neither knew it nor believed in its existence. In their ignorance they still urged on Sir Edward, whilst the widow not only kept her secret, but, if all was true that was told to Sir Edward, she and Mrs. Norton had the wit or the cunning to mislead Sir Edward's feed friends of the widow's household by words intended to be reported to him, words which might still give him hope, and draw off his attention from the person whom she really favoured. Sir Edward's manuscript is unfortunately incomplete at its close, but the very last entry contains an example of this designed misleading: " Yesternight," Sir Edward writes under the date of the 25th February, " at supper she was in a merry plight; and, when they were taking away, she said, ' Well, Thomas, I must have one glass of beer more.' Then turned to Mrs. Norton, ' Here's,' said she, ' to all that love you.' R.—' Then you drink to some that love you too.' R.—' Nay, who knows that?' R.—' Yes, better than me, and that doth Sir E. D.' R.—' Well!' said she, and so drank." This incident was reported the next morning to Sir Edward, and is chronicled as if an evidence in his favour.

We have said that the curious manuscript from which we have derived these details is imperfect at its close. A hope of discovering the remainder of it kept back this publication for a considerable time; but, as the lost portion seems irretrievable, we have determined to use it as it stands, adding the conclusion of the romance from another and less interesting source. The lost portion, containing Sir Edward's comments upon what actually did occur, would have been worth a Jew's eye.

We have noticed, among the widow's early suitors, the distinguished lawyer, Sir Heneage Finch, Recorder of London, and late Speaker of the House of Commons, and we have mentioned how Sir Edward Dering paid Mr. Recorder a visit on a Sunday evening shortly after he had committed Dr. Raven for trial. Sir Heneage, as we have remarked, on that occasion related the story of his courtship and withdrawal, " disclaimed any desire or purpose of proceeding, and promised me [*i.e.* Sir Edward] as occasion served to give me assistance." Two days afterwards Sir Edward mentions that Mr. Recorder told him that he had said to Mr. George Loe that he had heard that a Kentish gentleman was then a suitor. Mr. Loe confessed so, and named Sir Edward. The Recorder replied, " If she be wise let her not refuse him; she will be happy if she have him." On subsequent occasions we find Sir Edward again calling upon Mr. Recorder, and Mr. Recorder interposing, although ineffectually, on his behalf with Mr. Justice Croke, and Sir Edward dining with Mr. Recorder, who informed him that Lord Lumley had become a suitor. This friendly intercourse continued upon the same footing and basis of Sir Heneage's withdrawal throughout the whole of Sir Edward's suit. The loss of the conclusion of Sir Edward's manuscript renders us unable to discover when or how it was that he first found out that Sir Heneage was really the widow's accepted suitor, and that, either in the dictionary of Mr. Recorder, the word withdrawal, and all the other words he had used upon that subject, meant that, having the widow's acceptance of his proposals in his pocket, he (no doubt with her consent, and possibly, for some cause connected with that business with Steward in which Sir Heneage may have been her adviser,) withdrew from any public suit or display of his conquest until it was convenient to her to marry him; or else, (the more charitable supposition) that the widow, having made up her mind, concealed her decision from the object of her choice, until a settlement with Steward put her in the position to marry. Be this as it may, it seems unquestionable that, after Lumley was got rid of, a preference for the Recorder was the concealed obstacle in Sir Edward's path, and the proof of the fact lies in this, that the widow became Lady Finch almost immediately after the time of which we are treating.[a]

Before dismissing this lady, it may be as well to add, that her son Simon, the boy whom Sir Edward entertained with cakes, became a man of very great wealth, which was carried by his three daughters and coheiresses into several noble families. His great-uncle Richard Bennett, or rather Bennet as they all came ultimately to spell their name, was the ancestor of the Earls of Arlington and Tankerville. Of Mrs. Bennett's second marriage all that is known is favourable, except its brief continuance. Among the many widowers who besieged her she seems undoubtedly to have taken the best. Of the issue of Sir Heneage's former marriage, three sons and one daughter survived their mother, who died on the 11th of April, 1627. The eldest of these sons, named after his father, became Lord Chancellor and Earl of Nottingham. By Mrs. Bennett, Sir Heneage had two daughters,—Elizabeth, who became wife to Edward Madison, Esq., and Anne, married to Edward the third Viscount and first Earl of Conway. Sir Heneage Finch died on the 5th December, 1631.

Annoyed as Sir Edward must have been by failure under such peculiar circumstances, he instantly set about retrieving his lost time. No journal explains the ups and downs of this his last courtship, but it was successful and happy. Unton, daughter of Sir Ralph Gibbes, of Honington, in co. Warwick, was the lady who

---

[a] They were married shortly after Easter, on the 16th April, 1629, at St. Dunstan's in the West. (Nichols's Collect. Topog. et Genealog. v. 218.) At the same time, and in the same church, were also married Mr. Harbottle Grimstone, afterwards Sir Harbottle and Master of the Rolls, and the widow's niece Mary Croke, daughter of Sir George, the Judge. (Ibid.)

became Sir Edward's third wife. She had evidently none of the
wealth which distinguished the widow Bennett, but the connection
was highly respectable and the marriage one of mutual affection.
Some of his letters which are printed in the present volume speak
upon this subject unmistakeably. They had four children, named
Henry, who settled at Pevington, co. Kent; Edward, who was a
merchant in London, and was knighted; Dorothy, married to Thomas English, of Buckland in Maidstone, Esq.; and Frances, married
to Thomas Cowper, Esq. Unton Lady Dering survived her husband upwards of thirty years. She died in 1676.

Sir Edward Dering's family position being once more settled, he
now resumed his endeavours after advancement in the world. We
have seen that before the death of Buckingham he had been in
treaty, with the Duke's approbation, for the purchase from Sir
John Hippisley of the Lieutenancy of Dover Castle. Under the
new Lord Warden, Theophilus Earl of Suffolk, the treaty was
resumed and carried into effect. As an eminent office, which
had already been in his own family, and was to be executed in his
own county, we may well suppose that this Lieutenancy was an
object of attraction, if not of ambition, to Sir Edward Dering.
But he soon discovered that in procuring it he had made a great
mistake. In time of war, the rough Sir John Hippisley had found
it extremely profitable, and he was a man to make it so at any time.
Peace ensued almost immediately after Sir Edward's appointment.
The importance of the office was thereby greatly diminished; it
yielded comparatively little profit, but it required constant attention,
and involved its holder in continual litigation and disputes before the
Council and elsewhere with people of the most unscrupulous class.
With a high sounding title, and a commanding position, Sir Edward's
principal occupation was to be the comptroller, and often the
gaoler, of pirates, privateers, and smugglers, who were continually

on the look-out for some cause of complaint against him or his officers, or for some way of escape from his custody. Term by term he was dragged up to London to defend himself in disputes with such persons respecting questions which with his own good will he would never have approached. No occupation on earth could be less congenial to a man whose tastes were domestic and whose studies were antiquarian and theological, nor less convenient to one who could ill afford the expenses to which he was thus put, and who, having bought his office at a war price, could not find any body to take it off his hands in time of peace. His correspondence with his wife, during his compulsory visits to London at this time, is full of regrets upon these subjects. His ambition had misled him, and he had to pay the penalty.

At length there came a day of release. The Lieutenancy was transferred to Capt. Thomas Wentworth, and for four or five years Sir Edward devoted himself to the care of his family and to the literary pursuits which were congenial to his taste. This was the happiest period of his life. His collections were studied and methodised, he formed many schemes of literary labour, and entered into that curious agreement with Dugdale, Sir Christopher Hatton, and Sir Thomas Shirley, for their mutual assistance in antiquarian researches, which has been recently printed in the Archæologia Cantiana (i. 55).

During this time the state of public affairs grew more and more unsatisfactory. People of Sir Edward's way of thinking were especially displeased at the changes introduced into Church and State under the influence of Archbishop Laud. The anti-ceremonial and anti-hierarchical spirit of his namesake of the reign of Elizabeth revived within him. Conscious of talent, and anxious for an opportunity for its display, old stirrings of heart after distinction and power began again to make themselves felt. The papers published

in the present volume (Nos. I. to XI.) relate to his endeavours to procure his return to Parliament, and his ultimate success in securing
his unopposed election to the Long Parliament as a knight of the
shire for Kent.

Highly gratified by the honour conferred upon him, he proceeded
to Westminster with an intention to bestir himself. In the opinion of
the party opposed to the administration, the whole machinery of the
government had gone wrong, during the suspension for eleven years of
the meeting of Parliament. The church, the law, the finances, the
government of Ireland, and even many of the ordinary ministerial
branches of the civil administration, had, according to their notions,
been perverted in ways at variance with ancient usage and with the
fundamental principles of the constitution. A searching inquiry, to
be carried into every office of the executive, was determined upon. No
branch of this inquiry was deemed of greater importance than that
which affected the Church. It was chiefly as a church reformer that
Sir Edward had been returned, and he instantly put himself
forward as a leader in this important scrutiny. Within a few
days after the commencement of public business he presented
a petition from a Kentish minister, whom Archbishop Laud had
sent for by a pursuivant, and in the course of his speech on that
occasion publicly expressed his hope, that ere the expiration of
a twelvemonth, " His Grace would have more grace, or no Grace
at all." [a] Within a few weeks he moved for a sub-committee of
religion, to examine complaints of oppressed ministers, and abuses
in licensing and forbidding the publication of books.[b] He presented
a petition from the county of Kent, in which it was prayed that the

[a] Speeches, p. 10. On this case of Mr. Wilson, see the present volume, p. 19.

[b] Sir Edward Dering's minutes of the proceedings of this sub-committee (which from
its importance was shortly afterwards made an independent committee), will be found in
this volume, at p. 80.

hierarchical power might be totally abrogated, and on that occasion he declared himself the representative of the opinions of the petitioners, and avowed his belief that it might be said of the Hierarchy of the Church of England, as a Pope Adrian said of the clergy in his time, " *A vertice capitis ad plantam pedis, nihil est sanum in toto ordine ecclesiastico.*" [a] He delivered a learned argument against the recent canons, which he averred that the prelates desired to obtrude upon the people [b] on the ground of the pretended divinity of episcopacy, and the temporal power granted by princes. He was active in reporting from the committee of which he was the chairman, and in one of those reports, on the case of M^r. Wilkinson, he stated that reading the King's Book of Sports in churches, bowing before the Altar in divine service, and bowing at the Name of Jesus were " disciplinarian [questions] in the [then] present way of Novellism." [c]

These speeches, and a great many others of the same kind, with his constant votes on the popular side, procured for him the position he desired. He was looked up to as an acknowledged leader upon all questions relating to the Church, and his acquaintance with the theology of the points in dispute, the clearness with which he stated his arguments, and the eloquence and learning with which he enforced them, secured him not only the attention of the House, but a high degree of popularity out of doors. We learn from the present volume that, during the tumultuary proceedings before the execution of Strafford, the citizens who thronged the House regarded his advice, as he assures his wife, perhaps more than that of many other members, and many took him by the hand whom he knew not, and many said to one another, "There goes Sir Edward Dering," " That is Sir Edward Dering," and " God bless your worship, &c."

Before matters in parliament had made any considerable progress,

[a] Speeches, p. 19.   [b] Ibid. p. 25.   [c] Ibid. p. 41.

the party of Church Reformers began to divide. The extreme section professed themselves to be for "Root and Branch," that is, for the total abrogation of the hierarchy and of all episcopal and cathedral officers; another section would have been satisfied with the exclusion of the Bishops from the House of Lords, and the removal of the clergy from all secular jurisdiction. In which of these sections, or parties, as they ultimately became, stood Sir Edward Dering? Such speeches as that on presenting the Kentish petition were considered as determining the question in favour of the extreme party, but still there existed a suspicion. He tells us that he was stopped in Westminster Hall, and catechized by a Root and Branch man in plain terms, "Art thou for us, or for our adversaries?"[a] He records the question, but does not give his answer.

That answer might well be thought to be found in his conduct in May 1641. He was sitting in the gallery of the House of Commons by the side of his friend Sir Arthur Haselrig. The House was in no good humour with the House of Lords, through which there was labouring heavily a Bill for disenabling all persons in Holy Orders from the exercise of any secular jurisdiction. A petition out of Lincolnshire, upon some cognate subject, had been presented by Sir Edward Ayscough, and was being spoken to by Mr. Strode, when Sir Henry Vane the younger and Oliver Cromwell came into the gallery, bringing with them a brief Bill, drawn, it is said, by Oliver St. John, and contained in less than two sheets of paper, for the utter abolishing of archbishops, bishops, deans, and chapters, with all their officers. The Bill was communicated to Sir Arthur Haselrig, who pressed it into the hand of Sir Edward Dering. "He told me," remarks Sir Edward, "he was resolved that it should go in, but was urgent that I would present it." Sir Edward hastily perused the Bill. The comments on the Lincolnshire petition gave

[a] Speeches, p. 2.

an opportunity for its introduction with effect. At that moment
Strode sat down, Dering rose in haste, caught the eye of the
Speaker, and from that unwonted position [a] astounded the House by
presenting to it this daring Bill without any preliminary motion for
leave. He described it as very short but very sharp. " It is a purg-
ing Bill. I give it you as I take physic, not for delight but for cure.
A cure now, the last and only cure. If, as I hope, all other remedies
have first been tried, then

*   *   *   Immedicabile vulnus
Ense recidendum est, ne pars sincera trahatur,

but " Cuncta prius tentanda." I never was for ruin, so long as I
could hold any hope of reforming. My hopes that way are even
almost withered."

Clarendon says, [b] that the application of the quotation from Ovid
was the greatest motive of Sir Edward for presenting this Bill,
and that he was a man of levity and vanity, easily flattered by
being commended. Whether his conduct sprang from any such silly
feeling, from a love of hearing himself talk, from a fondness for
popular applause, or from a determination to be in the forefront of
the battle at whatever cost, whatever may have been its cause, he
probably repented what he had done long before the popular applause which was called forth by so bold a proposal had subsided. In
a moment of inconsideration, he had not only taken his stand among
the advocates of " Root and Branch," but had gone beyond any of
them. He had hitherto been merely coquetting with that party;
speaking, as in the case of the Kentish petition, words which seemed
to support their views, but which he evidently uttered with qualifications existing in his own mind, which were perhaps suspected by

---

[a] Martin of Galway's Bill against Cruelty to Animals is said to have been the only other
Bill ever introduced from the gallery.

[b] Hist. Rebellion, lib. iii.

those who knew him best, but which passed unobserved by the majority of those who merely heard him speak. It is quite clear that Dering was not prepared to go the length which his adopted Bill suggested. If his own report of his speech on this occasion may be altogether depended upon, which from internal evidence seems a little questionable, he introduced into it various qualifications of his proposal which mark the unsettlement of his own mind, and when he subsequently published his speech, he took credit to himself for the faintness with which he had commended his own proposal.[a] After a little calm consideration, and when the remonstrances of friends had come to the aid of the uncertainty, or perhaps rather of the certainty, of his own adverse opinions, the position in which he had placed himself became apparent.

What was to be done? A bad man would have thrown himself into the vortex, towards which he had descended, regardless of the warnings of friends or the reproaches of conscience. A coward would have fled from the mischief he had inadvertently done. A wise man would have accepted the mistake as a proof of incompetency for occupying a leading position, and on a proper opportunity would have partially retired. Dering was none of these. To have continued in such a course would have been monstrous to him. Cowardice was no part of his nature. The wisdom of partial withdrawal probably never occurred to him. He sealed his ruin as a politician,—his ruin every way,—by determining on the earliest possible occasion to contend, in the face of his speeches and his Bill, that his intention had never been to abolish Bishops, but merely to reform their offices; not to get rid of them, but to reduce their greatness to a presumed primitive model.

The Bill he had introduced was for a time laid aside. It was not until a month after its introduction that he found an opportunity

a Speeches, p. 3.

to explain his meaning. When he did so, the whole aspect of affairs towards him, both in and out of the House, was at once changed. Within, he found himself arrayed against the very men by whom he had lately been courted, and to whom he had been giving his support, men greatly his superiors in intellect and perseverance, no less conscientiously convinced on their own side of these questions than he himself was on his, and of far more sturdy and unyielding temperament. As before he had taken one side of the house by surprise, now he took the other. Some he says expostulated, others condemned, some advised, others would seem to condole. Without the House, no man now cried God bless him; he was stigmatized as a renegade and a pervert, and all his popularity was at an end.

Thus began a quarrel which was fatal to him. Once in opposition to the movers in this great controversy, points of divergence soon multiplied, and Sir Edward lost no opportunity to proclaim his disagreement. One of his most celebrated published speeches, although never actually spoken, was in favour of bowing the knee on the occurrence of the name Jesus in divine service. That which he had before stigmatised as one of the recently introduced novelties he now solemnly upheld, and declared that it was horror to him to think of its non-observance. Another of his most celebrated speeches was upon the subject of the Grand Remonstrance,[a] on which he took his stand in direct opposition to the movement party. On this occasion he made a speech which Pym thought it right to answer, and which we shall find that Sir Edward was subsequently pleased to bring under the notice of the King. As to his late friends of the Root and Branch party, a paper published in this volume shows to

[a] See, for this speech and Pym's reply, Mr. Forster's admirable volume on the Grand Remonstrance, pp. 289, 303.

what extremity of anger against them he soon ascended. He vowed
that he would never cease to oppose them, by word, by writing, and
by prayer.

Painfully alive to his change of position, he had recourse in
January, 1641-2, to a device which at that time was novel. One or
two of his speeches had been published without his concurrrence,
and had been extensively read. He determined to collect and
publish all those, either spoken or intended to be spoken, which
related to matters of religion, with the addition of a running vin-
dicatory commentary, the object of which was to prove that he had
never belonged to the party of the Root and Branch, and that his
conscience and his tongue had ever been in accord. A letter
written at this time to his wife proves with what avidity pamphlets
of this kind were read, and shews something of Sir Edward's then
present public position.

Sir Edward Dering to his wife.
[Surrenden MS. 24 January, 1641-2.]

My deare sweet heart, Comming late in, and Richard to have my letter
away presently, I must desire leave to be briefer then I would be. I had
so strongly received hope of seeing thee heere that itt troubles me now to
loose my joyous expectation. Too morrow is a physick day for Betty, and
perhaps the last. I hope they (my Lady Darell and Sir John) do not look
for any ceremonious shew of love from her, he using so little, indeed too
little, and too little civility, in not seeing my sister Cornwallys * after she
had knighted him, which she complaynes of in a letter to me. If, occa-
sionally, you can touch him for itt, well ; his parting heere was course
also.

Feare not the extreamityes of the time. Before danger do grow dreadfull,
I shall not fayle to be with thee, but do not perplex thy selfe and me with
more selfe-accusing of thy selfe then needes.

* Eliza, wife of Sir Frederick Cornwallis. She was a daughter of Sir John Ashburnham,
and sister of Sir Edward's late wife. She held an office in the Queen's Household.

You write of a speech of Mr. Hamden's, but no word of itt was sayd heere, nor of that poore phrases ascribed to Sir Benjamin Rudyard. I have moved for meetings, but can gett none.

I have not pursued nor do intend the Leuitenancy of the Tower. If I did, I think I might have itt.

My speech you write of [a] crept out from his fellowes by stealth. Some faultes are in itt. The rest will all out about Tuesday, viz. to morrow seavenight. This evening I received two letters from my sister Cornwallys ; in one these words, "I was yesternight (which was Thursday night last) much pleased with hearing my Lord Marquesse Hertford speak your prayses to the King and Queen, who as readily confirmed them. Itt was occasioned by your speech, which the Marquess had given to the King in the afternoon, and the King gave itt to the Prince's tutor to read to the Queen, and said he wondred they did print any thing so good, and both their Majestys did highly prayse itt. I gave the Marquesse thanks, &c."

The other letter was in answer of one from me, wherein I signifyed some passages of the time heere. She writes :—"I told the Queen the effect of your letter, and gave itt the King to read. He swore your speech and this both witnesse an honest heart." So much for courtship; but I will be thy country-fellow again.

I am almost tyred out with swimming against the streame, but I am silent allmost of late. If I and my birth-day cannot bring thee up, nothing will.

There are above forty-five hundred of that speech sold, and more in printing: never any thing sold like that.

Your provision was bestowed as you wish.

The King stays att Windsor, and means to pursue the five gentlemen in a legal way. [He is] in greate necessitys, but the Court, I hear, [did fall?] yesterday very full.

I cannot write to little Poll now. God's blessing and my heartes love to thee and them.

From thine,

24 Jan. 1641. EDWARD DERING.

[a] Probably his speech on the Remonstrance.

Itt comes into my head that if you come up the charge will be but half a journey, for I must be att the rest of the charge to send the girle downe.

> To my best and dearest, the Lady Dering,
> att Surrenden Dering.

As soon as Sir Edward Dering's volume of his collected speeches was completed at the press, which was a few days earlier than the preceding letter gave promise of, two copies of it were sent to Lady Cornwallis. The use she put them to appears in the following letter :—

ELIZA LADY CORNWALLIS TO SIR EDWARD DERING.

[Surrenden MS. 3 February, 1641-2.]

Dear Brother,—I reseuede your letter and too Books, for which I gife you kinde thanks. His Majestie hade one to reede, the Marquis of Harforde the other, hoo approufs rite well of them, and I think wondringe wheare the offens lis. The King was smillinge at your enttry and clous, which shurly thay licke not, nor have not much reson, being a smarte truth. But I hope, brother, the worst of your suffrings are paste, and that you will be very well aquite of this and all troble, for your just desirs to God, your King, and conttry can neuer want consolation. Onely I feare your Lady and Jepeie will bee fritted and troubbled at the hering of it, but I hope not when they know the cas. My saruis to them I pray when you see them, for I feare I shall not a greate whils, for thay say the Quene is presently going for Holland, and I have not scene some of my barns this too years. God helpe me, but it tis a time of all afflicktion to all. I pray God in his good time to amend it, and, if it bee his good pleasure, gife us a happye meeting, to the joy of me, your trw louing sister,

> and humble saruante,
>
> E. CORNWALLIS.

I hade the eill lucke to make Capten Connisby stay to lounge. I thanke you, sir, for the fauor of your letter. I shoud it to the King.

I was one nite in towne, and thout to asseene Betty, but coulde not, nore my ounc litle barne nether. Winsor, the 3 of February, 1641.

Winsor affords noe better pappar.

Sweet brother, make my excus to Capten Connisby for my not seing him; for I was abede, and thout it not feete to make him stay lounger, ore send him my letter with thout seing him, for it wantted only scalling.

> For my deere brother Sir Edward Deringe,
> knite and barranete, these.

Sir Edward Dering's collection of his speeches, and more especially the running commentary with which he accompanied them, cannot be read without seeing that the object of the book was not simply his own vindication. He was aggressive as well as exculpatory; or perhaps, rather, he strove to justify himself by damaging the party of Pym and Hampden. The time of publication was critical in the extreme. The confusion occasioned by the King's demand of the Five Members was just then at its height.[a] Both parties were eying each other in anticipation of the near approach of another description of struggle. The King was surprised, as we have seen, that any thing so " good," in his sense of that word, was at that time permitted to pass the press. His Majesty's judgment was formed on seeing only a separate copy of one speech, probably that on the Remonstrance; but his surprise was well founded, and not less so the glee with which he read " the entry and close," of the completed book. The persons whom Dering desired to depreciate viewed the book precisely in the same manner, but not with the same pleasure, as the King. Even before it was actually published, a committee of the House of Commons, formerly appointed to consider the subject of unauthorised printing with reference to the somewhat similar case of Lord Digby, and of which committee Sir Edward Dering

---

[a] No better account of this confusion has ever been published than that in Sir Edward's letter of the 13th January, 1641-2, printed in this volume at p. 66.

was a member,[a] was directed to meet on the morrow and consider Sir Edward's volume.[b] This order was made on the 20th of January, 1641-2. Whether the committee reported or not does not appear; probably it did. On the following 4th February, the Book again came under the consideration of the House. Sir Edward was present in his seat. "Divers passages" were pointed out to him, and he was heard in answer and explanation. Finally, the book was voted to be against the honour and privilege of the House, and scandalous to it, and was ordered to be burned—that poor mode of confutation, borrowed from the old custom in cases of presumed heresy—by the hands of the common hangman, in Westminster, Cheapside, and Smithfield. It was further resolved, that Sir Edward should be disabled to sit as a member of the House during that parliament, and the speaker was directed to issue his warrant for a new election for Kent. All this passed without opposition. It was then moved that Sir Edward should be sent to the Tower. On a division the question was carried in the affirmative by a majority of 85 to 61.[c] He remained in custody until the 11th February, when he was discharged on his own petition.[d]

Of his temper and feelings after his discharge the paper printed in this volume, and before alluded to, contains ample evidence. "As for Root and Branch," he remarks, "I am resolved by word and by writing to do you all the mischief I can, and I make no doubt but that my book and I shall do you more mischief out of the House than if I were still among you." With this bitter feeling in his heart he retired into Kent, and in fulfilment of his pledge began almost immediately to bestir himself. At the assizes, in the following month, he procured a number of his political friends to join him on the Grand Jury, and by their assistance succeeded in

[a] Commons' Journ., ii. 136.
[b] Ibid. p. 387.
[c] Ibid. vol. iii. p. 411.
[d] Ibid. p. 426.

carrying, against a stout opposition, a decidedly anti-Hampden and
Pym petition to the House of Commons.[a] The facts being reported
to the House by one of the persons who sate on the Grand Jury,
the House summoned Dering and the other leaders to appear before
them. Sir Edward delayed, but at length obeyed the summons.
His appearance was registered, but he slipped away before interrogatories could be prepared for his examination, addressing a letter
to his brother-in-law, Sir Henry Gibbes, one of the members, to
excuse his flight. The House of Commons procured an order to
stop the ports, with a view to his arrest, and shortly afterwards
carried up to the House of Lords an impeachment against him,[b] probably for conspiracy to raise the county of Kent against the Parliament.

For some months after this time he is thought to have lived in
seclusion in the neighbourhood of Surrenden, which had become
his seat by the death of his father; and to this period may be
assigned a story which is commonly told of him, that, to lay asleep
the vigilance of some officer of the Parliament, Sir Edward
donned a surplice, and read prayers in a neighbouring church
before a congregation of his friends and neighbours.[c]

We next hear of him at Nottingham at the setting up of the
royal standard in August, 1642. Sir Edward raised a regiment of
horse at his own expense, and was among the first to obey the royal
summons. The portrait which, through the liberality of the present
head of the house, Sir Edward Cholmeley Dering, graces the present
volume, exhibits Sir Edward in his martial character. In the back
ground is represented a military action upon a bridge, which,
bearing in mind the brief period of Sir Edward's service, can
scarcely refer to any other encounter than that which took place at
Powick near Worcester, on the 23rd September, 1642. It was the
first occasion on which the cavalry of the two parties crossed swords.

[a] Ibid. p. 502.
[b] Comm. Journ. pp. 507, 511, 513, 514, 533, 535, 536, 537.   [c] Nalson, ii. 249.

The parliamentarians were advancing towards Worcester. In a dashing charge Prince Rupert drove them back in confusion over Powick bridge, and finally put them to ignominious flight. Clarendon mentions the action as one which proved of unspeakable advantage to the King and rendered the name of Prince Rupert " very terrible." (Hist. Rebell. lib. vi.) Round his waist, loosely wrapped, after the manner of a sash, Sir Edward wears what seems to be a flag of some kind ornamented with *fleurs-de-lys*. Two conjectures have been made as to the meaning of this remarkable decoration. One finds its explanation in an armorial atchievement for Sir Edward certified by Segar, who was Garter in the time of James I. In this representation of the Dering arms, the mantle in which the shield is placed is sable, lined or, semé of *fleurs-de-lys* sable, probably in allusion to the bearing of a family named Pluckley, whose arms the Derings quartered. The other conjecture is, that the sash was probably a trophy taken by Sir Edward, and hastily folded round his person whilst the fight was going on. The arms represented in the picture are, 1. Dering, anciently De Morinis. 2. Dering. 3. D'Ipre. 4. Badlesmere. 5. Bohun; and 6. Pennington. The collar of SS is observable as a late example of its use by a private gentleman. The pendant badge is no doubt intended for that of the order of Baronets. The portrait represents Sir Edward as a handsome man of middle age, intelligent, gentle, kindly, but with perhaps something of a touch of womanly softness in the expression of his long oval countenance. Particular attention has evidently been paid to the collar, the hair, the armour, and the sword-hilt. Probably this was characteristic. We should judge Sir Edward to have been nice in his dress and personal ornaments, and attentive to all the proprieties of costume. The portrait is indeed in all respects intended to be that of a true cavalier.[a]

---

[a] The original is at Surrenden. Our etching, which is an admirable representation of it, is the work of Mr. Herbert L. Smith.

But that was a character which can scarcely be claimed on behalf of Sir Edward Dering. In heart he was but faintly attached to the side of the great contest which he had been driven by his unhappy blundering to assume, and a few months' experience of the hardships and difficulties of actual warfare convinced him how little that way of life was suited to his taste or his physical powers. His letters from 1639 make mention of his suffering from almost continual headache. The fatigues of soldiership aggravated the tormenting ailment. The pain extended to one of his shoulders, with such violence that he could not lift his hand to his head. For all military action he was soon entirely disabled.

Whilst the armies of the King and Parliament were first engaged on a great scale at Edge Hill, Sir Edward was striving to make his peace with the House of Commons. From some place probably in London, where he was hiding from the spies or agents of the opposite party, he applied to Sir Richard Skeffington to pave the way with the Parliament for his permitted return. Sir Richard replied, in a letter addressed by way of blind to Lady Dering at Surrenden, that he had made Mr. P[ym?] acquainted with Sir Edward's letter. He was much joyed at it, and was very willing to secure Sir Edward, provided he would " render himself, or make some submission by letter to him."[a] The terms were probably too mortifying to be then submitted to; but after six months' service he obtained the King's

[a] Letter in Surrenden Collection, which is altogether of so great importance that it will be best to give it as it stands. " Deare Cosin, This Tusday night at 5 a clock I made Mr. P. acquainted with your letter. Hee is very willing to secure you, and is much joyed with your letter, and so am I in my hart. But you must first render yourselfe, or make some submission by your letter to him, that thereupon hee may move the Houso in your behalfe. This is all I can do in these buisie times. Things are not so bad with our armies upon Sunday's fight as wee heard them. The Lord Linsse his son, Lunsforde, Vaviser, and Ashurnam taken prisoners. The[y] begane on Monday again to fight, but the certen effect of that day and this wee heare not. I besecch the Lord to bring peace out of warre and stanch our bleeding woounds. And thus, with my hartie affection unto you and your Lady, I rest yours assured to my power, R. Skeff. [P.S.] Pardon my last and excuse mee if I come not yett to you. [2nd P.S.] Excuse my haste and scribling.

permission to resign his regiment and retire from active service. The question now was whither could he go? His estate had been sequestered, Surrenden had been four times plundered by the parliamentary soldiers, " his goods and stock " had been seized and taken away, his farm houses and fences destroyed, his woods felled, and his rents abated.[a] Under these circumstances, it is said that he strangely applied to the King for a grant of the Deanery of Canterbury,[b] one of the very dignities which he had moved to abolish. One does not very well see how he could have derived any advantage from the appointment, Canterbury at that time being in the hands of the Parliament; but one fact gives a colour of probability to the statement, which is, that his relative [c] Dr. Isaac Bargrave, Dean from 1625, died in January, 1642-3,[d] just at the moment when, if any profit could have been made out of the deanery, it must have most suited the circumstances of Sir Edward Dering to have procured it. The King, it is added, refused the request, as it was very right in him to do.

Sir Edward's ultimate course must have been in every way most distressing to him. On 30 January, 1643-4, the Parliament issued a Declaration permitting persons who had been in arms against them to return to their homes, upon taking the Covenant, and paying a composition for the restoration of their estates. Sir Edward Dering, who was with the King at Oxford at that time, was the first person who petitioned to take the benefit of this Declaration. The permission was granted.[e] He submitted to the conditions, and returned into Kent in February, 1643-4, at liberty, but, as he himself said, it was the liberty of starving in good company—that of his wife and children. Until the amount of his composition could be settled with the proper authorities, he was not permitted to inhabit Surrenden, nor was he put

[Dated] This Tusday night, 8 a clock. [Addressed] To my much honnored Lady Deering, att Surnden in Kent, give these with speed I pray you. [Indorsed by Sir Edward Dering.] 8 [a mistake for 25th] Octob. 1642. Sir Richard Skeffington.

[a] Sprotti Chron. ed. Hearne, p. xlv. [b] Nalson, ii. 249.
[c] See post, p. 7. [d] Le Neve's Fasti, ed. Hardy, i. 33.
[e] Comm. Journ. iii. 390.

into possession of his estates, but he found refuge in one of his own ruinous farm-houses. He lived there in the extremest poverty,[a] whilst the question of his composition was in agitation. It had to be settled by a local committee, and afterwards to be confirmed by Parliament. The former body returned the value of his estates at 800*l.* per annum, and recommended the payment of 1,000*l.* as composition; an amount considerably less in proportion than in the majority of similar cases, perhaps in consideration of the great damage done to his estates whilst under sequestration. The 1,000*l.* was confirmed by the House of Commons on the 27th July, 1644, but before that day Sir Edward had passed beyond the jurisdiction of sequestrators and committee-men. He had found a quiet resting-place in the church of Pluckley. The disease in his head, which is stated to have been an imposthume, terminated his melancholy career on the previous 22nd June. On a representation of the circumstances to the Parliament, the composition-money was forborne, and the young heir admitted to his estates without any payment.[b]

It is unnecessary for us to attempt any summary of the character of Sir Edward. In peaceable times the " *uberrima omnigenæ eruditionis copia,*" which is commemorated on his monument in Pluckley church, would have made him usefully and honorably distinguished. In the days in which he lived, nothing sufficed to carry any man through life with safety, but steadiness and perseverance in a settled and conscientious course. To be uncertain, or to waver, from whatever motives, was to be lost. So many persons found it, and among them few were more to be pitied than SIR EDWARD DERING.

JOHN BRUCE.

5, *Upper Gloucester Street, Dorset Square,*
    7 *November,* 1861.

---

[a] Sprotti Chron. ed. Hearne, p. xlv.   [b] Commons' Journ. iii. 603.

PROCEEDINGS,

PRINCIPALLY IN THE COUNTY OF KENT,

IN CONNECTION WITH THE

TWO PARLIAMENTS CALLED IN 1640.

———————————

I.

Letter from Sr EDWARD DERING, Bart, to Sr ROGER TWYSDEN, Bart, of Roydon Hall, in East Peckham, inviting him to stand for the County of Kent, in the New Parliament.*

1639,
15 Car. I.

HONOURABLE SIR,

    I have wanted a letter from you, and you have wanted mine, but the reason hath beene, because I have had a daely resolution to come over to you. Now, I am called so earnestly eastward that I cannot (as I entended) be with you, being immediately for Canterbury.

    I were guilty of a weak freindship if I did not lett you knowe that, heering of a Parliament (att the first by my casuall being att Dovor), I did, with some easterne freindes, then, and next day, name you for a knight's service to the house, which

20 December.

———

* This is not the letter itself, but the original draught of it.

was received with a cheerefull desire. Beleeve me, heere is in these partes a very strong party indisposed, nor will they take any impression (for aught I can discerne) for them who stand; onely Mr Knatchbull hath good strength. You are doubly pretious with them now, once in your self, and againe in being obliged to particular greate ones above. Itt shall not be vanity with so neare a freind to say, that I have had from the meny many serious and hearty invitements; but I hope to appeare in that court in a lower sphere. In the meane time, I observe a most free alacrity of voyces for your selfe, if you would but owne them. You are better beloved then your modesty will suffer you to beleeve. If you be not fettered beyond all freedome, appeare for your selfe.* If you love Mr Treasurer† perswad his desistance. Sr Tho. Walsingham‡ and Sr George Sondes§ have left many more voyces free then they have taken. If Mr Treasurer should desist, joyne with Mr Knatchbull. If you be not sure of a burgesse place, you shall be guilty of a greate fault not to owne the country which seekes after you. If you desire to speak with me I shall come home on Christmas eve, and, on Saterday following, will attend you att Peckham. In the meane while, lett me heere something from you. I shall leave one to bring itt into East Kent. I hope, att the least, you are sure of Ry, or Winchelsea; ‖ send me word else.

* These expressions seem to imply that Sir Roger Twysden was deemed to be tied hand and foot to his cousin-german Sir Henry Vane, whose mother was sister to Sir William Twysden, Sir Roger's father:—

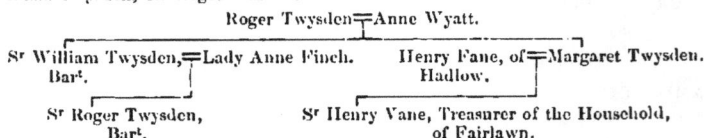

Roger Twysden⹋Anne Wyatt.

Sr William Twysden,⹋Lady Anne Finch.　　　Henry Vane, of⹋Margaret Twysden.
Bar^t.　　　　　　　　　　　　　　　　　Hadlow.

Sr Roger Twysden,　　　　　　Sr Henry Vane, Treasurer of the Household,
Bar^t.　　　　　　　　　　　　　　of Fairlawn.

† i. e. Sir Henry Vane of Fairlawn, Treasurer of the Household.

‡ Sir Thomas Walsingham, of Scadbury, in Chislehurst.

§ Sir George Sondes, of Throwley.

‖ Sir Roger sat for Winchelsea in the parliament of 1625.

Hearty service to your noble lady and your selfe from my other selfe and from me.

1639.
15 Car. I.

Your affectionate and ever faithfull cosen* that loves you,

E. D.

Surrenden Dering,
20 December, Friday morning, 1639.

[Endorsed by Sir Edward Dering, "1639. To Sr RogerTwisden, 26 Dec."†]

II.

Letter from Sr ROGER TWYSDEN to Sr EDWARD DERING in reply, canvassing him for the Treasurer of the Household Sr Harry Vane.

NOBLE SIR,‡

As to some other of my very worthy friends, so am I much bound to your self for this your kind invytation, who must confesse I can not tell any way how to deserve it, though I never will fayle of doing the best service I can to the country whenever they call me to it; but the truth is, I am at this tyme all together ingaged to doe to the Treasurer, who is named, the best I can in it; and I should bee sory (if he or any of hys stand) they should not cary it, but with out all opposition, and therefore am resolved never at all to appear, where there may bee any contestation with such a friend,

24 December.

* They were second cousins:—

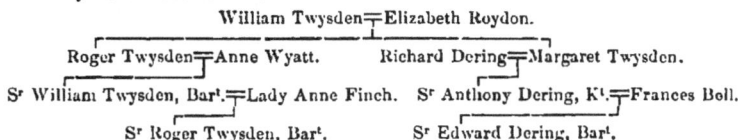

William Twysden⸗Elizabeth Roydon.

Roger Twysden⸗Anne Wyatt.   Richard Dering⸗Margaret Twysden.

Sr William Twysden, Bart.⸗Lady Anne Finch.   Sr Anthony Dering, Kt.⸗Frances Boll.

Sr Roger Twysden, Bart.   Sr Edward Dering, Bart.

† Sir Edward had originally written "20 Decr.," which was subsequently altered to "26th Decr." The date at the foot of the letter is "20th Decr.," which, by the context, it palpably must have been.

‡ Vide note, No. III. p. 5, infra.

who I doe know hath as true an hart to God and the kingdom's good as any they can bestow it on.   And I would bee glad hee might have that pledge of affection from us that wee thought hym so; but I think that hee stands is rather hys friends desires then any declaration is made by hymself to any as yet.   I am not provyded for of any other place; for Winchelsea I have laboured to get my brother Thom,* but I know not with what successe it will bee.   If the Treasurer give out, I am free, and there will bee tyme enough to speak of it, for the Parlyament beegins not tyll the 13 Aprill,† nor will the writs bee out tyll 1 March; but where you speak of coming over hyther (though with an if) on Saturday, I intreat you, if it please you, to doe me that favor; or rather, beecause I feare if it bee on Saturday you will bee going on Munday, defer your journey tyl Munday, and stay to goe on Saturday.   Wee shall spend the tyme in reading, walking, or somewhat else that will beeguile it; and I doubt not but to give you suche reasons for the Tresurer's election as shall with willingnesse perswade you to interest all your friends. I can not in this winter dead season seeke my ladies company, to whom all wee desire to be rememberd, and in some better tyme of the year shall hold our selves favord if shee will look on us.   Your man much hasts to goe back this night a very long journey, which makes me break of, only adding that this is the hand of your

poore kinsman that truly loves you,

ROGER TWYSDEN.

If you take so much paynes as to visit your affectionate cosen,‡ pray bring your history of William Thorne,§ and I will shew you an

---

* Thomas Twisden, for so he spelt his name, Sir Roger's brother. He was not returned to this Parliament. On the Restoration, being then a serjeant-at-law, he was made a judge, and was appointed one of the commissioners for the trial of the Regicides. He was created a baronet in 1666.   His seat was Bradbourne in East Malling.

† Sir Roger makes a mistake here.   Parliament was summoned for the 3d April, 1640.

‡ " Cosen," vide note, p. 3.

§ Thorne, a monk of St. Augustine's, Canterbury, in the 14th century.   His history here alluded to was published by Sir Roger Twysden in his *Decem Scriptores*.

old MSS. sometyme of the same Abbeys, conteyning many prety Miscellaneas, writ about Ed. 3 hys tyme, out of which perhaps Thorn took some part of hys History.   Mr Knatchbull is an honest gentleman, and I beeleeve will have many voyces, both for hys oun worth, and S^r Ed. Scot's sake.

1639.
15 Car. I.

     [Superscription.]
To my honourable good friend Sr Edward Deering,
    at hys howse at Surrenden in Pluckley.

[Endorsed by Sr Edward Dering, "24 (? 26) Decr. 1639.   Sr Roger Twisden."]

III.

Note of Sir ROGER TWYSDEN relating to Electioneering Manœuvres in the County of Kent.

[Among the MSS. at Roydon Hall* was a note relating to this election so illustrative of the preceding letters, and so interesting in itself, that I cannot refrain from subjoining it.]

Memorandum.—The 16th of March, $163\frac{9}{40}$, I was chosen knight of this shire for the parliament summoned to beegin the 13th of Aprill following; which, beecause it was carryed with great contestation between my self and a neere kinsman of myne, Sr Edward Deryng of Pluckley, I have for posterytys sake thought good a little to note the manner of the carying of it.

When first the speech of a parlyament so long expected beegan, about the end of Mychaelmas terme 1639, many men were spoken

* Now in my possession. This Note of Sir Roger Twysden's is so strictly illustrative of the preceding letters, and so interesting in itself, that I venture to insert it here, although it has already been printed in the charming biography which my valued and accomplished friend Mr. Kemble inserted in his learned preface to Sir Roger's Treatise on the Government of England.

of as fit to stand to bee knights for Kent.   Amongst the rest, myselfe
was invyted to be one, which I declyned, as beeing a matter of great
expence, and indeede not thinking the country would chuse me ; so
I ever put it off as alltogether unworthy of it, yet professing I would
bee most glad to doe the country all service.   Some weeke after
this, Sʳ Henry Vane, the treasurer of hys Majestys howsehold, my
cosen germin, came to hys howse at Fayrlane,* and opened hymself
so far unto me that hee had a purpose of standing for it, that I
promised hym all the assistance lay in me, knowing hym a man
truly devoted to God and hys countryes good, and that had perswaded the King to this course.   And so I exprest myself unto hym
that I did not doe it with the least intentyon hee should diminish in
ought the religion now establisht by law, nor the liberties of the
subject ; beesides, he promised me, that if hee were knight of the
shire, I should serve in that burges place which he, as a pryvy
counsellor, would not bee destytute of, in which I could doe my
country as much service as in this or any other, all being equall
in the howse.   Trwly the common people had been so bytten with
shippe money they were very averse from a courtyer.   I dealt with
all my neighbours effectually, and had promis of many, yet could I
not bee confident of hys beeing elected ; I did therefore think the
best way of facilitating it was to get all elce but hymself and one
more sit downe.   Mʳ Knatchbul of Mersham Hatch, Sʳ George
Sonds, and Sʳ Thomas Walsingham, did stand from the beeginning ;
all these but the first, who had the greatest vote from the beeginning,
out of their affectionat respect to Mʳ Treasurer, sate downe, beeing
both deputy lieutenants.   Sʳ Edward Dering had at the first writ to
me to stand to bee one myself, which I refused, and gave hym all
the arguments lay in my power for doing so ; afterward, coming to
London, finding hym there, I did with strong importunyty presse hym
to bee for Sʳ Hary Vane, and did then conceive hym as firme for

* In Wrotham.

hym **as** any man; and, if the affirming hee was a little ingaged to 1639. 15 Car. I. Sr Thomas Walsingham, and a profession he held the Treasurer a fitter man to doe the country good, that he would not stand hymself, but would doe reason, yet he could not absolutely give a promis tyl the assizes, becaus 16 gentlemen of them had affirmed sollemnly he was not one that did beefore that ingage hymselfe any way, and this on assurance Sr Thomas Walsingham would sit downe—if, I say, all these were tyes, it is most true hee had promised me to bee for Sr Henry Vane.

At the assizes Sr Henry Vane writ unto me to understand the sence of the country. I went thither, as satisfyed he would be chosen without opposition, seeing Sr George Sonds and Sr Thomas Walsingham, out of respect to him, sate downe, as ever I did anything in my life; but, coming thither, I found Sr Edward Dering speak more cooly of it then I expected; after supper there was certainly some pryvate consultation beetween hym, Mr George Stroude of Westram, and Isack Bargrave,* Dean of Canterbury; and the next day a resolution publisht that he would stand. I must needes remember that, beeing prest in my hearing to say whether he would stand or not, he, the first night, sayd he could not tell; it seemes he resolved on it that night.

I tooke this so unkindly, to see so little respect of that which I tooke hym to have promised me to assist me in the atteyning of, for a kinsman allmost as neere hym † as myself, I could not refrain myself, but told hym of it very playnly, and acquainted Mr Treasurer with all the proceedings, who instantly resolved not to stand hymself, but writ to me, with all the rest of hys friends heerabouts, to set up

---

* Dean Bargrave married a first cousin of Sir Edward Dering's father, Sir Anthony :—

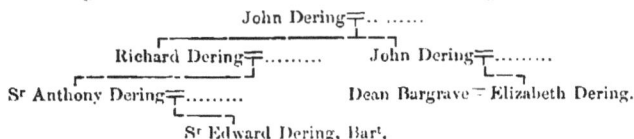

John Dering⊤.. ......
Richard Dering⊤........   John Dering⊤........
Sr Anthony Dering⊤........   Dean Bargrave ⊤ Elizabeth Dering.
Sr Edward Dering, Bar^t.

† Both were cousins of Sir Henry Vane, but by different lines :—Sir Roger Twys-

myself and oppose Dering. This was a troublesome taske; all the gentlemen of Kent were ingaged already for Knatchbull. Dering, after the assizes, did never lye still, but ride up and downe solliciting every body, yea, such as were for Sr Henry Vane he strove to get a promis of, that, he giving out, they should bee for hym. What should I doe? To publish to friends by letter that I intended to stand was to meet with a certayn denyall from them whose assistance I desired. I could doe no more but this, to give out to my friends that if I were chosen I should take it for a great favor, and doe the country all service lyeth in my power; that I could not conceive they would chuse so worthlesse a man as myself am, and such like; but never write or send purposely to any man for to procure me any voyces.

IV.

Letter to Sr EDWARD DERING, from GEORGE STRODE, Esqr, promising his support.*

NOBLE SIR,

2 September.

I conceave you doe your selfe a great deale of right in resuminge your pretencon (which in my aprehencon was most unequally carried in the last election). I have found an ill health since I sawe you, and to worse it with a fall lately taken in Sussex,

den was first cousin to Sir Henry Vane, and Sir Edward Dering and Sir Henry were second cousins, *i. e.* children of first cousins:—

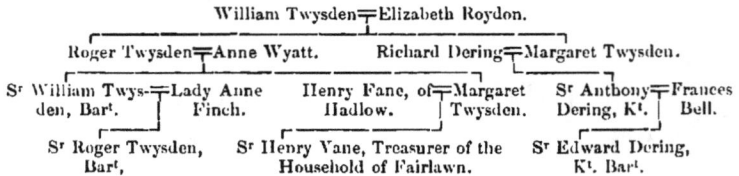

William Twysden=Elizabeth Roydon.

Roger Twysden=Anne Wyatt.   Richard Dering=Margaret Twysden.

Sr William Twys-=Lady Anne   Henry Fane, of=Margaret   Sr Anthony=Frances
den, Bar^t.   Finch.   Hadlow.   Twysden.   Dering, K^t.   Bell.

Sr Roger Twysden,   Sr Henry Vane, Treasurer of the   Sr Edward Dering,
Bar^t,   Household of Fairlawn.   K^t. Bar^t.

* Though not so specified, it is evident that this promise is with reference to his election as knight of the shire to the Parliament summoned for the 3rd Nov.

and doupt my abilletye sodainly to ride, which is the cause of my not attendinge the sessions.

I wilbe ingaged for noe man in the county but Sr Edward Deringe, and I will imploye my sonne to supplie my place in doinge you service.

I may promise noe farther, but as soone Sr Jno Cullpeper as any other; you will discover the designe at the sessions, and bee assured of him that is

Your reall freinde and redy servant,

George Strode.*

Squerries, the 2d of Sept. 1640.

My service to your noble lady.

[Superscription.]
To my ever honored friende Sr Edward Deringe, Barronett,
at his howse these presente.

Surenden.

[Endorsed by Sir Edward Dering—" 1640. 5 Oct.   Mr Strode."]

V.

Letter to Sr EDWARD DERING, from Sr PETER HEYMAN,
promising his support.

Noble Sir,

Till this morninge, I heard nothing of any matter wherin good fortune might make me fitt for an ingagement to doe yow

---

* George Strode, Esq. of Squerries, in Westerham, afterwards knighted; he was a fellow-sufferer with Sir Roger Twysden, Mr. Richard Spencer, and Sir Edward Dering, from the wrath of the Parliament against the promoters of the Kent Petition, and was imprisoned for it, with them, in March, 1642.   Sir George Strode is in the list of the unfortunate victims who had to compound for their estates, for which he had to pay 2,814l. Mr. Spencer had to compound at 300l.; Sir Roger Twysden, at 1,700l.

1640.
16 Car. I.

service ; but if now your occasion require any neighbourlike respect, I shalbe reddy to doe it, when tyme and place shall require. And, for my sonns, I know not but yow may use them as your servants, and my self as your frend, and respective neighboure.

PET. HEYMAN.*

29 7bris, 1640.

[Superscription.]
To my honored frend, Sr Edwarde Derynge,
Knight and Baronet, these.

[Seal.]   A Traveller with Cornucopia on back.   Legend—" Copia fecit."

[Endorsed by Sr Edward Dering—" 1640.   29 Sept.   Sr Peter Heyman."]

VI.

Letter to Sr EDWARD DERING, from Sr EDWARD BOYS,
conditionally promising his support.

HONOURED SIR,

1 October.

I am ingaged unto two of my friends ; soe that yf they stand, I cannot goe from my promise ; but, yf either of them doe not stand, I wilbe for one of my voices for you.   I am perswaded that neither of them will appeare in it.   I have bin solicetted by some of my friends for Sr John Culpeper,* and have hade a letter from him selfe for that purpose ; but have given them a flat deniall. My son is not with me ; but I doe expect him very shortly.   I have

* This was Sir Peter Heyman, Knt. of Somerfeild, in Sellindge.   He had been member for Dover in the Short Parliament just dissolved.

† Sir John Colepeper, of Leeds Castle, the Royalist faithful unto death ; afterwards created by Charles I. Lord Colepeper.   He was returned, with Sir Edward Dering, as knight of the shire to this Parliament.

shewed Ned Swane your letter, who is very zealous for you. And thus, with my best respects, I rest

Your lovinge friend,

EDW. BOYS.*

8ber. 1, 1640.

[Superscription.]
For my honored friend Sr Edward Dearinge,
Knight & Barronet, presente these.

[Endorsed by Sr Edward Dering—" 1640. 3 Octob.   Sr Edw. Boys."]

VII.

Letter to Sr EDWARD DERING, from GEORGE HAULE, Esqr,
urging him to make his appearance at Maidstone.

NOBLE SIR,

Yf you intend to stand for one of the knights of the sheire, you must speedily appeere in these parts, either in person, or by letter. Sr John Culpeper† stands, and many here have passed their voces for him. Mr. Spenser‡ intends to stande; here are many very glad of it. Sr John Sydley§ stands for burgisse of our towne; he is very lickely to carrie it. I have spoken to some of our towne of you ; they wish they had your letter to publish; you will loose many by it else. I doubt Sr John

---

* Sir Edward Boys, of Betshanger, member for Dover in this Parliament.

† Sir John Colepeper, vide note p. 10.

‡ The Hon. Richard Spencer, second son of Robert Lord Spencer of Wormleighton ; he had a seat in Orpington, vide note p. 9.

§ Sir John Sedley, of St. Clere, in Ightham, Bart.; vide p. 12.

Culpeper's voices in these parts will not be very fast to you.   So in hast I rest,

Your servant to commande,

GEO. HAULE.*

[Superscription.]
To my honorable good frinde Sr Edw. Deeringe,
    Knight and Barronet, these.

[Seal.]   On a saltire 5 mullets, impaling a saltire.

[Endorsed by Sr Edward Dering—" 1640.   2 Octob.   Cosen† Hawle."

VIII.

Letter to Sr EDWARD DERING from Sr JOHN SEDLEY, promising his support, and asking Sr Edward's at Hythe, &c.

NOBLE SIR,

If you hadd not appeared, I was resolved to sitt quiett in my howse; but I cannot refuse your commands, assuringe you still the clayme of the choycest share in my affections, which that my active endeavors may the better manifest nothing shalbee wantinge within my spheare to support you from any thinge that is like a fall.   I hadd (before your letter arryved mee) engaged many of my freinds for you, and will doe more ; to bringe with them the same constancye, I intend to wayte on you with my selfe, at the election.

---

* George Haule, Esq. of Digons, in Maidstone, and Knight-Rider Street.
† He was cousin of Sir Edward Dering :—

Richard Dering⊤Margaret Twisden.

Sr Anthony Dering=Frances Bell.	Henry Haule, of Bigons alias Digons,=Jane Dering. in Maidstone.
Sr Edward Dering.	George Haule.

I fynde some of these parts, especially about Maydstone, so poysoned with faction, and so full of falshood and treachery, that I knowe not howe to judge of theyr integritye, unlesse I did see theyr hearts, which it were happy that some of them were anatomized to that purpose. Sʳ, I resolved (longe before the newes of this parliament), knowinge that within a whyle one there must bee, to appeare for one of theyr burgesses at Maydstone, havinge hadd the commande of that towne, as captayne, above 12 yeares, declyninge in the meane many overtures from my freinds of other places, that I myght with confydence have embraced; but, restinge there, and havinge obtayned such a free and full vote to mee to have carryed it for one undoubtedly, I went on Weddenesday last to Maydstone, to the nowe Mayor, to request but the curtesie hee denyeth not to any cobler or tynker that will solicitt him, to sweare mee a freeman of the towne, which hee refuse, seduced and perswaded to this unmannerly affront by Sʳ Francis Barnham,* whose malice, were it not in howrely machination buysyed against one or other, hee cowld not live; his plott beinge, as I discover, to sett upp there younge Sʳ Henry Vane,† Mʳ Treasurer's sonne, a courtyer as well as his father nowe, though lately, as you knowe, Governour at Newe Englande; and I thinke you will accompt it as unneighbourlye in younge Sir Henry Vane to embrace the motion (where he knewe I was preingaged) as malitious in Barnham to offer it; but Mʳ Treasurer pleaseth himselfe in this revenge on mee, for my profession at the last election to you, yett shall my freindshipp remayne imoveable where once desert hath fixed mee. Sʳ, I am nowe, by the mischeivous conspiracy of Barnham, cast asyde, that I feare my endeavours will come too supyne to any other place; yett I would desyre to knowe speedely from you, whether the townes of

---

* Sir Francis Barnham, of Holingbourne, to whom his brother-in-law Belknap Rudston (who had married his sister Anne) left the seat and estate of Boughton Monchensie, where Sir Francis Barnham's son Robert afterwards resided, having been created a Baronet by Charles II. Sir Francis himself resided at Holingbourne.

† The members who sat in this Parliament were, Sir Francis Barnham, Knt. and Sir Humphry Tufton, Knt.; so Sir Francis was probably manœuvring for himself.

Hythe and Rumney bee already fast engaged for all theyr burgesses,* and what interest you and Sr William Brockman have in
any of them, the which, if there shall bee any advantadge left, or
gappe yett open, to stake presently for mee; and, as I heare from
you, I shall make my speedy repayre thither. The writts bee not
yett come to [the] sherriffe, nor to any port towne. What nowe
remaynes is our heartyest services to your selfe and noble lady
attested by

       Your affectionate freinde and kinsman to serve you,
                         JOHN SEDLEY.

St. Cleere, in hast, 5 Octob. 1640.

                   [Superscription.]
To my honorable freinde and kinsman Sr Edward Deringe,
   Knight and Baronet, at Surrenden Deringe, present these
   speedily.

[Seal.] Quarterly.—1st. A fess wavy between 3 goat's heads erased; on the fess
a crescent for difference. [Sedley.]†   2nd. A bend, in sinister chief a leopard's
face. [Isaac.]   3rd. Ermine, on a chevron 3 escallop shells. [Grove.]   4th.
On a chevron 3 birds [magpies?—Holdich]; on fess point, the Ulster hand.

[Endorsed by Sr Edward Dering—"1640, 5 Octob.; Sr John Sedley."]

---

* With all his eagerness Sir John Sedley could find no place to have him. Not being
returned to Parliament, he lorded it over the county at sessions and magistrates'
meetings.

† William Sedley, of Southfleet,⊤Anne, d. and h. of Roger Grove,
        Sheriff of Kent 1589.   of London.

1.	2.	3.
John Sedley, of⊤Anne, dau. of John Colepe-per, of Ayles-ford. Southfleet, s. & h. ob. 1581.	Robert =Elizabeth, dau. of George Da-rell, of Cale Hill. Sedley.	Nicholas⊤Jane, d. & heir. of Edward Isaack, of Howlett's, in Beaksbourne. Sedley.
Sr William Sedley,⊤Elizabeth, dr. of Stephen Darell, of Spelmonden, and widow of Henry Lord Abergavenny. of the Friars, Ayles-ford, created Baro-net 1611.	Sr Isaac Sedley, of⊤......... d. and heir. Gt. Chart; created Bart. 1621; Sheriff 2 Car. I. of ...... Holdich, of Runworth, Norfolk.	
	Sr John Sedley, of St. Clere⊤.........	

1640.
16 Car. I.

IX.

Letter to Sr EDWARD DERING from Mr JOHN PLAYER * with Intelligence as to Electioneering Movements.

NOBLE SIR,

Your letters came to my hands this day, and I durst not 15 October.
be soe uncivil as not to returne my humble service to your selfe (though my infelicitie in writing would have witholden my penne), and thankes for your acceptance of my indeavours, which, besides fayttfullnesse, can have noe acceptablenesse. I heare daylie from abroad good and comfortable incouragement, upon letters to Canterbury, and elsewhere. As for that Westerne knight, Sr Robert,† his fame doth scarce reach us; his relations lesse affect these parts, and his assistants not soe powerfull with anye; what his confidence may be I know not, his hopes are like to prove desperate. For Sr John,‡ I heare of noe progresse greatlie, nor accrument to the indeavours this way; I think his friends know his utmost strength, which is like rather to decline to a consumption than anye healthy augmentation, for that hopes give to conceive not onely that prioritie which is soe much indeavoured, to fayle, but to think it his happiness (if it might be) to have a second. §

This afternoone it came to mine ears, that, in the Weale, Sr Roger Twisenden is voied much, and therefore (under correction) think it not amisse to advise whither (if not before, if he be not at Great

---

* In all probability this was the John Player who was Vicar of Kennington, the small parish next to Ashford, in 1643.

† This " Western Knight" was Sir Robert Mansell, vide p. 16.

‡ This, of course, is Sir John Colepeper, who was returned.

§ The writer's acknowledged "infelicity" in writing is exemplified in this incomprehensible sentence. The only sense I can pick out of it is that—"inasmuch as hopes give (*i. e.* allow us) to conceive, not only that he will fail in being at the head of the poll, for which such strong efforts are made, but that he may think himself lucky if he comes in second."

Chart,* as I heard he was latelie expected there) to take him in your iournye westward, to reinforce his affection to you, and renew your correspondenge, that soe you may perceive whither (as I am confident he hath not) he have anye thought. Your competitor's activitie will make your self and your well wellet vegelant. I should be glad that opportunitye might serve me to wayte on you; but, as this weeke I shall not, and next weeke cannot, by reason of business calling me westward as farre as London, yet, with purpos of returning before the choys, and, in the meane time, shall not fayle to adde my best indeavours that the truth it self, and such as love it, may rejoyce in you, and the honour of God by you, which he unfeinedlie wisheth, who is

　　　　　　　　Your humble servant,　　　　Jo. Player.

Ashford, Octob^r 15, 1640.

　　　　　　　[Superscription.]
To the honorable Sr Edward Dering, at his house
　　　Surenden Dering, present these.

[Seal, not armorial.]　A Bee or Fly.

[Endorsed by Sr Edward Dering—"1640, 15 Octob.　Mr Player."]

X.

Letter to Sr EDWARD DERING from Mr GEORGE STRODE about the Election, and his fear of being named Sheriff.

NOBLE SIR,

　　　　　I have yours by this bearer, and wee heare that all sitt downe but your selfe, Sr John Culpeper, and Mr Browne.‡　I have

---

　* Chelmington in Great Chart was the seat of the Twysdens before their acquisition of Roydon Hall by marriage with a coheiress of the Roydons.

　† (*sic*) Well-willers.

　‡ Probably Mr. Richard Browne, of Great Chart, who sat for Romney in this Parliament.

intreated the knight to leave me free untill the time. I doe allsoe
belive Mr Spencer* is quit of from the hops that the cuntry would
cast it uppon him; wee live not in such an age. S^r Ro. Mansell's
pretence was decayinge ere begone, and soe sodainly vaneshed. I
have a very great creeke in my backe that doth not suffer me to
ride on a horse; yf I am any whet better I may not fayle to wayte
on you. When not, my sonne shall (God willinge). I give out to
goe, and they shall knowe noe other.

I must now returne you a greater thanks for your love and care
of me in my perticuler. It is possible the Keeper† doe not love
me; I knowe he doth hate my brother; it may bee he expects that
I should use means unto him. Yf the parlament did sitte but two
months right ere the choyce of sherrives,‡ I might hope he could
doe me noe preiudice in that way. Yf things weare as they should
be, I would not much dispute it, and as they ar noe gratification
to bee kept of only on your kinde notice, I may use the mor diligence
to prevent a mischefe; yf I must be, I wish that I weare now in
place, to bee your servant at the county court; but I am very
confident that the cuntry heare eyther wilbe for you or not apeare.

1640
16 Car. I.

* Mr. Spencer, of Orpington, son of Lord Spencer of Wormleighton: vide p. 11,
note.

† The Lord Keeper was Sir John Finch, Lord Finch of Fordwich; he was son of Sir
Henry Finch (the brother of Sir Moyle Finch), and therefore first-cousin of Lady Anne
Twysden: his seat was the Moat, near Canterbury, now the property of Earl Cowper, but
neither mansion nor park remains. Flight saved him from the fate of Strafford and
Laud.

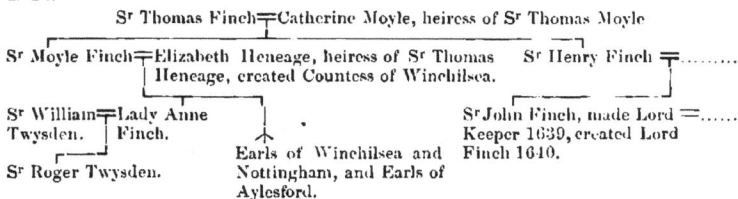

Sr Thomas Finch⊤Catherine Moyle, heiress of Sr Thomas Moyle

Sr Moyle Finch⊤Elizabeth Heneage, heiress of Sr Thomas   Sr Henry Finch ⊤.........
         Heneage, created Countess of Winchilsea.

Sr William⊤Lady Anne   S^rJohn Finch, made Lord ⊤......
Twysden. | Finch.   Keeper 1639, created Lord
                 Finch 1640.
Sr Roger Twysden.   Earls of Winchilsea and
              Nottingham, and Earls of
              Aylesford.

‡ He escaped the shrievalty. James Hugessen, Esq. of Sewards, in Linsted, was sheriff
the next year, and Strode never served the office.

1640.
16 Car. I.

My sonne will wayte on you in the feeld, and give you an acompt of his intencion of a second voyce. Trobled with nothinge mor then the feare that I cannot in person doe you the service I soe much desire, but that you would ever comand

Your humble servant,   GEORGE STRODE.

Squerries, the 19° 8ᵇᵉʳ, 1640.

[Superscription.]

To my ever honored freind Sʳ Edwarde Deringe, Baronet,
at his howse, these present.
Surenden Deringe.

[Endorsed by Sʳ Edward Dering—"1640, 20 Octob. Mʳ Strode."]

XI.

22 October.

Letter to Sʳ EDWARD DERING from Mʳ HUGESSEN * saying that he will attend with his son and tenantry to vote for him and Sʳ John Colpeper.

HONORID SIR,

Your Lettre by this bearer wel receaved, and, accordinge to the service and love wich bear unto your self, you shall fynd, by God's helpe, that my self, my soon, and as many of my tenants as I cann procure, will gyve owr attendance and owr voyses for your self and for Sʳ John Colpeper, howe ever I receaved a Lettre from my respected nayghbour Sʳ Edward Haels † to stand for Sʳ John Colpeper and your self. I conseave that Sʳ Edward Haells hath

---

* James Hugessen, Esq. of Sewards, in Linton. He was sheriff the following year.

† Sir Edward Hales, Bart. formerly of Hales Place, in Tenterden. He had removed his residence to Henden, in Woodchurch, of which he became possessed in right of his first wife, heiress of Harlackenden. He married for his second wife Martha, daughter of Sir Mathew Carew the elder, and widow of Sir John Cromer of Tunstall, where he seems to have been now living—"my respected neighbour." He died and was buried at Tunstall in 1654. His son John, who died "vita patris," married Christian the daughter and co-heiress of the same Sir John Cromer, by the said Martha—the father thus marrying the widow, and the son her daughter.

requested dyvers other gentlemen and others to the same effect, so that I hoope you will fyend the greatest part of this contrye to stand accordinglye. Not else at present, beinge in haest; but, wishing your helth and happenesse, I remayne

Your servant to be comandid,

JAMES HUGESSEN.

From my house at Linsteed,
   22, 8^{tob}. 1640.

      [Superscription.]
To my honnorid ffrend Sr Edward Deringe, Kneyth
  and Baronett, at his house, Surenden Deringe,
  in the parish of Plockley.

[Seal.*] On a mount an Oak between two Boars erect, affrontés against it. And Crest: an Oak tree between two wings erect.

[Endorsed by Sr Edward Dering—" 1640, 22 Octob. Mr Hugessen."]

XII.

Letter from Sr EDWARD DERING to his wife,† announcing his arrival 31 October.
in London for the Parliament.

MY DEARE SWEETE HEART,

    I came well too London this day between 2 and 3 of the clock. I lay att my cosen Hawles.‡ Mr Willson§ came along with me, for whom a pursivant was sent; but the messenger missed of him, and he came now voluntary. I like his conversation.

---

  * The coat of Hugessen, of Linsted, was Argent, on a mount vert an oak tree proper between two boars combatant azure. Crest: An oak tree between two wings erect.

  † His third wife, Unton, daughter of Sir Ralph Gibbes, Kt.

  ‡ George Haule, Esq. of Maidstone—note p. 12.

  § This was Thomas Wilson, Rector of Otham, a great Puritan. He had been presented to that rectory by Mr. George Swinnock, who had purchased the next presentation. He was suspended by the High Commission Court, 1635, and restored 1639. Mr. George Swinnock published his life. When Robert Barrell was ejected from the perpetual curacy of Maidstone by the Parliament, Thomas Wilson was appointed in his stead. See more of him pp. 38, 39, *infra*.

The King came yesterday, my Lord keeper tooday. The King will go privately to the Parliament.

Jo. Pitman sayes that yesternight Sr John Meldrom sent purposely to my sister's * house to signify that my brother was sett att liberty that morning when the King came away; and Jo. sayth, that Mr Johnston did send word that his master desired that my sister would come to London. Therefore, Jo., with a coach, entendeth to be there, att Surenden, on Tuesday next.

My service to my deare sister; my love to my sweete cosens; and, to thy best selfe, the heart of

Thine owne
EDWARD DERING.

Saterday night, last Octob. 1640.

[Superscription.]
To my best and dearest freind the Lady Dering
att Surenden Dering.

[Seal.] A Saltire, with the Ulster hand.

[Endorsed, not by Sr Edward Dering, but probably by Lady Dering—
" My dearest, Octo: the last, 1640."]

XIII.

Letter to Sr EDWARD DERING from WILLIAM BARRET, pointing out the National Sins which subject the kingdom to God's wrath, as calling loudly for the interference of Parliament.

NOBLE SIR,

With all respect, my best desires remembred unto you, ernestly praying unto our good God that he would be pleased to

* Sir Edward Dering had a sister Margaret, married to Sir Peter Wroth, of Blendon Hall, in Bexley, 28 Feb. 1624-5.

furnish your soule with the graces of his sperit, that you may want neither wisedome, courage, nor bouldnes, to stand it out for the inlargment of the Gospell of Jesus Christ; and that God would now be pleased to give unto you, and the rest of that noble house, zeale, courage, and bouldnes for God and his truth, and to fight it out against the Goliaths of these times, that doe rayle against the liveing God, and to batter downe those underminers of the glorious Gospell, and they that stopp the mouths of God's preachers, and, by this means, make waye for Popery. Sir, I am bould, as with a friend, to offer three or foure things to your wise consideration which I take to be leading sinns unto judgments.

1640.
16 Car. 1.

1. The first is, the profanation of the Lord's daye. For this sinn he threatens hee will kindle fire at our gates that shall not be quenched. This sinn opens the flodgates. Wh . . . and distractions have there ben and are, since that booke* come forth. Jer. 17, 27.

2. Secondly. The suppressing of the word of God. One would thincke that no man were so w . . . . . to doe such a fearefull thing: it is a sinn that is rancked with the crusefying the Lord of glory. 1 Thessal. 2 chapter, 15, 16. The persons that committed this sinn was Annas, the high priest, and Caiephas, and Allexander, and as many as were of the kindred of the high priest. Acts 4 and 6. Whose servants or children they are that doe those things. Our Saviour tells us (John 8, 44), You are of your father the devill, for his workes yee doe.

3. Thirdly. The imprisoning of God's servants. 2 Cron. 36, 16. Luke 20, 9—16.

4. Fourth. That damned sinne of Idolletry; this is that sinne which maketh God to give a bill of divorce unto his people. Math. 19, 9. May wee not now see who they are that are the hatchers of these sinns? Is it not Annas, and Caiphas, and Allexander, and as many as are of the kindred of the high priest?

---

* The Book of Sports, first published by James I. 24 May, 1618; and republished by Charles 1. 18 October, 1633.

Surely, if our Prelates were appointed of God for the good and building of his Church, their names would be found in the word of God. It is to be feared that, if these sinns be not purged, and these persons, that God will, before it be longe, purge and refine us by his Judgments. My prayers shalbe unto Almighty God, to blesse your meeting with our noble Joshua, and you the elders of Israiell; and that there be unity betweene the head and the members; and, for your particuler, whose good my soule much desireth, God hath now put a price into your hands; and what neede there is of your best indeavours you well knowe. O that God would be pleased to double his sperit upon you, that your faithfulnes may appeare for God and your country, that so your friends that have ingaged their creddit for your faithfulnes may have just cause to blesse God for you, and that those that are not as yet perswaded of your sincerety may be of another mind.

Yours to command in all humillety,

WILLIAM BARRET.

Ashford, this 2d daye of
November, 1640.

[Superscription.]
To the Right Worshipful and well respected friend
Sr Edward Dearing, Knight and Barron-Knight,
at his lodging in London, these present with trust.

[Endorsed by Sr Edward Dering—" 1640.   4 Novr. Wm. Baret."]

XIV.

1640.
16 Car. I.

15 December.

Letter to Sr EDWARD DERING from Mr EDWARD KEMPE * about
a petition for restoring Edward Ranger as foot post of Dovor.

HONORED SIR,

 The much busines I have had for my daughter Curtis,
my long absence from home, with my feare of being troublsome to
you in your waightie affaiers, hath bine the cause I have not before
this time presented my service to you, which I beseech you now to
except of from your humble servant.

About three weeks since a report came to Tenterden that you
were dangerously sicke, past recovery: I sent to Surenden and
found the contrary. (I blest God for it.) 'Tis since reported by
some small divines about the Cathedarall that you have bine
dangerously sicke in mind (in plaine tearms madd), otherwise you
would never have uttered such things as you have done in Parlament. I need not send to London to satisfie myselfe, for that the
cuntrye hath latly bin satisfied 'tis otherwise. I beseech God blesse
your labors, and give good sucsese to it; 'tis the prayers, I hope,
of all good men. In this towne, now, 'tis not "Sir Ed. Bo." †
but "S^r Ed. Dering, that God hath sent from Heaven:" the scene
is changd.

* In the Visitation of Kent, Philipot 1619, is this pedigree and coat, by letters patent
under hand and seal of William Segar, Garter:—Gules, a fess between three garbs in a
bordure engrailed or ; and for Crest, a demy gryffon or, winged gules, siezing on a garb or.

  Edward Kempe, Major=Alicia, relicta Johannis Tenche,
     erat Dovor.   filia Thome Legent.

  Edward Kempe,=Catherina, filia Christopheri Bacheler de civitate
  de Dovor.   Cantuar.

Anthonius Percevall, armiger, capitaneus=1. Alicia. 2. Anna. 3. Maria. 4. Phœbe.
  de Archcliffe.

 This letter was doubtless written by Edward Kempe, son of the Mayor.

 † "Sir Ed. Bo." i.e. Sir Edward Boys, the Member for Dovor and Lieutenant of the
Castle.

1640.
16 Car. I.

Sir, one Edward Ranger, that was foot post of this towne, and outed by Wythering, we heare intends, by the Burgesses of this towne, to petition the Parlament for his place againe; he hath indevored to gaine a certificatt, under the towne scale, of his good carag (but hath caried himselfe so foully to the magistrats, and to the better sort of the towne, as he cannot gaine it). I know what* he may doe of the Rable, which are the best men in the repute of Sir B. and Sir H.† Therfore, my humble sute to you is, that, if any such thing be presented to the House, you will remember your freinds here in Care of it.

I am this day commanded by my Lady Brockman to present her love and service to you and your Lady; the like I beseech you both except from my wife, daughter, and from him that will ever be,

Your faythfull servant, Edw. Kempe.

[Superscription.]
To the Honorable my Honored freind Sir
Edward Dering, Knight and Baronett,
these present at London.

[In another hand.]
15 December, 1640. Dovor.

[In another hand, as if directing it on after
arrival at the wrong place.]
Att Sr Henry Gibbes his house in St. Martins Lane,
neare Charing Crosse.

[Endorsed by Sr Edward Dering—" 1640. 18 Decr. Mr Kempe."]

---

* Originally written " know not what," but " not " afterwards erased.

† Do these initials stand for Edward Boys, present Member for Dovor and Lieutenant of the Castle, and Sir Peter Heyman late member ?

1640.
16 Car. I.

December

XV.

ADDRESS to Sr EDWARD DERING from the Inhabitants of the Weald, with the Kent petition against Episcopacy, sent to him through Mr RICHARD ROBSON, of Cranbrook.

RIGHT WORSHIPFULL,

In all due respect, these are to intimate unto youe, that, hearing of late of a certeyne petition which was, with good advise and deliberacion of divers cittizens of London, and inhabitants of the suburbs therof, drawne and composed, and by them intended to be exhibited to the Commons howse of Parliament; and, desirous to have a veiw of a Copye therof, by the helpe of some freinds, obteyned it, and, approving therof, thought fitt to make knowne the same in this county of Kent, to the inhabitants therof, who generally gave good approbacion therto, and have sett to their hands, who, with us in the Weale of Kent, desire it may be in due tyme exhibited up unto the said house: Wee, therefore, of the weale of Kent, whose names are subscribed to the said petition, thought fitt to present the said petition of this our County (with the names of many other inhabitants in the said County subscribed and annexed thereto) unto your worship, humbly beseeching your worship to exhibit the same on our behalf to the said honorable howse (wherof your selfe is a worthy member), and to further the gratious acceptacion therof, and that the contents therof may be seriously considered of by that honorable assembly, and that the greivances therin exprest may be rectified and reformed, as that honorable assembly in their deepe and singular wisdomes shall thinke meet, wherto we humbly submitt; and being not unmyndfull of that worthy and memorable service youe have begun in the said howse, and further progress therof hitherto to the uttmost of your power, (as we conceave) for the good both of Church and Commonwealth, wee render unto your worship humble and hearty thanks therefore, and doe ingenuously confess that wee and others have cause to praise God for youe, and rest obliged to your worship for your service. And thus, nothing dowbting of your worship's best endeavour heerin, wee present our said petition to youe, and leave the success to Allmighty God, whose ayd wee dayly ymplore for an happy success uppon the ymployments of this honorable and hopefull Parliament; and commend your worship to the grace of God, and rest

> Your worship's in all obliged respect, who dayly
> pray for your health and eternall happiness:
> many inhabitants in the Weale of Kent.

Dated at Cranebrooke, in Kent,
the first of December, 1640.

[Superscription.]
To the right worshipfull S[r] Edward Deering,
k[nt] and Barronet, one of the Knights of
the Parliament for the County of Kent.

[Endorsed by S[r] Edward Dering,—
"1640. Dec. Weild of Kent, per Rich. Robson of Cranbroke."]

The presentation by Sir Edward Dering, in consequence of this address, of a petition against Episcopacy was a circumstance frequently alluded to, and of considerable importance, in his after life. The following extract from his "Collection of Speeches," ed. 1642, p. 16, will give his own explanation of his conduct on this occasion, and form an apt introduction to the petition itself; or rather to the petitions, for Sir Edward, it will be seen, did not present the petition actually transmitted to him, but a condensation or abridgment of it.

" I come now to the likeliest tryall wherein to find my self guilty. A petition was brought unto me out of Kent, in "terminis terminantibus," as that from many Citizens of London, which is in print. This, indeed, if it were not the Spawne of the London petition, yet, finding it a Parat taught to speake the syllables of that, and by roate calling for Root and Branch, I dealt with the presenters thereof, and with other parties thereunto, untill (with their consents) I reduced it to lesse then a quarter of its former length, and taught it a new and more modest language.. Upon delivery of this petition I thus prefaced :—

" January 13, 1640.

" Mr. SPEAKER, Yesterday we did regulate the most important businesse[s] before us, and gave them motion, so that our weighty affaires are now on their feet in their progresse, journ[y]ing on towards severall periods, where some I hope will shortly find their latest home. Yet, among all these, I observe one, a very main one, to sleep 'sine die:' give me leave to awaken it ; it is a businesse of an immense weight and worth ; such as deserves our best care, and most severe circumspection. I mean the Grand Petition long since given in by many thousand Citizens against the domineering of the Clergy. Wherein (for my part), although I cannot approve of all that is presented unto you, yet, I do clearely professe, that a great part of it, nay the greatest part thereof, is so well grounded, that my heart goes cheerfully along therewith. It seems that my Country (for which I have the honour to serve) is of the same mind ; and, least that you should think that all faults are included within the walls of Troy, they will show you—' Iliacos intra muros peccatur et extra.' The same grievances which the City groans under, are provincial unto us, and I much feare they are nationall among us all. The Pride, the Avarice, the Ambition, and Oppression, by our ill ruling Clergy, is Epidemicall, it hath infected them all. There is not any, or scarce any of them, who is not practicall in their own 'great cause in hand,' which they impiously doe miscall ' the piety of the times;' but, in truth, so wrong a Piety, that I am bold to say, ' In facinus jurasse putes.' Here in this Petition is the Disease represented—here is the Cure intreated. The number of your Petitioners is considerable, being above five-and-twenty hundred names, and would have been four times as many if that were thought materiall. The matter in the Petition is of high import: but your Petitioners themselves are all of them quiet and silent at their own houses, humbly expecting and praying the resolution of this great Senate upon these their earnest and their hearty desires. Here is no noyse—no numbers at your door : they will be neither your trouble nor your jealousie ; for I do not know of any one of them this day in the Town : So much they do affie in the justice of their petition, and in the goodnesse of this House. If now you want any of them here, to make avowance of their Petition, I am their servant. I do appeare for them and for my selfe, and am ready to avow this petition, in their names, and in my own. Nothing doubting, but fully confident, that I may justly say of the present usage of the Hierarchy in the Church of England, as once the Pope (Pope Adrian, as I remember) said of the Clergy in his time—'a vertice capitis ad plantam pedis, nihil est sanum in toto ordine ecclesiastico.' I beseech you, read the petition—regard us,—and relieve us."

XVI.

The KENT PETITION against Episcopacy, in the state in which it was forwarded to Sr EDWARD DERING by Mr RICHARD ROBSON of Cranbrook.*

To the honourable the Commons howse of Parliament.

The humble Peticion of many of his Majesties Subjects in the County of Kent,

Humbly sheweth,

That, whereas the governement of Arch Bishopps, Lord Bishopps, Deanes, Archdeacons, &c. with their Courts, and administrations in them, hath proved prejudiciall, and very dangerous, both to the Church and Common Wealth ; They themselves having formerly held, that their Jurisdiction or Governement is of humane authority ; till, of theis later tymes, being further pressed about the unlawfulnes thereof, they have claymed their Calling ymediately from

* This I state by conjecture ; I did not find it actually tied up with Mr. Robson's communication from Cranbrook, p. 25, supra—but it is evidently the petition which accompanied his letter, and is that which Sir Edward presented to the House after a little con-

our Lord Jesus Christ, which is against the Lawes of this Kingdome, and derogatory to his Majestie, and his estate roiall.   And, whereas the said governement is found by wofull experience to be a mayne cause and occasioner of manyfold Evills, pressures, and greivances of a very high nature, unto his Majesties Subjects, in their Consciences, liberties, and estates, as by an Indenture of perticulers hereunto annexed may in part appeare—

We, therefore, most humbly pray and beseech this honourable Assembly (the premisses considered), That the said governement, with all its dependances, Root and branch, may be abolished, and all Lawes made in favour thereof made void; and so the government, according to Gods word, may be rightly planted amongst us.   And we your humble Suppliants (as in duty we are bound) will daily pray for his Majesties long and happy reigne over us;

1640.
16 Car. I.

densation. For advantage of collation, I subjoin the condensed Petition as actually presented to the House by Sir Edward .—"The Petition," he says, " it selfe speaks thus :—

" To the Honourable the Commons House of Parliament.

"The humble Petition of many the Inhabitants within His Majesties county of Kent.

" Most humbly shewing, that by sad experience we doe daily finde the government in the Church of England, by Archbishops, Lord bishops, Deanes, and Archdeacons, with their courts, jurisdictions, and administrations, by them and their inferiour Officers, to be very dangerous, both in Church and Common-wealth, and to be the occasion of manifold grievances unto his Majesties Subjects, in their consciences, liberties, and estates, and likely to be fatall unto us in the continuance thereof. The dangerous effects of which Lordly power in them have appeared in these particulars following.

" They doe with a hard hand overrule all other Ministers, subjecting them to their cruell authority.

" They do suspend, punish, and deprive many godly, religious, and painfull Ministers, upon slight and upon no grounds : whilst, in the mean time, few of them doe preach the Word of God themselves, and that but seldome ; but they doe restraine the painfull preaching of others, both for Lectures and for afternoon Sermons on the Sabbath day.

" They do countenance and have of late encouraged Papists, Priests, and Arminian both bookes and persons.

" They hinder good and godly books to be printed : yet they do licence to be published many Popish, Arminian, and other dangerous tenents.

" They have deformed our Churches with Popish pictures, and suited them with Romish altars.

and for the prosperous successe of this high and honourable Court of Parliament, &c.

A Perticuler of manyfold evills, pressures, and grievances, cawsed, practiced, or occasioned by the Prelacy, and their dependances.

1. The subjecting and inslaving of all Ministers under them and their authority, and so, by degrees, exempting of them from the temporall power.

Whence followeth—

2. The faintheartnesse of Ministers to preach the truethes of God, least they should displease the Prelates, as namely, the doctrynes of Predestination, of free grace, of perseverance, of originall sin remayning after Baptisme, of the Saboth, the doctrynes against universall grace, Election for faith foreseene, freewill, against Antichrist, non residence, humane Inventions in God's worshipp, &c., all

"They have of late extolled and commended much the Church of Rome, denying the Pope to be Antichrist; affirming the Church of Rome to be a true Church in fundamentals.

"They have practiced and inforced antiquated and obsolete ceremonies, as standing at the Hymnes, at Gloria patri, and turning to the East at severall parts of the Divine Service, bowing to the altar, which they tearm the place of God's residence upon earth; the reading of a second service at the altar; and denying the Holy Sacrament of the Eucharist to such as have not come up to a new set Rayle before the altar.

"They have made and contrived illegall Canons and Constitutions, and framed a most pernitious and desperate Oath; an Oath of covenant and confederacy for their owne Hierarchicall greatnesse, beside many other dangerous and pernicious passages in the said Canons.

"They doe dispence with plurality of Benefices; they do both prohibite and grant marriages, neither of them by the rule of Law or conscience; but do prohibite that they may grant, and grant that they may have money.

"They have procured a licencious liberty for the Lord's day, but have pressed the strict observation of Saints holidaies; and do punish, suspend, degrade, deprive godly Ministers for not publishing a book for liberty of sports on the Sabbath day.

"They doe generally abuse the great ordinance of Excommunication, making some times a gaine of it, to the great discomfort of many poore soules, who, for want of money, can get no absolution.

which are generally withheld from the people's knowledge, becawse not pleasing to the Bishopps.

1640.
16 Car. I.

3. The incouragement of Ministers to dispise the temporall Magistracy, the Nobles and Gentry of the Land, to abuse the Subjects, and live contentiously with their Nighbours, knowing that, being the Bishopps' Creatures, they shalbe supported.

4. The restraint of many godly and able men from the Ministery, the thrusting out of many Congregations their faithfull, diligent, and powerfull Ministers, who lived peaceably with them, and did them good, only becawse they cannot in conscience submitt unto and maynteyne the Bishopps' needles devises; nay, sometyme, for no other cawse but their faithfull zealous preaching, or great auditoryes.

5. The suppressing of that godly designe (sett on foot by certeyne feoffees, and furthered with many great gifts by sundry well affected persons) for the buying in of Impropriacions, and placing of able Ministers in them, maynteyning of Lectures, and founding free schooles, which the Prelates could not endure, least it should in tyme darken their glory, and draw the Ministers from their dependance upon them.

6. The great increase of idle, lewd, dissolute, ignorant, and erro-

"They claime their Office and jurisdiction to be jure divino, and do exercise the same (contrary to law) in their own names, and under their own Seales.

"They receive and take upon them temporall honours, dignities, places, and offices in the Commonwealth, as if it were lawfull for them to use both Swords.

"They take cognisance in their Courts, and elsewhere, of matters determinable at the Common Law.

"They put Ministers upon Parishes, without the patron, and without the people's consent.

"They do yerely impose oaths upon Churchwardens, to the most apparent danger of filling the land with perjury.

"They do exercise oathes ex officio, in the nature of an Inquisition, even into the thoughts of men.

"They have apprehended men by Pursivants, without citation or missives first sent: they break up men's houses and studies, taking away what they please.

"They do awe the Judges of the Land with their greatnesse, to the inhibiting of prohibitions, and hindring of habeas corpus when it is due.

"They are strongly suspected to be confederate with the Roman party in this land, nious men in the Ministry, which swarme like locusts of Egypt over the whole kingdome; for, will they but weare a Canonicall Coat, a Sirplus, a hood, bow at the name of Jesus, and be zealous for supersticious Ceremonies, they may live as they list, confront whome they please, preach and vent what errors they will, and neglect preaching at their pleasure without controle.

Whence proceeds—

7. The discouragement of many from trayning up their Children in Learning; the many Schismes, Errors, and strong opinions in the Church; the great corruptions of the Universities; the grosse and lamentable ignorance, almost every where, among people; the want of preaching Ministers in very many places, both of England and Wales; the loathing of the Ministery; and the generall defection to all manner of prophanes.

8. The swarming of lascivious, idle, and unprofitable bookes, Pamphletts, Playbookes, and Ballades; as namely, Ovid's Art of Love, the Parliament of Women (come out at the dissolution of the last Parliament), Carewes Poems, Parker's Ballades, in disgrace of Religion, &c. to the increase of all Vice, and withdrawing of the people from reading, studdying, and hearing the word of God, and other good Bookes.

9. The hindering of godly bookes to be printed, the blotting out, or perverting (in those which they do suffer) all or most part of that which strikes either at Arminianisme, or Popery,—the adding of what and where pleaseth them; and the restraint of reprinting bookes formerly licensed, without a relicensing.

and, with them, to be authors, contrivers, or consenters to the present commotions in the North; and the rather, because of contribution by the Clergy, and by the Papists, in the last yeer, 1639, and, because of an ill-named benevolence of six Subsidies, granted, or intended to be granted, this present yeare, 1640, thereby, and with these moneys, to engage (as much in them lay) the two Nations into blood.

"It is therefore humbly and earnestly prayed, that this Hierarchicall power may be totally abrogated, if the wisdome of this Honourable House shall find that it cannot be maintained by God's Word, and to his glory.

"And we your Peticioners shall ever pray, &c."

1640.
16 Car. I.

10. The publishing and venting of Popish, Arminian, and other dangerous bookes and tenents; as, namely, that the Church of Rome is a true Church, and in the worst tymes never erred in fundamentalls:—That the Subjects have no propriety in their estates; but that the King may take from them what he pleaseth,—that all is the King's—and that he is bound by no Law—and many others.

From the former whereof hath sprung—

11. The great growth of Popery, and increase of Papists, Preists, and Jesuites, in very many places of the Kingdom, such as hath not byn since the Reformacion; the frequent venting of Crucifixes and Popish pictures, both ingraven and printed, and the placing of such in Bibles.

From the latter hath byn occasioned—

12. The multitude of Monopolies and Pattents (drawing with them innumerable perjuries), the large increase of Customes, imposicions upon Commodities, the Shippmoney, and many other very great burdens upon the Commonwealth—under which all groane.

13. Moreover, the Office and Jurisdiction of Arch-Bishopps, Lord Bishopps, Deanes, Arch-deacons, &c., being the same way of Church governement which is in the Romish Church, and which was in England in the tyme of Popery (little change thereof being made, except only the head from whence it was derived), and the same arguments supporting the Pope which do uphold the Prelacy, and overthrowing the Prelacy which do pull downe the Pope; and other reformed Churches having upon their rejection of the Pope cast the Prelates out also as members of the Beast: hence it is, that the Prelates in England, by themselves, or their disciples, plead and maynteyne that the Pope is not Antichrist—that the Church of Rome is a true Church, hath not erred in fundamentall points, and that Salvation is attayneable in that Religion: and, thereupon, have

1640.
16 Car. I.
restrayned Ministers to pray for the conversion of our sovereigne Lady the Queene.

Hence also hath come—

14. The great conformity and likenes (both contynued and increased) of our Church to the Church of Rome, in Vestures, gestures, Ceremonies, and administrations ; as, namely, the Bishops' Rochett, the Lawne sleeves, the fower-corner'd Capp, the Cope, the Surplice, the Tippett, the Hood, the Canonicall Coat, the Pulpitt Cloathes, especially now of late with the Jesuites Badge upon them, &c.

15. The standing up at Gloria Patri, and at reading of the Gospell, the praying towards the East, the bowing at the name Jesus, the bowing to the Altar, and towards the East, the Crosse in Baptisme, the kneeling at the receiving of the Communion, &c.

16. The setting up of Altars, turning of Communion Tables Altarwise, setting Images, Crucifixes, and Canopies over them, and Tapers and bookes upon them, and bowing and adoring to, or before them ; the reading of a second service at the Altar, and forcing people to come up thither to receive, or ells denying the Sacrament to them ; stiling the Altar to be the mercy seate, and the place of God Almighty in the Church, which is a playne devise to usher in the Masse.

17. The Christening and consecrating of Churches and Chappells, the consecrating of Fonts, Pulpitts, Tables, Challices, Churchyards, and many other things, and then puting holynes in them ; yea, reconsecration upon pretended pollutions, as though every thing were uncleane without their consecrating ; and for want of this, sundry Churches have been interdicted, and kept from use, as polluted places.

18. The Liturgie for the most part framed out of the Romish Breviary, the Rituall, and Masse booke. Also the Booke of Ordinacion of Archbishopps, Bishops, Ministers, &c. framed out of the Roman Pontificall.

1640.
16 Car. I.

19. The multitude of Canons formerly made, wherein (amongst other things) Excommunication, ipso facto, is denownced for speaking a word against the devices aforesaid, or subscription thereto (although no Law enjoyne it), a restraynt from the ministery without such subscription ; an appeale is denyed to any that shall refuse subscription or (unlawfull) Conformity, though he be never so much wronged by the inferior Judge.   Also, the Cannons made in the late sacred Synode (as they call it), wherein are many strange and dangerous devices to undermyne the Gospell and the Subjects Liberties, to propagate Popery, to spoile God's people, ensnare Ministers and other Students, and so to draw all into an absolute subjection and thraldom to them and their government, spoiling both King and Parliament of their power.

20. The dispencing with and countenancing plurality of Benefices, prohibiting of marriages without their lycence, at certeyne tymes, almost halfe the yere, and lycensing of marriages without banes asking.

21. The prophanacion of the Lord's day, pleading for it, and enjoining Ministers to read a declaration sett forth (as is thought by their procurement) for the tollerating of Sports upon that day, suspending and depriving many godly Ministers for not reading the same, onely out of Conscience that it was against the Law of God so to do, and no Law of the Land enjoyning it.

22. The pressing of the strict observacion of Saints' holly daies, whereby great sumes of mony are drawne out of men's purses for working on them, a very heavy burden upon most people, who, getting their livings by their daily imployments, must either omitt them, and bridle, or part with their mony, whereby many poore families are undone, or brought behind hand ; yea, many Churchwardens are sued, and threatned to be sued (by their trowblesome ministers) as perjured persons, for presenting the parishioners who failed in observing holly daies.

23. The great increase and frequency of whoredomes and adul-

teries, occasioned by the Prelates' corrupt administracion, who, taking upon them the punishment of such things, do turne all into mony for the filling of their purses ; and, least their Officers should defraud them of the gayne, they have in their late Cannons (in sted of remedying the Vices) decreed, that the Commutacion of pennance shall not be without the Bishop's privity.

24. The generall abuse of the great Ordinance of Excommunication, which God hath left in his Church, to be used as the last and greatest punishment the Church can inflict against obstinate and great offendors: and yet, the Prelates and their officers (who of right have nothing to do with it) do daily excommunicate men, either for doing that which is lawfull, or for vaine, idle, and triviall matters; as working or opening a Shopp upon a hollyday, not appearing at every beck upon their summons, not paying a fee, and the like: yea, they have made it (as they do all other things) a hooke or Instrument, wherewith to empty men's purses, and advance their owne greatnes: and so, that sacred ordinance of God, by their perverting of it, is become contemptible unto all men, and seldome, or never, used against notorious Offenders, who, for the most part, are their favourites.

25. Yea, further (the Pride and Ambition of the Prelacy being boundles, unwilling to be Subject to either man or Lawes), they clayme their office and jurisdiction to be *Jure divino,* exercise ecclesiasticall authority in their owne names and rights, and under their owne seales, and take upon them temporall dignities, places, and offices, in the Common Wealth, that so they may sway both swords.

Whence followes—

26. The taking Cognizance in their Courts and Consistoryes, and where ells they sitt on matters determynable of right at Common Law; the putting of Ministers upon Parishes, without the Patron's or people's consents.

1640.
16 Car. I.

27. The imposing of oathes and various and triviall Articles yerely, upon Churchwardens and Sydemen, which, without perjury, they cannot observe, unles they fall at Jarrs contynually with their Minister and Neighbours, and wholly neglect their owne callings.

28. The exercising of *Ex officio* oathes, and proceedings, by way of Inquisicion, reaching even to men's thoughts; the apprehending and deteyning of men by Pursivants; the frequent suspending and depriving of Ministers; the fyncing and imprisoning of all sorts of people, breaking up of men's howses and studdies, and taking away their bookes, letters, and other writings; seizing upon their estates, removing them from their callings, separating betweene them and their wives, against both their wills; the rejecting of Prohibitions, with threatnings; and the doing of many other outrages, to the utter infringing of the Lawes, the Subjects liberties, and ruyning of them and their families. And, of later tymes, the Judges of the land are so awed with the power and greatnes of the Prelates, or otherwise perverted, that neither Prohibition, habeas corpus, nor any other lawfull remedy, can be had or take place for the distressed Subject, in most cases: onely Papists, Jesuites, Priests, and such others as propagate Popery, or Arminianisme, are countenanced, spared, and have much liberty.

And from hence have followed (among others) theis dangerous consequencies—

1. The generall hope and expectacion of the Romish party, that their supersticious Religion will, ere long, be fully planted in this kingdome againe; and so they are incouraged to persist therein, and to practice the same openly in divers places, to the high dishonor of God, and contrary to the Lawes of this Realme.

2. The discouragement and distraction of all good Subjects, of whome multitudes, both Clothiers, Marchants, and others, being deprived of their Ministers, and overburdened with their pressures, have departed the kingdome, to Holland and other parts, and have drawne with them a great part of the Manufacture of Cloth, and

1640.
16 Car. I.

trading, out of the Land, into the places where they reside; whereby, Wooll (the great Staple of the kingdome) is become of small value, and vends not,—trading is decayed, many poore people want worke, Seamen lesse imployed, and the whole Land much impoverished, to the great dishonor of the kingdome, and blemish of the governement thereof.

3. The present Warrs and Commotions happened betweene his Majestie and his subjects of Scotland, wherein his Majestie, and all his kingdomes, are endangered, and suffer greatly, and are like to become a Prey to the Common Enemie, in case the Warrs go on, which we exceedingly feare will not only go on, but also increase, to an utter ruyne of all, unles the Prelates, with their dependances, be removed out of England also; for they, and their Practices (as we, under your honors' favor do verily beleive and conceive) have occasioned all the quarrell.

All which we humbly referre to the grave consideracion of this honourable assembly, desiring the Lord of Heaven to direct you in the right way to redresse all theis Evills.

---

4 February.

XVII.

Letter to Sr EDWARD DERING from REVD THOMAS WILSON,* with commendation and counsel.

Non sine magna bonorum et veritatis amantium virorum voluptate et lætitia.
Zan. Epist. Junio. [Zanchii Hieron. Operum Theologic. Tom. VIII. fol. Heidelb. 1613. p. 291.]

MUCH HONORED SIR,

'Tis occasion of great gladnes to me, and to all that be the true lovers of Zion's peace, that you were called of God, and raised

* See page 19, *supra.* Sir Edward Dering there writes to his wife, that he had taken Mr. Wilson (for whom a pursuivant had been dispatched, whose clutches he had contrived to escape,) with him to London, and was pleased with his conversation. I have stated in a note thereto that this Mr. Wilson was the Puritan Rector of Otham. By Sir

up by him, at this day, to put to your hand (yea, head and heart) to the present work, wherunto, God (who set you apart) hath gifted, and wherein he hath honored you,—for thos that honor him he wil

Edward Dering's Speeches, p. 9, it appears that on 10 November, 1640, (that is, just ten days after Mr. Wilson had accompanied him to London,) Sir Edward presented a petition to the House from Mr. Wilson, speaking as follows :—

"Now, Mr. Speaker, in pursuit of my own motion [*i.e.* on the settling of Religion,] and to make a little entrance into this great affaire, I will present unto you the petition of a poore oppressed minister in the county of Kent. A man orthodox in his doctrine, conformable in his life, laborious in the ministery as any we have or I doe know. He is now a sufferer (as all good men are) under the generall obloquy of a Puritan ; (as with other things was excellently delivered by that silver trumpet at the barre.) The pursivant watches his doore, and divides him and his cure asunder, to both their griefes : for it is not with him as (perhaps) with some that set the pursivant at worke, gladded of an excuse to be out of their pulpit. It his delight to preach.

"About a week since, I went over to Lambeth, to move that great bishop (too great indeed) to take this danger off from this minister, and to recall the pursivant. And withall I did undertake for Master Wilson (for so your petitioner is called) that he should answer his accusers in any of the King's Courts at Westminster. The bishop made me answer (as neere as I can remember) in hæc verba, ' I am sure that he wil not be absent from his cure a twelvemoneth together, and then (I doubt not) but once in a yeer we shall have him.'

" This was all I could obtaine ; but I hope (by the help of this house) before this yeere of threats runs round His Grace will either have more grace, or no grace at all. For our manifold griefes doe fill a mighty and a vast circumference, yet so that from every part our lines of sorrow doe lead unto him, and point at him the center, from whence our miseries in this church, and many of them in the Commonwealth, do flow.—

" Let the Petition be read, and let us enter upon the worke."

After quoting his speech, Sir Edward, in his vindication, continues thus :—

" What is here for ' Root and Branch?' I cannot find a line that I can wish unsaid ; nor do I read a letter that I would go lesse in. It is replied, that the petitioner, Mr. Wilson is a man for ' Root and Branch.' If he be, that was no part of his petition ; nor indeed any part of my knowledge then : I am no more obliged to answer herein, then I am bound to own and defend Mr. Wilson, if he should hereafter cast aside the Common Prayer. What were that to me, or to what I then did say ?—sure I am, that I was well assured, that he did not allow of separation then, and that he had been a powerfull per-swader of others not to withdraw from our publike service ; and I thinke so well of his goodnesse, temper, and conscience, that he will not easily be led away to these mistaking excesses."

1640-1.
16 Car. I.

honor. The country loves you, askes mercies of the God of heaven, and blesseth him for you; for how can our hearts be but towards you, who offered yourselfe so willingly, and have done so worthily for the house of the Lord ? " Mihi videris huic potissimum rei natus, ut de omnibus bene merearis." O that all men were of the same mind, " ut omne tandem aliquando ex ecclesia tollatur scandalum,"— that the pure word, sound doctrine, may be heard every where, and the troubles of the church cured, bridled, or cast out. " Quanti te fecerim, non est operæ pretium multis verbis explicare, præsertim quoniam summopere odi adulationis vitium; hactenus ad te, me a scribendo pudor retardavit, quis enim ego, ut ad talem, tantum virum, vereque nobilem, scribere auderem? nunc cogor pudorem illum tandem deponere." Let the zeal of God's glory and his house eat you up; let your spirit be stirred within you, while you see the manner of God's worship so marred with superstitions (albeit, with pretence of wisedome and humility), and the whole right of the law for the time of God's worship alleviated with profession of Christian (most un-Christian) liberty. Resolve what you are, or may be, and can doe, to be God's and his churche's, the king's, the kingdome's, and your countrie's. Mind that of Zanchy—" Sicut Christus sui facti rationem reddens, attulit in medium verbum Dei, et juxta illud, se repurgasse templum probavit, dicendo, ' scriptum est, Domus mea Domus orationis vocabitur, at vos fecistis eam speluncam latronum ;' ita ecclesiarum reformatores adferre debent verbum Dei, et juxta illud ecclesias reformare :" adding this in the same Epistle, "Si volumus esse æqui judices, debemus ita pronuntiare ecclesias esse verbo Dei tum errores dedocendas, tum in vera pietate instituendas."—Admire not all that can plead antiquity (without the adjunct sacred), for so somewhat may be said for the mystery of iniquity:—it was in the Apostles' daies, 2 Thes. ii. 7 ; and things grew to a love of primacy in the time of purest lights, 3 John, 9. Let God's law be your light; it was David's, Ps. cxix. 105 ; it was a lamp on the night, and

O beatam rem-
publicam
Christianam,
si tuum consi-
lium locum
habere apud
omnes possit.

a light on the day, Pro. vi. 23.   Christ tels his church, desirous to be directed what way to take, how to walk by the footsteps of the flock (Cant. i. 7, 8).   The way of other churches is to be minded and gone in (1 Thess. ii. 14).   You have learned "consuetudinem veritate majorem non esse."   We are to beware of the subtilties in disputation in the time of reformation.   I shall transcribe you the mind of Amesius, a man of singular piety and learning (lib. ii., c. 13, n. 19, 20):— "Deus suo proprio cultu toto ac solo est a nobis colendus; nihil hic addendum, detrahendum, aut mutandum (Deut. xii. 32).   Futilis admodum est illa distinctio quâ nonnulli suas additiones excusare conantur, quod additio tantùm corrumpens prohibetur, et non additio conservans, quoniam additio quævis æque ac detractio expresse opponitur observationi vel conservationi mandatorum Dei tanquam corruptio."   And further, he dislikes that distinction and evasion, " quâ essentialium tantùm additionem prohiberi dicunt, non accidentalium:" and addes, for his reason, " sicut minima mandata Dei etiam ad iota et apices sunt religiose observanda (Mat. v. 19,) sic etiam additiones quæ videntur minimæ eâdem ratione sunt rejiciendæ." Consult with God, not vain wits.   Walk humbly with God; exalt him, and he will exalt you, and bring you to honour (Pro. iv. 8).   Mind that spirit in him who would enjoin nothing wherby to cast a snare upon the Church (1 Cor. vii. 35).   " Hoc scripsi, ut meis literis incipiam illo ad te aditu quem mihi tua patefecisti clementia, frui:" for beleeve it, godlines is greatest gain; piety is followed with sweetest pleasure, and that all under the sun be but trifles compared with the fear of God; for this is the whole of man; this makes up a complete man; and he is but the shadow of a man that wants this. Pardon my prolixity.   I know " non vacat exiguis, tuæ tantùm tribuo prudentiæ, ut de omnibus actionibus tuis bene sentiam."   I doe but put you in remembrance, who both know and beleeve the Scriptures.   The Father of Lights shine on you, and upon your tabernacle, with the light of his countenance!   The Lord of Glory keep you blameles in soul and body, until the comming of the

1640-1.
16 Car. I.

Nimium altercando amittitur veritas.

Ames. Medul.
[12mo. Ams.
1652. p. 280.]

Lord in glory, whos spirit be with you, to direct, to strengthen, and give you everlasting consolation, and good hope through grace.

    Your worship's most bounden,

      and ready to be commanded in the Lord,

          THOMAS WILSON.

Otham in Kent, February 4, 1641.

[Superscription.]
To the right worshipful Sir Edward Dering, Knight and Baronet, at his lodging in St. Martin's Lane, London, present thes.

[Endorsed by Sʳ Edward Dering—"1640. Feb. Mr. Wilson."]

XVIII.

Letter from Sʳ EDWARD DERING to his Lady with parliamentary intelligence.

MY EVER DEARE NUMPS,*

  Thy pretious and hearty letter I received with that ardor that itt was written. Sʳ Edward Hales is cleared, and that is all, (but tak heed how you say so), his man is found faulty. I doubt whether this mayd will stay another week; but now you have ventured, send what word you will.

The scaffolds are up in Westminster hall, and Strafford comes to the barre on Monday morning.† The tryall (I suppose) will last 3 or 4 dayes.

---

* A term of affection which Sir Edward almost always used to this his third wife, to whom he seems to have been passionately attached to the last.

† This would be March 22, on which day Strafford first appeared at the bar. Instead of three days, the trial lasted seven weeks. The Court sat March 22d, 23d, 24th, 25th, 26th, 27th; Monday 29th, 30th, 31st; April 1st, 3d; Monday 5th, 7th, 8th, 10th;

1640-1.
16 Car. I.

I shall hardly be so good as my word, nor can I see thee so soone as I wish. I cannot guesse when to come doune. If you saw my almanack of busines, itt would satisfy.

I desire that Harry would signify to Sir William Brockman,* that I wish for all my odd money in.

I pray, send over to my cosen John Dering † (to whom I ow a letter) and lett him know, that my lady promised, and the keepers promised me some white deere (if itt be possible) att this time.

I do not heare how many deare of mine are dead. I can hardly think they all scape. Tell the keeper, he must now, att our Lady Day, watch my deare, that, att some time, when best advantage is, he may leave a brace of buckes, or a leash, in my lower park, and shutt of the rest.

I can not buy the latches and lock for thee.

I entend to suppe with my sister too night.

God preserve my pretty children, and send thee ease of thy troublesome cough.

If I could tell what to send or bring Mr. Bradshaw, I would. The footman I will think on; in the meane time (if Jo: Hunt shew him) he may tend all those gardens.

Tuesday 13th, on which day the Earl finished his defence. The 14th, 15th, 16th, 17th, 29th, and 30th were occupied in discussions as to the law. May 1st, the King came down to the House of Lords at 10 A.M., and, in his speech, declared, that, in conscience, he never could be persuaded to deem it a case of statutable treason. May 8th, the Bill passed the Lords. May 12th, he was executed.

* Sir William Brockman, of Beechborough in Newington, near Hythe. He was the gallant defender of Maidstone, and a stanch royalist.

† I suppose this was the son of George Dering, who was a younger son of Anthony Dering of Charing, a younger brother of Richard Dering :—

John Dering.╤......

Richard Dering.╤Margaret Twysden.	Anthony Dering, of Charing.╤......
Sr Anthony Dering.╤Frances Bell.	Three sons. George Dering.╤......
Sr Edward Dering, Kt. and Bart.	John Dering.

You have seen 3 of my speeches, besides my reportes. You may comfort up Baker, if you please, for I think not on him; his danger will be at the assises.

Remember me to Harry; itt seems I shall shortly see him.

We shall have some statutes to regulate the Councell table, the Starre chamber, and the High Commission.

I thank thee for the length of thy wellcome letters, wherein I confesse that I cannot equall thy love.

Thine more and more if possibly,

EDWARD DERING.

Westminster, 18 March, 1640.

Heere is a new dedication, which I neither see nor knew of untell this morning (as you may guesse by the title); this he brought for you, and one for my selfe.

[Endorsed, not in Sr Edward's hand, but apparently Lady Dering's, "My Dearest. March 18, 1640."]

XIX.

Letter from Dr VANE * to Sr EDWARD DERING, entreating him to postpone his summons to appear before the Committee, as he was under commands to attend on the Princess Mary, during the visit of the Prince of Orange.

NOBLE SIR,

       Pardon, I beseech you, my intrusion uppon your patience,

---

* By his mention of " cousin Monings " it would seem as if Dr. Vane were a brother of the Treasurer of the Household, Sir Henry Vane; he evidently held some office about the household. The connexion between the Vanes and the Moninses was as follows:

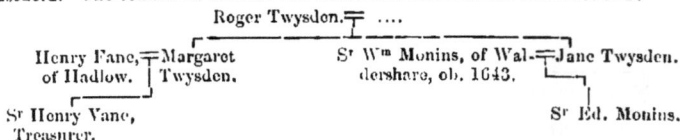

Roger Twysden.

Henry Vane,＝Margaret	Sr Wm Monins, of Wal-＝Jane Twysden.
of Hadlow. Twysden.	dershare, ob. 1643.
Sr Henry Vane,	Sr Ed. Monins.
Treasurer.	

and (beeing at this time) on your piety. Yet, what I sue for, being a deed of charity, it doth (I hope) well sort with this day,* and your disposition. I have no title to sue under, but your owne goodnesse, for my cosen Monyngs sake formerly exprest unto me. By that I entreat you to retard my summons before your Committee,† as long as possibly may be, both, because I am at this time very sick, and when I shalbee well (if God grant it) I am commanded to waite on the Princesse Mary,‡ until the Prince of Orange bee come over, and returne againe. What prejudice to mee, what hinderance in that employment (on which I alone am to attend) my calling away will be, you can well judge; what favour you shall doe me in preventing it, I can and will ever acknowledge. And, seeing all attendance must give place to that on you, if you please to grant mee this favour, you will soe much the more mightely oblige,

S^r, your most humble servant,
Tho. Vane.

April 4, 1641.

[Superscription.]
To the most Honoured Sr Edward Dearinge, knight and
    baronet, one of the knights of the shire for the county
    of Kent, present these.

[Seal.] 3 right-hand gauntlets, backs affrontés, 2, 1. A crescent for difference; and for crest, a dexter gauntlet, holding a sword pointing sinister way.

[Endorsed by Sr Edward Dering—"1641, 5 April. Dr Vane."]

---

* The 4th of April was on Sunday in 1641.

† *i. e.* "The Committee on Religion" of which Sir Edward Dering was Chairman. He says, in his vindication p. 42, "Upon my motion Nov. 23, 1640, it pleased the Grand Committee for Religion to appoint a sub-committee to receive complaints from oppressed ministers, which sub-committee was shortly after made a committee by order of the House. It pleased the gentlemen of this committee to put the honour and the burden of the chaire upon me."

‡ The marriage between the Princess Mary (who was born 1631), and the Prince of Orange, took place on the 2d May this year, less than a month after the date of this letter. She could have been barely ten years old, and was a widow at nineteen in 1650.

XX.

Letter from Sr EDWARD DERING to his Lady, with parliamentary
intelligence.

2 May.

MY DEARE LOVE,

I came well to London by 4 of the clocke, somewhat
weary, and my head a little out of order; but, after I had supped
with my sister Gibb, very well. I went first to the Parliament
house; there was nobody. The King had in the morning told them,
he could not in conscience concurre to sentence the point of treason:
the sullen boys therefore brak up schoole at 11 of the clocke, and
went to play, not suffering so much as the Committee for Religion * to
sitt. We shall meet sullen too morow. God send good issue; but
my despayres begin to go above my fayth in that. Yett (as I said
att Christmas, and often since) we shall be cured with a confusion. If the French play not the devills with us, the confusion will
be short and safe.

There lyeth on my table 6s. 9d. for Richard. Besse gave me not
my yellow silk stockins. The boy shall go on Wensday to Cambridge. Send Derby to London on Saterday, to carry back those
horses on Monday following.

Att dinner with my mother. My sister Wroth is ill again. God
bless thee and my deare little ones !

Thine in hast, but heartily,

2 May, 1641. EDWARD DERING.

[Superscription.]
To my best and dearest frend, the Lady Dering, att
Surenden Dering; dd.

[Seal.] A saltire impaling three coats arranged one above the other,† viz.: 1, In
chief, an eagle displayed within a bordure, for Tufton ; 2. In fess, a fess between
6 mullets—Ashburnham ; 3. In base, 3 battle axes paleways, 2, 1, for Gibbes.

[Endorsed, not in Sr Edward's hand, probably in Lady Dering's.—" My
Dearest, May ye 2d 1641."]

---

* Vide note, p. 45 *supra.*

† These are the arms of his three wives, Tufton, Ashburnham, and Gibbes.

1641.
17 Car. I.

XXI.

Letter from Sr EDWARD DERING to his Lady, with parliamentary
intelligence.

MY DEAREST LOVE,

20 May.

Yesterday, I made a motion, that, by reason of 8 monthes
session (allmost), the sicknesses of the poxe and plague encreasing,
the necessity of composing the state and church in those things
wherein this house had (upon just groundes) disjoynted them, we
might have a committee to oversee all our worke, and to present to
the house what must be done before we part, and to turne aside all
that may stay till we meete again ; a committee was by the house
most gladly appointed, for perusall of the clark's books, and of all
the chayres.   I will endeavour to shorten all that may, or else the
service att parting will be broaken and imperfect, and I shall have
no patience to stay itt out, especially if new afflictions be with thee.

God in heaven blesse our little boy; indeed, love, they are all
pretious to me.

There are 6 severall copys of Strafford's speeches, none very right.
I thank Mr. Bevin for his care and love.

We did appease and send away the citizens; and they did regard
my advice as much, perhaps more, then any of the rest; but there
was no such violent kindnes : but many tooke me by the hand whom
I knew not; many said to one another, " There goes Sr Edward
Dering," " That is Sr Edward Dering," and " God blesse your worship," &c.

I know not what to do for money.

You may thanke Sherwood for want of the syrup.   I will send
him again too day.

Notwithstanding the currishnes of Copley, * he had the face to

* There had been interminable quarrels between Mr. Copley, the Vicar of Pluckley, and
Sir Edward Dering, and his father Sir Anthony, in which there was the most envenomed
rancour called forth on both sides.

come to me (before I had thy letter) and to desire me to be a meanes that he might be abated in the subsidy.

Harry Betnam * will serve the devill, to gett his father's fortune.

In hast, God blesse us and ours.

Thy truely loving

EDWARD DERING.

20 May, 1641.

Send Derby to Mr. Pulley with his booke: it is licensed.

[Endorsed, not by Sr Edward Dering; but probably by Lady Dering.—" My Dearest, May 20th, 1641."]

XXII.

Letter from Sr ANTHONY WELDON † to Sr EDWARD DERING, and Sr JOHN COLPEPER, the Knights of the Shire, complaining of the insolent tyranny of persons described as " base ministers."

20 May.

HONOURED SIRS,

Your greater busines being overpast, give me leave to present our grevance; a grevance to us far more pressing than shipmonie; or any other that I knowe: whether you consider it in the insolent carriage, or the charg, or both. The grevance is soe much the greter by being executed by base ministers; and hath raged more since they understoode our intentions of petitioning the honourable Parlament then before; which, in my opinion, is an insolencye far beyond all other; to threten, abuse, and beate men for complaining (as they have expressed). Be pleased to know, at the beginning of Parlament, out of my respect to Sr Henry Vaine, I sentt to him both a letter and coppye of the articles. Truly, not desyring to

* Probably Bettenham, of Shurland, in Pluckley, close to Surrenden.

† This was Sir Anthony Weldon of Swanscombe, a strong parliamentarian, and a persecutor of all who opposed his opinions, in Kent.

1611.
17 Car. I.

complayne of eyther, wee might have seene amendment, or he had bynn nerly concernd in it.   Butt his answer was, he had nothing to doe with it.   And since, they have raged in much more violence, and, even now, are as insolent as ever in this parte.   I have now putt it in to the right hands to ease the cuntry.   Myself having now performed the uttmost of my endevors: and must leve the rest to you, who, I am confident, will doe the cuntry that right that may bynd them to a thankfull memorye, and make me in my expressions

Your freind and servant,

ANTHO: WELDON.

[Superscription.]

" To the honourable K⁰ᵗˢ, Sʳ Edward Dering, Kⁿᵗ and Baronet, Sʳ John Culpeper, Kⁿᵗ, Kⁿᵗˢ of the shire for the county of Kent, present these."
[Endorsed, " Gunpowder-men."]

XXIII.

Letter from ROBERT CODRINGTON,* [to Sʳ EDWARD DERING †] pleading for mercy from the Parliament, for unintentional offence given in one of his Poems.

24 May.

SIR,

I am grown an impudent begger, and, if you relieve me not with your mercy, I am in danger to be lost for ever.   You are not ignorant what troubles are come upon me by making an unfortunate choyce, (to pleasure a poore fellow now in prison,) to personate

---

* Robert Codrington, a miscellaneous writer and translator, was born in 1602, of an ancient family in Gloucestershire.   He was admitted a demy of Magdalen college, Oxford, in 1619, and M.A. in 1626.   He lived afterwards in Norfolk as a private gentleman⸱ Wood says that he was always accounted a Puritan.   He died in London of the plague in 1665.

† There is no superscription, but I conjecture it to have been addressed to Sir Edward Dering, from its being found among his muniments.

the late Earle of Strafford, speaking in those characters which I
thought came neerest to the vehemence and the vastnes of that
unruly spirit. For my owne part, I never saw the man in all my
life. When I heard he was committed by the Parliament, there was
no man that entertayned the newes with a more perfect joy; and
when, agayne, the sentence of death did proceed against him, there
there was no man concluded that it was more justly done. As for
the word "Anarchy," in the poem, (for that word I am taught gives
the first offence,) the word signifies, "without a prince;" by which I
understand, the commotion of the citisens who came downe with
swords and staves demaunding justice; undoubtedly intimating thereby, that if the state (by which I understand the upper and lower
Houses of Parliament) should not forthwith comply with theyr desires,
they would be a law and a prince unto themselves; and a direct relation
unto that have those verses which follow in the third clause, "allthough
this scanted age vents none," &c. by which I truely understand the
Senate of the Citty, who, being armed in the same designe, came
downe with the younger sort of merchants, theyr cholerick and
spruce companions. For my owne parte, I protest before the
Majestie of Allmighty God, that I have allwayes with a deliberate
and solemne joy affirmed, and, from my heart, I doe verily believe,
that there was never a more hopefull parliament than this, never an
assembly mette of more able and more excellent men in a more need-
full time, for the establishing of the kingdome, which now indeede
beginnes to hold up her head in earnest, to feele new health in her
veynes, and to enjoy all those blessings which a flourishing and
glorious age can eyther promise or produce. With the like sincerity
and zeale I doe protest, that I had not the least intention whereby
I might therein incurre the displeasure of the Parliament, or of any
parliamentary, whom, with all the indeavours of my soule, with all
my feares and hopes, I have precisely honoured, and for whose
union and prosperity I doe dayly and devoutly pray; but most
humbly and most obnixely I must beseach both them and you (who,

I heare, is particularly intrusted in this busines,) that what errours my ignorance and my rashnes have therein committed, your most noble wisedomes, and your mercyes, would vouchsafe to pardon. I have been a long time sick, and my sicknes is attended with a greate lamenes. I am brought by a consumption even to the grave allready. I should be loath to breath out my last in a prison, from whence neyther the weakenes of my body, nor the burden of my ensuing debts, would suffer me to returne alive. In the meane while, my poore wife and children take theyr full share in my sorrowes, the charge of whom doth looke directly on me; and it is a new anguish of heart unto me, that so many noble familyes, to whom I neerely am allyed, should bleed in my wounds, and suffer in my dishonour, with me. Amongst the many hundred of Poems which I have written, this is the first that hath given me an occasion to repent, from whence there is nothing to be receaved but the ignominy of it.

Sir, being thus hung round with sorrowes, it is a new affliction to me to torment you (being so greate a stranger to you) with the tediousnes of these lines, which may improve themselves into my happinas, if, on the perusall of them, you shall be pleased to descend from your more high and greate imployments, to relieve from danger him who is, and whom the Parliament and your selfe shall ever find to be,

Your most humble, most faithfull,
and most devoted Servant,
ROBERT CODRINGTON.

May 24, 1641.

1641.
17 Car. I.
26 July.

XXIV.

Letter to Sr EDWARD DERING from Dr HOLDSWORTH, * Master of Emanuel College, Cambridge, on hearing that he was to be brought before the Committee of Religion.

NOBLE SIR,

I perceive I am under a cloud in the House of Commons, by some misreports which have bene cast upon my speech at the last commencement. The news thereof was very unwelcome to me;

---

* This was the celebrated Dr. Holdsworth, who was educated at, and was afterwards Fellow of, St. John's college, Cambridge, where he was tutor to Sir Symonds d'Ewes. In 1625 he was a Professor of Gresham College, in 1631 Prebendary of Lincoln, and in 1633 Archdeacon of Huntingdon. In 1638 he was a candidate for the Mastership of St. John's; but neither he, nor his competitor, was acceptable at court, and the King, by mandate, ordered Dr. Beale to be appointed. In 1637 he was elected Master of Emanuel College, and created D.D. In 1639 he was elected President of Sion College. In 1641 he resigned the Professorship of Gresham College. While Vice-Chancellor of Cambridge, he supplied the King with money contributed by the University, a crime not easily forgiven by the Parliament. When the Assembly of Divines was called, he was appointed one of them; but never took his seat. Soon after, in obedience to the King's mandate, he had such parts of His Majesty's declaration as were formerly printed at York, printed at Cambridge; for which, and for a sermon then preached by him, he was forced to leave the University before the expiration of his office of Vice-Chancellor. He was concealed awhile, but was ultimately apprehended near London, and was imprisoned ;—first, at Ely House, and afterwards at the Tower. So highly regarded was he at Cambridge, that, while a prisoner, he was elected Margaret Professor of Divinity, although neither able to attend to its duties nor receive its profits. He held the office till his death; but the rectory of St. Peter-le-Poor, in the City of London, and the mastership of Emanuel College were taken from him. It is uncertain when he was released from prison. He attended the King at Hampton Court in 1647; and, in January following, when Parliament voted that no more addresses should be made to the King, he preached a bold sermon against the resolution, for which he was again imprisoned ; but, being released, he assisted, on the King's part, at the treaty of the Isle of Wight. He did not long survive his master, dying August 29, 1649, his death probably hastened by that melancholy catastrophe. He was buried at St. Peter-le-Poor church. He was a staunch royalist and episcopalian ; devout, charitable, and an excellent scholar. His sermons, " Prelectiones " &c. have been published.

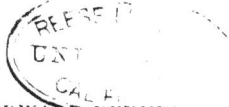

1641.
17 Car. I.
26 July.

therefor, hearing it was referred by the house to that Committee where your selfe are the worthy Chayreman, I thought it concerned me near to offer to your wyse consideration the generall knowledge of the truth, which being concealed might breed me sore prejudice. —Sir, the maine scope of my oration was to bemoane the sad condicion of the Church, and soe of the Vniversity, which the indiscreet and offensive practises of some of our owne order, by their introduction of superstitious rites, and preaching of unsavory doctrines, hath brought upon both ; whereby, they stirred up the displeasure of the common people of this lande against us. In the prosecution hereof, I did not in the least manner reflect upon any proceedings in Parliament, but laboured to doe them all the honour which became me: nay I did not soe much as glance at any other person which did oppose himself to the government established, because I would be sure not to give offense ; soe farr I was from any undutifull carriage my selfe, that I took as strict order as was possible to prævent it in others, as well preachers and disputants, as prævaricators, all which I shall make evident if there be cause. Only, I intreat you, Sir, to shew me the favour of a speedy hearing if I must be called to answer, not doubting but that I shall give you full satisfaction. In this assurance, with the præsentment of my most regardfull respect to your selfe, I commend you to God's grace, and rest

Your obliged friend and ready servant

RI: HOLDSWORTH.

Em: Coll: July 26, 1641.

    [Superscription.]

"To the right worshipfull his much honoured friend
  Sr Edward Deering. These present."

[Seal,] A stag's head erased.

[Endorsed by Sr Edward Deering—" 1641, 28 July, Dr. Holdesworth."]

XXV.

1641.
17 Car. I.
16 September.

Petition to the House of Commons, complaining of the establishment of paupers in the farm-houses, by the non-resident farmers—from the parishioners of Rucking.

To the honourable house of Commons nowe assembled in Parliament.

The humble Petition of the parishioners of the parish of Ruckinge, adjoyninge to Romney Marsh, in the county of Kent,

1. Your Petitioners shewe, that, whereas the said parish of Ruckinge is of large extent, and that parte of it lyeth in Romney Marsh, and parte of it in the sheire, and that there are divers antient farmes, and sufficient farme houses, in the said Parish, in which formerly sufficient able men have lived in, such as have bin able to give and alowe towards the mayntenance both of Church and poore in the said parish, as alsoe to finde armes in defence of his Majestie. The said Marsh not beinge soe populus as other places, and lyinge to the mayne sea in the face of the Enymie.

2. Nowe, soe it is, may it please you, that Mathew Whitinge, Richard Baker, and Thomas Fishenden, of Ruckinge aforesaid, have 8 severall farmes betweene them, in the said parish, in theire hands, and doe use the lands belonginge to the said farmes, themselves, but doe place poore people in the farme houses, not able to give releife, as heretofore, but to receave; and not able to contribute, eyther to Church or poore, or to find armes to serve his Majestie ; and that Thomas Cuckowe, John Smyth, and Thomas Haffenden are men that live in other parishes, and fare remoate Townes, and doe likewise ingrose and take divers severall farmes in the said parish into theire hands, and doe use the land themselves, and place poore people in the houses, and bringe in poore out of other parishes, and place them there ; besids many cottags that have bin and are of late erected uppon the wast grounds in the said parish :—All which things have and doe daylie soe much impoverish the said parish, that the said

parish is soe much gon to decay, and soe much poore increased, and daylie more and more is liklie to increase, that the feawe rich that are in the said parish are not able so supporte and releceive the poore, but them feaue rich that nowe are left, by reason of theire heavie burdens, will be forced to leave the said parish, unlesse som other course be taken.

1640.
17 Car. I.
16 September.

3. May it therefore please this honourable Court, the premisses considered, soe to order it, that the parties abovesaid may place such tennants in the said severall farme houses as are able to use the lands to the severall farmes belonginge, as formerly they have bin letten and enjoyed together; and that none of the parties abovesaid may bee suffered to use any more or other farme or farmes than what they dwell uppon; and that noe cottags, for the tyme to com, may bee erected on the wast grounds, or else wheare in the said parish; and that such cottags as have bin erected of late, contrary to the Statute of Queene Elizabeth, may bee pulled downe; and that whatsoever other thinge concerninge the premisses may seeme fitt and expedient to your grave wisdomes may bee ordered.

And your petitioners shall humblie pray, &c.

JOHN BARMAN.   JOHN COOPAR.
THOMAS AWCHLEY.   JOHN × ROGERS, Churchwarden,
DANIEL § RAZELL, his marke.   his marke.
JOHN AUCHLEY.   EDWARD WATTES.

[Endorsed by Sr Edward Dering—"1641. 16 Sept. Petition, Rokinge."]

XXVI.

Letter from Sir Edward Dering to his Lady with parliamentary
intelligence.

MY DEAR AND MY COMFORTABLE NUMPES,

My happines is (for the greatest part of itt in this world)

circuited in the same sphære with thine.   Love and cheerefullnes are blessings invaluable; and if, perchance, some excentricke motion interpose, all att last (as in the sphæres) helpe to make up the harmony.   So (I hope) with us, every motion shall mend the tune.

Thy letter found me well att my Sister's: we did presently (as you wished) reade over the 91 Spalme (as you call itt).   I did thinke to have returned you a text; but I am in hast.

Yesterday we resolved that our house shall daily sitt from 9 to two or three.   Newes from Scotland not good.   Hamilton, Argile, and Lanricke are fled to theire strengthes.   No newes of the King's returne.

This day a bill * was read to take away Bishops' votes in the House of Lords.   To morrow is sett for the debate of it; and will, quæstionles, go cleare away with us, and (I thinke) with the Lordes also.

Remember me heartily to the good boy-begetting couple.   Tell my brother, that I mett a gent by chance, who wished me to certify him, that, on Wensday next, the Lords of the Councell do intend to proceed upon his silver businesse; and the gentt wished that my brother would come up.

My coming downe againe is now uncerteyn.   I have sent the boy to Cambridge (thorough I hope) this day.   I have appointed Richard to go from thence directly home.

---

* This was not the original Bill which he himself had introduced 21 May, 1641 ; but a new one ; c. his Speeches, p. 90. He spoke upon it, urging the omission of the words "and that it is inconsistent with their function," as likely to lead to a debate on doctrine. " I have formerly," said he, " and againe I pray you, that we may not engage ourselves into the determination of doctrinall points in Divinity,—perhaps it is not proper for us, and for my part, I doe think we are not herein 'idonei et competentes Judices.'   Was it ever heard or seen, that a set of laymen, gentlemen, souldiers, lawyers, merchants, all professions admitted but the profession of professions for this worke, divines alone excluded, that we should determine upon doctrinall points in Divinity ?   Theology is not so low, so facile a trade.   Let us maintaine the doctrines that are established ; to declare new is not fit for our assembly, and, for my part, I do think I have found daily cause to wish these resolutions recommended unto other resolvers."

God blesse us with a comfortable returne together, and preserve our little flocke.

Thine owne, as ever, for ever,

EDWARD DERING.

London, 21 Octob: 1641.

[Superscription,]
To my best and dearest friend the Lady Dering,
at Arcliffe fort, neare Dovor.

[Seal.] Dering, impaling Tufton, Ashburnham, and Gibbes, as before.

[Endorsed, not by Sʳ Edward, Dering but probably by Lady Dering:
"My dearest, October 22, 1641."]

XXVII.

Petition to the House of Commons from JOHN READING, the Minister, to endow with regular Tythes the Parish of St Mary Dover.*

To the most honourable High Court of Parliament.
The humble Petition of John Reading, Minister of the parish of St. Marie, Dover,
Sheweth that, whereas

* This is only a fragment of the Petition, and, being without date, I can only supply the date conjecturally. I conclude this to be about the proper place for its insertion, owing to the following passage in a speech of Sir Edward Dering (p. 93), 23 October, 1641 : "Many mournfull sad complaints I have of late received from ministers the ablest and every way the worthiest that I know. I could willingly name you two, one at Dovor, the other at Cranebroke in Kent. Men, upon whose merit let my credit stand or fall in this house. He that hath preached least of these hath preached severall thousands of excellent sermons to his people." In the margin, Sir Edward supplies the names—"Mr. Reading," "Mr. Abbot."

Before the Reformation, there was a rector, curate, &c. to this parish ; but how they were paid is uncertain. Afterwards, the parishioners seem to have hired the services of their minister by contract. Sometimes it was 20 marks and the Easter-book, some times 10*l.* and the book and fees, sometimes 5 marks. Walter Richards 1601-1608 had 30*l.* This John Reading was brought to Dover in 1616, by Lord Zouch, the Lord

CAMD. SOC. I

1. There are remayning in .... only two Parish Churches, viz., the Parish of St. James the Apostle, and this Parish of St. Marie. The Minister of the said St. James Parish hath for his maintenance a setled meanes from tithes on lands, and 2s. in the pound, according .... the rents of the houses and edifices being within the said parish; but the minister of St. Maries Parish hath no settled meanes, there being only 10 or 12 acres of land within the Circuite of the same (besides streets and howses), and no tithes upon the rents of houses are paid unto him; but the Parishioners, instedd thereof, have payed the minister for the time being, sometimes one summe per annum, and sometimes another, as they pleased.

2. Divers parish Churches in Dover, some ages past, decaying and falling downe, the parishioners have betaken themselves to the parish of St. Marie; some very few excepted, who went to the said parish of St. James.

Warden, as his Chaplain. The parish was then without a minister, and he took the duty, for several weeks, to oblige the parishioners, whereupon they asked him to accept the cure at 100*l*. per annum. He was chaplain to Charles I., and was, for a time, very popular with his new flock; but when Republicanism prevailed among them his popularity fled. Probably his salary of 100*l*. was not then maintained, and thence this petition. We are thus aided in our conjectures as to the date. His house was plundered in 1642, and in the next year, while employed on his Paraphrase of St. John's Gospel, Sir Edward Boys had him seized and imprisoned. The King, hearing of this, obtained for him from Archbishop Laud the Rectory of Chartham, and he was appointed Prebendary of Canterbury. In 1644 Sir William Brockman gave him the living of Cheriton, and he was appointed by the Assembly of Divines one of the nine persons to write annotations on the New Testament. He was seized by Major Boys, at Cheriton, and carried prisoner to Leeds Castle. During this confinement, he wrote his "Guide to the Holy City." On May 10, 1650, he disputed publicly in Folkestone church with Samuel Fisher, a Baptist. He was a rigid Calvinist, as supposed by many. He was the first minister of the parish who had 100*l*. per annum. Probably, after the Restoration, he returned to this parish, for we find him the spokesman of the Corporation, in addressing Charles the Second, on his landing on the beach at Dover, and in presenting his Majesty a Bible with gold clasps. He published several sermons and controversial tracts, chiefly against the Anabaptists. He died at Chartham 1667.

The Inhabitants of St. Mary's Dover had always been backward in raising money to pay their minister. The church was often, for long periods together, without one.

1641.
17 Car. I.

The parishioners of St. Marie have usuallie (by cessers thereunto yearely chosen) taxed the ministers mayntenance according to
the several . . . . . of the parishioners; which being not easily
known to the said cessers, or willingly mistaken, by reason of their
particular . . . . , many discords and contentions
about the inequalitie of the cesse have arisen among them, insomuch
as sundrie complaints have been made to the Lord of Canterbery and
the Lord Warden and divers suites in Law have beene commenced
amongst . . . . differences.

4. The Mayor, Jurates, and most prudent and peaceable inhabitants
heere, then being, in the yeare 1620, weary of their contentions.
. . . . uncertainty of charge (it being according to the
pleasures and affectiones of yearely cessers) presented two petitions,
one to the Lord Bishop of Canterbery then being, and the other to
the right honourable Lord Zouche, then Lord Warden of the Cinque
Ports, entreating their Lordships' assistance in the reducing them into
the forme of a Rectorie, they thereby consenting, for themselves, and
their posterities, to pay to theire minister . . . the time . . . .
in the pound, for and according to the rents of their several houses
and edifices scituate and being in the parishe, for everie house or
edifice letten, or worth to be letten at 40s rent per annum . . . 1s in
the pound for all howses and a . . . . and also the oblations or Easter booke, with other usuall and accustomed fees appertayning to the Minister, as by one of these petitions by themselves presented to the Lord Bishop of Canterbery may more particularly
appeare.

5. Your Petitioners, being thereunto commanded by the said
Lords, presented this whole affaire to the Parliament held the said
yeare at Westminster, . . . bill . . . . . . into this house, which
was read and committed, and after much debate, in respecte of the
greate opposition there made by many of the parishioners of the said
St. Maries (who it seemed loved liberty more then . . . .
equity) the Knightes and Burgesses of the Committy (whereof some
yett live, and are now members of this honourable howse), being first

well enformed that the said St. Maries . . . . was anciently and before
the memory of man, a parish and parsonage (which . . . . . , without any appearing law, impropriated) . . . . unanimously to
endow the same with tithes for the Ministers livelihood . . . . . the
rents of the houses and edifices, and messuages . . . . be
builded on the ground or wasts scituate and being within the said
Parish of St. Maries, as it is and antientlie hath been taken . . . . .
. . . . . .   2s in the pound, for all the said rents, without exception,
with the oblations, or Easter booke, and all the accustomed . . . . .
. . . . appertayning to all Ministers . . . .
. . . . . . before the said bill could be transmitted . . . .
. . . . . . confirmation, the said Parliament was dissolved, and . . .
. . . . ner discowraged with loss of . . . . . . Coste and . . . . . .
. . . . ed any more herein.

[The rest of this Petition is wanting.]

XXVIII.

Petition from the County of Kent, to the House of Commons, for Reformation not Abrogation of the Liturgy.*

[No. 1.]   .

[There are three copies of the same petition, made evidently for circulation in different
districts. I have numbered them by way of distinction.]

Douer.

To the Honourable the House of Commons now assembled in
Parliament.

The humble Petition of many of the Gentrie, Ministers, Free-
holders, and Subsidie-men within the Countie of Kent,

Humbly shewing,

Whereas divers Petitions have beene addressed to this Honourable

---

* The annexed three Petitions are almost verbatim the same. The difference between
them is only such as would easily occur in transmitting copies of any one petition to

1641.
17 Car. 1.

House, earnestly praying Releife and Ease from many Pressures, both in the Civill and Ecclesiastical state of this Kingdome.

And further, whereas it hath beene desired by some that there * be an utter abolition of all government by Bishops, and an abrogation of the Publike forme of Common Prayer. May it please this Honourable House, wee doe earnestly and heartily concurre with the sayd Petitioners, for Releife and Ease against the many exorbitancies and pressures generally suffered of late, both in the Church and State.

But wee doe, withall, earnestly and heartily, as possibly wee can, beseech and pray this Honourable House, both in the Church Government and in our present Liturgie, † to give us a severe Reformation, not an absolute Innovation.

And, because truth and peace can meete togeither but uppon one side (although there be strong confidence on both sides), wee most humbly pray, even for God's sake (whose cause it is, and frome whome onely wee must have both Peace and Truth), that you will either commande ‡ a free nationall synod to be forthwith called, of Persons irreproveable in Life and Doctrine; or else, that you please not to conclude us up unhearde (which wee are confident you will not), but grant us a solemne, free debate, by chosen

different districts for signature. The variations, as they respectively occur, are noted *infra*.

As there is no date to these petitions, we can only obtain it by approximation. The first signature to the Dover petition is that of Thomas Cullen, Mayor. By the Corporation Records, it appears that he was elected to the Mayoralty 8 September, 1641, and on November 20, 1641, we find Sir Edward Dering speaks boldly and powerfully in defence of the much assailed Liturgy (Speeches 96-107). We shall not befar wrong, therefore, in inserting these petitions at this place, as dating between September and November 1641.

* In No. 3, instead of " there be," it is " there might be."

† In No. 2, these words are added after Liturgy—(" if upon just and lawfull disquisition by learned men, anie errrors shall be found in either.")

‡ In No. 3, " command" is erased, and " use meanes that " substituted, and the word " to" after " synod" erased ; the whole sentence running thus, " will either use meanes that a free nationall synod be forthwith called," &c.

Persons to be held before you, whereuppon you may please to settle such Resolutions as may deservedly binde all our obedience for the times to come.

And we shall ever most heartily pray, &c.

Gentlemen.	Ministers.	Freeholders.	Freemen of the Port of Dover.
Thomas Cullen, maior		Michaell Burnley	John Perrott
* Step. Monins		Fra. Raworth	Richard Foord
* Will. Leonard	Jo. Reading	John Youngez	John Benger
* Jon. Pringle	Jos. Alleyn	William Hatton	W. Pepper
* Tho. Teddeman	Francis Marshe	Will. Waad	Henry Teddiman
* Luke Pepper	Thomas Graunts	William Eldred	John Kenton
* Luke Braylsforde		Humfrey Mantlle	Richard Neales
* Hen. Booth		John Foord	John White
Dan. Porten		Geo. West	Thomas Wim . .
* Jo. Golder		Tresham Steveins	Richard Knight
* Nycholas Roberts		Thos. + Stoke his	Robert + Venitar
* John Loome		mark	Jacob Willer
Paull Wymond		Nicholas Hatton	Thomas Dawkes
Anth. Perceual		Edward Baylline	Abraham Upton
F. Fairfax		John Whitt + mark	Thomas Rudder
W. Fowler		Cockrell Harwod	Edw. Worthington
Edw. Kempe		Tho. Mason	Robert Anderson
Ja. Skynner		Robert Wickenden	John Barly
Isaack Cotton		J. Jacob	Thomas Miles
Luke Burden		William Hedgant	Giles Smith
Bartho. Wins		William Eastone	Thomas Edge
John Browne		Edw. + Nash, mark	John Keen
Willm Waldeg		William Dawkes	Nathaniel Burges
Will. Fox		John Morris	Thomas Heringham
Giles Goddard		Roger Hutson	William James
Charles Elwood		Roger White	Richard Clarke
John Harrison		Eleazer + Kirton	Henry Hart
Will. Stratfeld		George + Turke	Thomas Pepper
		Edward Ranger	

Gentlemen.	Ministers.	Freeholders.	Freemen.
Thomas Garritt		Richard Jacob	John Fryer, + mark
Robert Wickenden		George Edge	Gilbert Wand
Hugh Morrell		William Radgant	Thomas + Hardume
Amb. Goddard		Francis Lulham	Roger Partridg
William Fordred		Thomas Osberne	James Bardwell
William Turner		Thomas Barrington	Will. + Otlainger
Timothie Jaye		Richard Phillips	Edw. White
John Bockinge		Richard + Summers	Richard Blisse
Giles Rawlines		William Cronx	John Croup
		John Rolfe	Thomas + Mantle
		Jeremye Pattisson	Edmun Hammon
		Joseph + Louper	Robart Baylie
		Richard Dawkes	Rafe + Pen
		Anth. Keylocke	Simon Barden
		George Eppes	Thomas Lovell
		John Wallop	William Poole
		Bennet Hickson	Robert Fanton
		John + Barrat	John Edge
		John Burden	John Willams
		Peeter Nepuen[?]	James Costen

[No. 2.] *

Gentlemen.	Ministers.	Freeholders.	Subsidie-men.
Bube. Webbe	Rich. Bond of Frit-	Tho. Buckherst	Thomas Bayly
Fran. Webbe	tenden	Robert Wood +	William Igelden
George Webbe		Henry Bourner +	Christopher Cooper+
		John Drayner	John Munne
		Richard Pattenson	John Payne
		Nicholas Brissenden	Simon Drayner
		William Crompe +	
		John Water	
		Thomas Water	
		Ri. Taylor +	

* The same Petition as No. 1, only differing in a single sentence, as noted p. 60.
Therefore it is not necessary to insert it again. I merely give the signatures. It is evidently the portion signed by the Frittenden people.

1641.
17 Car. I.

[No. 3.]*

Gentlemen.	Ministers.	Freeholders.	Subsidie-men.
Francis Marshe Thomas Marshe, senr. Thomas Marshe, junr. Robert Marshe	William Osborne	Richard Brookman John Gardner Thomas + Adams Thomas + Brook Isaak Adames	William Smith

XXIX.

Letter from Sr EDWARD DERING to his Lady, with Parliamentary Intelligence.

17 December.

DEARE SWEET HEART,

If I do willingly fayle thee in returne of my letters, which I perceive so wellcome to thee, never trust me. Besse is willing to go downe, but afraid of the tides, which indeed have of late beene desperately bad.

My affectionate returne to my owne deare sister, and, when my brother returnes, to him.

I cannot but somewhat wonder att Sr William Brockman,† who knew my intentions, and did set me on, with enticing me to have

---

* The same petition as No. 1, differing only in two instances, which I have noted, p. 61. This is evidently the portion signed by the East Langdon people. The Marsh family was a very ancient one in the hamlet of Martin in this parish. Thomas Marsh devised the family estate to his son John, who in 1646 conveyed it to John Burvill of Sutton, clerk ; and William Osborne was Rector of East Langdon, 1616, and died 1641 ; his son, William Osborne, succeeded him as Rector, being instituted Oct. 6, 1641.

† Sir William Brockman, of Beechborough, see p. 43. n.

some of the curious coloured deare, which he knew me fond of. He
told me I should have all them.   He sayd, of himselfe, " I know you
do desire no other, lett me alone to fitt you, I know you do not
desire above 6 or 7." Well, that market cannot now be mended.

I wish you had sent up the money, for my mother must have
73*l.* now.

I did not think to be so tyed as I am heere.   This day, Dovor
harbor businesse was againe debated.   S*r* H. Hayman* is peevish;
but I have prevayled with the rest, that my brother Perc. is not to
lay downe 500*l.* unlesse the duty be received by him.

Farewell, in furious hast,

Thy,

EDWARD DERING.

[Superscription.]
To my best and dearest the Lady Dering, at Surenden Dering.

[Seal.]   A saltire with the Ulster hand on fess point.

[Endorsed not by S*r* Edward Dering; but probably by Lady Dering—
" December 17, 1641.   My deare."]

XXX.

LIST OF RECUSANTS IN KENT.

Names of Recusants in Kent presented by the Knights for that
County.

S*r* Henry Guildeford, K*t*.	de Rolvenden.
Edward Guildeford, Esq.	de eadem.
Clement Finch, Esq.	de Milton juxta Sitingborn.
Richard Hawkins, Esq.	de Selling.

* Sir Henry Heyman, Bart., of Somerfield, in Sellindge.   He was, at this time, member
for Hythe.

† The exact date of this paper does not appear.   It may possibly have been prepared
before the time at which it is placed.

CAMD. SOC.   K

1641-2.
17 Car. I.

William Petit, Esq.	. . .	de Boughton under the Blean.
John Best, Gent.	. . . .	de St. Laurence juxta Cantuariam.
George Littleboy, Gent.	. .	de Byrling.
Ralph Loane, Gent.	. . .	de eadem.
George Loane, Esq.	. . .	de Sevenoke.
Henry Whetenhall, Esq.	. .	de East Peckham.
Benjamin Wyborne, Gent.	.	de Pepenbury.
Anthony Roper, Esq.	. . .	de Eltham.
Sr Anthony Roper, Kt.	. .	de Ferningham.
Henry Roper, Esq.	. . .	de eadem.
Thomas Turner, Gent.	. .	de Linsted.
. . . Stiche, Attorney at Law		de Orpinton.

[Endorsed by Sr Edward Dering—" Recusants names in Kent."]

XXXI.

Letter from Sr EDWARD DERING, to his Lady, with Notes about the King and Parliament.

MY TRULY DEARE SOUL,

13 January.

I did long for this letter, and the rather because John [*]
Darell came up without one; but I told him itt was his fault, not
to send a man unto you. I doubt he hath but a dullnesse of soul
in any thing but frugality, and, if there be too much of that, that is
a dullnesse too. If he had not preferred his twelvth market (which
every yeare he hath) before a knighthood, which no man in the
world takes above once in his life, he had been knighted on twelvth
day. If he had kept time and promise to be heere on Saterday
night, itt had been done (the Queen was moved again) on Sunday.
But, whether his own dullnesse, or Locker's joviality, or Harry's,
or all together, they came on Friday to Maydston, on Saterday to
Dertford, and on Sunday to Greenwich, and so to London, about

[*] Of Calehill in Little Chart.

4 or 5 of the clock, soon enough (for a necessity then), but came not to me untill Monday * (although I sent him word I would stay within till ten of the clock, and did so), between 2 and 3 of the clock afternoon. Indeed, he was looking for me before; but I sent him word, that att 9 I should go forth, yett would stay for him till 10, and did so. The issue is, that the King,† about two of the clock, went suddenly out of towne with the Queen and Prince, angered and feared with the preparation of armes to attend us the next day. Nor can I wonder at his purpose therein; but approve it.

Thus Mr. Darell is like to be Mr. Darell. Yesterday morning (for I saw him not nor heard from him on Tuesday) he sent to know when to come to me. I bid him come presently away, and, when he came, I gave him a letter, and sent him to Hampton Court : but by that time he was on horsebacke the King was gone to Windsor (if too Windsor); but gone he was. Some think to Windsor, and thence to Woodstocke, and farther: others think he well ‡ to Portesmouth. Jealousys are high, and my heart pitty's a King so fleeting and so freindlesse, yett without one noted Vice. The times are desperate, and 100*l.* in hand may quickly be worth 100*l.* per annum. Will. Gibbes wrote yesternight for my advice. He would faigne attend the King with his person, as other cavaliers do; but his purse is empty, and the King so poore he cannot feed them that follow him. I was told that the Prince one night wanted wine, and another candles. In the meane time, the Commons go high ; and, not onely the house, but a committee of the house, have armed and imbanded the King's subjects, not onely without his leave asked, but have

---

* *i.e.* January 10th.

† The King went to Hampton Court on 10th January, and on the next day the five accused members came from their lodgings in the city to Westminster, guarded by the sheriffs and trained bands of London and Westminster (under the command of Sergeant-Major-General Skippon), and attended by a conflux of many thousands of people, crying out, as they passed Whitehall, " What has become of the King and his cavaliers," and " where is he gone?" This was the " preparation of armes to attend us next day," the prospect of which drove the King from London.

‡ *sic.*

made a Sergeant-Major-General * to the King's terror; for thereupon he went out of towne, and not till then.

The Lieutenant of the Tower † (a gentleman of moderation and especiall worth) is voted a delinquent, and 'tis thought, must not hold it. The house would recommend one Sr John Conyers, one whom Strafford preferred to the government of Barwicke against the Scotts.

Heere have been 5,000 Petitioners out of Buckinghamshire (but I believe not above 2,000) to offer their lives to execute our commands. My mother will send down the petition.

If I could be Pym, with honesty, I had rather be Pym then King Charles.

The King is too flexible and too good natur'd; for, within two howers, and a greate deale lesse, before he made Culpeper Chancellor of the Exchequer, he had sent a messenger to bring Pym unto him, and would have given him that place.

By the help of God, you need not to feare my personall safety. Many thousands guarded us on Tuesday; ‡ and every day we have

---

* This was Captain Skippon, of whom Clarendon says, " That the Trained Bands of London might be under the command of a man fit to lead them, they granted a commission to Captain Skippon, who was Captain of the Artillery Garden, to be Major-General of the Militia of the City of London, an office never before heard of, nor imagined that they had authority to constitute. The man had served very long in Holland, and, from a common soldier, had raised himself to the degree of a captain, and to the reputation of a good officer; he was a man of order and sobriety, and untainted with any of those vices which the officers of the army were exercised in, and had newly given over that service upon some exceptions he had to it, and, coming to London, was, by some friends, preferred to that command in the Artillery Garden, which was to teach the citizens the exercise of their arms. He was altogether illiterate, and, having been bred always abroad, brought disaffection enough with him, from thence, against the Church of England, and so was much caressed and trusted by that party. This man marched that day at the head of their tumultuary army to the Parliament House."

† Sir John Byron.

‡ Vide as to dates, p. 67, *supra*. After the five members had been brought by the Trained Bands from the City to Parliament, Clarendon states that, after thanking them, the parliament appointed " Serjeant Major General Skippon every day to attend at Westminster, with such a guard as he thought sufficient for the two houses."

a sufficient guard against no enemy.   Mr. Bullock came, and offered, with his freinds, to be my personall guard : I refused itt, but could not persuade him from my side, from morning to night, unlesse in the very house.

Betty hath taken a glister and two potions: Besse says she is yett all one; the D^r says she must purge againe.   Thy goodnesse will not owne thine owne goodnesse : for, in saying she is now among her best freindes, thou dost wrong thy selfe, worth all of them, and more. I flatter not, I speake my very heart.   My sister Gibb wrote me word, that she would have the girle to dinner there this day, and desired me ; I can not go.   I have appointed your daynty goose and two capons, to be carryed by the girle in the coache.   The girle is with my mother att noone, such days as she takes no physick, and not else; but then, from morning to evening.

I have sent some pamphletts, and, for my love, a Spanish commodity choicely done : betwixt a bribe and a gratitude : I know not how I come by itt, but they are of the best.

I thank my love for her hearty prayers, and do not doubt of a blessed effect of them.   I owe thee mine, and thou hast them, as true as for thine owne,

EDWARD DERING.

13 Jan. 1641.

Sr Tho: Shirley* (now come in) commands a hearty remembrance to you.

---

* Sir Thomas Shirley of St. Botulph's-bridge, co. Huntingdon, knighted 22nd May, 1622. This was the antiquary and genealogist, whose principal collections are preserved in the British Museum and in the library of Queen's College, Oxford.   (See Shirley's Stemmata Shirleiana, p. 93-103.)

XXXII.

Letter to Sᵣ EDWARD DERING, with strong Remonstrances against Passages in his Parliamentary Speeches, from T.R.

SIR,

Uppon my perusuall of your last speech in Parliament,* I tooke to myself an humble purpose of signifyeing to your worthie self some animadversions and notes unto which the severall perticulers of your speech occasioned me.

In the first place, I shalbe bould to say ingeniously, that I heartily am sorry that the bias of your judgment, "in hoc die," after such a meridian light shineing uppon us, both from abroade, in the reformed churches, and at home, in soe many judicious, elaborate, and learned treatises, formerly, and of late, should seeme to sway soe much to that side, which will certainly expose your late honourable esteeme in the hearts of judicious and good men, to a great, at least, diminucion and distemper. I humbly conceave very many things in your speech doe labour of a verie great measure of affection. I shalbe bould to instance in some fewe for all.

It is surely true, that much of late hath been written and sayd to

* Sir Edward's " last " speech was 22 November, 1641, upon " the Remonstrance," in which he defends the bishops against the charge of idolatry, &c., and gives an emphatic "no" to the proposal (p. 111-119). This defence of the bishops seems to have offended T. R., who had expected more " root and branch " work from Sir Edward. He takes exception also to a passage in Sir Edward's speech, in defence of the liturgie, November 20, in which he says "Impudence, or ignorance, is now grown so frontlesse, that it is loudly expected by many that you should utterly abrogate all formes of publique worship ; and, at least, if you have a shorte forme, yet not to impose the use of it. Extirpation of Episcopacie, that hope is already swallowed, and now the same men are as greedy for abolition of the liturgie : that so the Church of England, in her publique prayers, may hereafter turne a babler at all adventure—a brainlesse, stupid, and an ignorant conceit of some." (p. 102.) A passage totally misrepresented in T. R.'s remonstrance. This passage was not in Sir Edward's " last " speech, but the last but one, perhaps it was the " last " that had come to T. R's. hands.

1641-2.
17 Car. I.

and fro, on both sides, about a right administration of discipline and worshipp; and truly, Sir, me thinkes, out of that diversitie of what hath been spoken and written, the Parliament hath a very faire overture given them, to discover and finde out the truth, which, without it, would be of more difficultie to them. It is your owne way, in your Parliamentary affaires; and, in all Judicatories concerning Episcopacie, soe much hath bin cleerly evinced against it, and nothing of any weight for it, that I shall say nothing at all in that particular, onely I shall beseech you to consider, whether it can possibly be beleeved that amongst any sort of Protestants, especially the conscientious partie (for the conceite of some giddy, silly people is inconsiderable), there be anie that doe protest against * the three undoubted signes of a true visible church. If you meane puritie of doctrine, sacraments, and discipline, I knowe, for my part, none that are (quoad esse) att any doubt in the former two, as concerning our church; and for the later, I knowe noe man of a right judgment, that can acknowledge it for other then such as it is: Romish and Antichristian. Sir, I doe not doubt, but that, upon search, some may be founde even amongst us, that denie the verie trinitie of persons; and of what number the Arminian, Socinian, and other hellish, popish errors are I knowe you are not ignorant; but, if theis, or any other of the like nature, should now presse into your presence, either in word or writing, I doubt not your care in your honourable house will shewe it self, in a sudden suppression of them.

---

* The passage here alluded to in Sir Edward's Speech is : " If I would deale with a Papist, to reduce him, he answers (I have been answered so already), To what religion would you persuade me ? What is the Religion you professe ? Your nine-and-thirty articles, they are contested against. Your publique solemne Liturgy, that is detested : and, which is more then both these, the three essentiall, proper, and onely markes of a true Church, they are protested against : what Religion would you perswade me to ? Where may I find, and know, and see, and read the Religion you professe ? I beseech you, Sir, helpe me an answer to the Papist " (p. 100) ; and then Sir Edward appends a note—' *Protestation protested* denies the Church of England to have the three marks of the true Church.' T. R. however, in taking the three points as Purity of Doctrine, Sacraments, and Discipline, begs the question, and argues sophistically.

Concerning the Liturgie, I shall say nothing. Much hath beene judiciously said about it; but am heartily sorrie, that such words as theis should ever have fallen from the learned lipps of Sr Edward Deering, that "the church of England, in her publick prayers, nay her offerture,* may be as a babbler, at all adventures, a brainles, stupid, and an ignorant conceite of some."

Sir Edward Deereing, yf conceaved prayers be a brainles, stupid, and ignorant conceit of some, and not most proper to the publicke ministracion of an able ministrie, I will not say,† that noble Lord's eyes that lately speake in the house of Peeres on this subject, but better eyes of multitudes then his or yours, doe faile them. Sir, I conceive you are, and are not, a competent judge in this matter.‡

* In Sir Edward's authorised version of his speeches, he gives the passage " in her public prayers may hereafter turne a babbler ;" and appends a note in the margin, sic — " In the false copy abroad, instead of ' may hereafter,' the silly transcriber put in ' nay her offerture,' which hath been some displeasure to me." (p. 102.) This note is a sufficient reply to T. R. Again, in introducing his Speech, Sir Edward says, " A coppy whereof, being stolen from me, issued lately forth, both unknown to me, and misprinted also, which hath beene entertained abroad both with applause and exception." (p. 96.)

† In the margin " Lord Say." This alludes to the well-known Speech which was answered by Archbishop Laud.

‡ In his so-often quoted speech of November 20, Sir Edward had said, " I must again propound my doubtfull ' quære,' to be resolved by the wisdome of this house ; whether we be ' idonei et competentes judices ' in doctrinall resolutions. In my opinion we are not. . . . The short close of all with a motion is but this: we are poisoned in many points of doctrine ; and I know no antidote, no recipe for cure but one—a well chosen and well tempered nationall synod, and God's blessing thereon : this may cure us ; without this (in my poor opinion) England is like to turne itselfe into a great Amsterdam. And, unlesse this councell be very speedy, the disease will be above the cure. Therefore, that we may have a full fruition of what is here but promised, I doe humbly move that you will command forth the Bill for a national synod, to be read the next morning. I saw the Bill, above five moneths since, in the hand of a worthy Member of this House. If that Bill be not to be had, then my humble motion is (as formerly) that you would name a Committee to draw up another. This being once resolved, I would then desire that all motions of religion (this about the Liturgy especially) may be transferred thither, and you will find it to be the way of peace and unity among us here." (p. 104-105.)

Sir, I heartily wish with you for a nationall Synod, well tempered with learning and pietie; that the wavering judgments of unsetled men's mindes might be rightly directed, about as well the doctrine of the Sabbath, as other matters of right worshipp and ecclesiasticall pollicie, which, by reason of the want of a present publicke competent determination thereof, suffer much in the mindes of very many. Sir, I shall now humbly desire but thus much of you, even that what I have written " ex animo et amore " may not be taken in any sinister or exasperate sense; onely, I desire you to be pleased to remember, that you now stand in a publicke designation of a most considerable trust reposed in you by God and your country, impartially, without passion, prejudice, or affection, for your part, to contribute your best abilities to make upp the hedge in the thorough reformacion of the church and kingdome, that soe the church of England may, by your blessed meanes, become that which it never was yet, the glory of the reformed religion: which is the humble and heartie daylie prayer of him who is

1611-2.
17 Car. I.

Your unfeignedly well wishing frend,
T. R.

Jan. 21, 1641.

Followe peace with all men, and holines, without which noe man shall see the Lord, lookeing diligently least any man fall from the grace of God ; lest any root of bitternes springing upp trouble you, and thereby many be defiled.—Hebr. 12.

God of his infinite mercie quench all unkindely heate in all your honourable assemblie.

[Superscription,]

" To the right worshipfull Sr Edward Deereing,
    Kt. & Baronet, be theis dd."

[Seal,] A Pelican, but hardly armorial.

[Endorsed by Sr Edward Dering—" 1641, 23 January. T. R."]

XXXIII.

1642.
17 Car. I.

Notes of an angry Conversation respecting the Circumstances of his Expulsion from the House of Commons, by Sr EDWARD DERING.*

D.—How happy and blessed had we been in this Parliament, if you, and five or six more that I could name, had never been born; or else, had never been of this house.

W.—We shall never be at peace, until five or six of this house be hanged.

M. P.—Your brother Dering would hang us if he could.

W.—You shall see, the way we go will be blessed, and will prosper.

D.—It will not be long (not many monthes) before all this mountayn of endeavour to root out Episcopacy, and to abolish our Liturgy, will fall downe, ly still and stinke, and shame the endeavourers thereof. I know thou art of that sence. And I will never cease, by word, by writing, and by prayer, to oppose itt: and thus I begin; God confounde thy purposes, and the way thou goest. God confounde the way the house goes.

M. P.—I would have the offence of Willmot, Ashburnham, and Pollard, made treason by a Bill.†

D.—I do not love this making of treason. Retrospective lawes are dangerous to our libertys and our lives. But thou art a superstitious fellow, a meere idolater; thou worshippest the brainless idoll of thine owne imagination.

M. P.—Wherein?

---

* I print these notes as I find them jotted down on a loose sheet. Sir Edward was expelled the House 2nd Feb. 1641-2, and his book burned, according to a vote of the House. Probably these notes were drawn up soon after that time. It would seem as if there had been three parties to the conversation, viz. Sir Edward Dering, perhaps one of his brothers-in-law (Sir Peter Wroth, or Gibbes), and a Member of Parliament. I have conjecturally assigned to each of these respectively the share he may be supposed to have taken in the conversation, by prefixing the letters D., W., M.P.

† They were charged with a plot to bring the army up to London, to overawe the Parliament.

1612.
17 Car. I.

D.—Thou makest an idoll of the omnipotent power of Legislation in this house.

W.—The Legislative power is the idoll of the house.

M. P.—The worst thing that ever you did was the speaking against the order of the house. Then you lost me*.

D.—That order (of the 8th September) is a wicked, injurious, irreligious order; and unparliamentary.

M. P.—Itt is fitt that this you say be reported to the house.

[Here ends the first page of the sheet. The second seems to have been written in different ink, and on some subsequent day. ED.]

D.—As for Roote and Branche, I am resolved by word, and by writing, to do you all the mischiefe I can, and I make no doubt but that my booke and I shall do you more mischiefe out of the house, then if I were still among you.

You have burnt my booke, and thereby raysed the price, and raised the desires of such as would have [it]. Alas, the burning of my booke cannot confute me, nor silence me in the way I go. Itt is not in the power of the house to confute me, though you should burne me with my booke; but itt is in the wisedome of the house to confute me; for I will ever be the servant, the slave of reason. Good reason (without any other power) shall ever convert me.

---

* Vide Sir Edward Dering's Speeches, pp. 78, 82, and 83, wherein, speaking against the order, he says, "Master Speaker—I shall be afraid to arraigne your orders: I have already been controlled (not for doing so, but as if I had done so), yet, Sir, I have often heard it in this House, that we '*are masters of our owne orders;*' and then (I thinke) we may in this place, arraigne them,—that is, question them, try them, approve, alter, reject, or condemn them . . . . Surely, Sir, I shall speake reverently of all your orders when I am abroad: I have done so of this. I am resolved that my obedience shall therein be found good, although my particular reason be rebellant to your conclusions. This is my duty abroad; but here, in this House, within these walles, freedome is my inheritance: and give me leave, I pray, at this time, to use a part of my birthright."

Then follows a splendid burst of eloquence against the order of the House "That all corporall bowing at the name of Jesus be henceforth forborne." This is the order, for speaking against which, Sir Edward is censured in the text; and which he, in reply, calls a " wicked, injurious, irreligious order, and unparliamentary."

I was unwilling that clause about my expulsion from the house should be inserted. I had not any thing to do therein. I did, att last, blott itt out with mine owne hand: but, had that clause concerned any man but myself, itt should not have been struck out, if I could prevayl; nay, though I were on the ground, I would ly untill you all went over my belly before I would consent to the expunging of itt. And, if my partner Culpeper should be so expelled, I would ride from east to west, and visitt all Kent, but we would petition him in again.

If you be a Deputy Lieutenant, by virtue of a vote of one or both houses, without the King, I tell you before hand, I will never obey you, but will undergo the penalty of my refusal.

To the ministers. Now you have a time, if you will make use of itt.

XXXIV.

Petition to the House of Commons from HENRY DARELL, to get the son and heir of his late brother, WILLIAM DARELL, Esq., out of the custody of the boy's mother, who was a Papist.

To the Honourable Assembly of the Commons House of Parliament.

The humble Petition of Henry Darell, Esqr.

Shewinge,

That, whereas William Darell, Esqr., the petitioner's brother, beinge seized in fee of the manner of Chingley and Scotney, amongst other lands, in Com. Kanc., of the yearly value of £400, or thereaboutes, and havinge six children, the eldest of them beinge not above the age of xij yeares, and beinge indebted in greate summes of money, did, by Indenture dated 19⁰ Julii, 13 Car., demyse Shingley Wood to the Petitioner and others, untill Michaelmas which shalbe anno Domini 1657; and the residue, untill Michaelmas which shalbe anno Domini 1652; in trust, and to such uses as he should, by his deed, or last will, limit and appoynt; and, for want of such limitations, to theis uses; viz., to pay his debts, to maintayne his children, and to rayse moneye, as much as might be out of the profitts thereof, for portions for his 3 daughters and 3 (*sic*) younger sonns : and to pay to his eldest sonne, from his full age until Michaelmas 1652, £100 yearly.

That the said William Darrell did, ultimo Augusti, 14 Car., by his will, ratifye and confirme the uses in the said indenture, and shortly after dyed : after whose death, the petitioner proved the said will, takeing upon him the execution thereof; and did, by office, entytle his Majestie to the wardship of the body, and of a third part of the lands of his brother's sonne, which [were] graunted unto the Petitioner, by indenture under severall scales of the court of wards, the rest of the lessees refusinge to intermeddle in the estate ; and the Petitioner, havinge noe children of his owne, did, out of the affection he beareth to his deceased brother, and out of a desire his sonne might live prosperously and plentifully in the world, beinge heire at lawe of the Petitioner's father's howse, take upon him the manadginge of the said estate, and hath paid or taken order for all, or the greatest part, of his said brother's debts, and did put his said brother's sonne to a schoole to be taught and bred by a Protestant schoolemaster ; the Petitioner indeavouringe to increase his brother's estate in all things, for the good of his sonne, and the rest of his children, and to have them bredd and brought up in learninge, and in the Protestant religion.

That Elizabeth Darrell, the widow and relict of the said William Darrell, beinge a vyolent Romanist, hath conveighed her sonne home unto her, and will not suffer him to goe back to schoole; but keepeth one William Applebee a popishe schoolemaster in her howse at Scotney Castle, to teach and instruct the said children in Popery; and, to that end, the said Elizabeth keepeth her out dores locked up, the house being walled and double moated aboute ; and keepeth the castle gates with gunnes and halbeards, to terrifie people from comeing there, imployinge the said William Applebee only to buy and sell for her, and to manadge her estate.

Yt may therefore please this honourable assemblie, to give order that the said Elizabeth may, accordinge to the statute of 3° Jacobi, capit. 5°, have but a third part of the lands of the said William Darrell, and that she may have noe part of his goods; and that by your honourable order to confirme your Petitioner's estate and trust, and to deliver his brother's children to the Petitioner without allowance for their keepinge, and he will take care that they shalbe bread and brought up in learninge, and in the Protestant religion; or that the Petitioner may be discharged of the trust, as shall seeme most fitt to this honourable assembly.

And the Petitioner shall, &c.

HENRY DARELL.

[Endorsed,—Darell's Petition.]

XXXV.

Letter to Sr EDWARD DERING, from his eldest Son Edward,* about the Difficulties he had in obtaining a Pass to go Abroad.

COLENDISSIME PATER,

Quod in me est feci; neque tamen abeundi veniam impetrare possum, nemini (aiunt) transfretandum, nisi qui prius fœdus Scoticum præstitit; neque ea quidem lege, quantum video, filio tuo. Omnes quos mihi alloquendi copia datur, Galliam Hollandiæ multum præferunt, argumentis ductis ex linguæ Gallicanæ præstantiâ, cui addunt, quod ibi minoris quam Lugduni Batavorum degere possumus: præsertim, si quis artem tripudiandi, equitandi, &c. neglexerit.

---

* According to family papers, he was born December 1625, therefore at this time was a few weeks over 18 years of age.

1643-4.
19 Car. I.

In Galliâ, urbem Aureliensem, Caenensem, Angiers, et Academiam Monpelier præcipuè laudant. Me quod attinet, utrumque pariter affecto, locumque quem tu aptissimum, eundem credam et ego jucundissimum. Tuum erit imperare,—auscultare

Obsequentissimi filii

Februarii 29.   EDUARDI DÆRING.

Amantissimæ matri obsequium nostrum præstes, rogo, fratribus et sororibus amorem.

If I should go over into France, my unkle Percivall can helpe me over at Rye.

I will endeavour to passe this weeke. If you would be pleased to write, either to the Speaker, or some parliament man, it may be it might be done.

Sr Peter Wroth * tells me, the Speaker (from whom alone a passe must be got) will give none but to those that will take the oath of allegeaunce, supremacy, and the covenant; and besides, maketh some scruple of me more then an other.

[Superscription,]

To his honoured Father, Sr Edward Dering,
   Knight and Baronett, at Surrenden Dering, in Kent.

   [Endorsed by Sr Edward Dering.—"1643 1o Martii—Ned."]

---

* Sir Peter Wroth was his uncle, having married a sister of Sir Edward Dering.

NOTES TAKEN BY SIR EDWARD DERING

AS CHAIRMAN OF THE SUB-COMMITTEE OF RELIGION
APPOINTED NOV. 23, 1640.*

23 NOVEMBER, 1640.—COMMITTEE.

Sr Edward Dering.	Sr Wm Masham.
Sr Simonds Dewes.	Sr Wm Bruerton.
S^r Jo. Clotworthy.	S^r Jo. Wray.
Sr Roger Palmer.	Sr Edw. Hungerford.
Mr Corbet.	Sr Oliver Luke.
Mr Knatchbull.	Mr Upton.
Sr Gilbert Pickering.	Mr Cromwell.
Mr Bagshaw.	Mr Goodwin.
Mr Purefoy.	Mr Bodwell.
Lo. Ruthen.	Mr Jephson.
Mr Moore.	Sr Robert Harley.
Sr Hen: Mildmay.	Sr Anthony Ireby.

Committee

To discover the many sufferings of ministers by ecclesiasticall proceedings: and for this, to survey registers.

To consider what quæstions have been propounded to ministers, when they come to receive orders.

To examine abuse in bookes, in licencing, in printing, in forbidding them.

---

* This is a small 4to. paper book wholly in the handwriting of Sir Edward. He gives the following account of the appointment of the Sub-Committee:—" Upon my motion November 23, it pleased the Grand Committee [i.e. the Committee of the whole house. ED.] for religion, to appoint a Sub-committee, to receive complaints from oppressed ministers, which Sub-committee was shortly after made a Committee by order of the house. It pleased the gentlemen of this Committee to put the honour and the burden of the chaire upon me." (Sir Edward Dering's Speeches, p. 42.)

24 NOVEMBER.

Sr Edward Dering.   Mr Jephson.
Mr Purefoy.   Sr Anthony Ireby.
Sr Henry Mildmay.   S^r Jo: Wray.
Sr Edw. Hungerford.

Sir Edw. Dering to the chaire.

Committee adjourned to Wensday, 25, *horâ consuetâ.*

25 NOVEMBER.—TREASURY CHAMBER.

Sr Edward Dering.   Sr Hen. Mildmay.   Mr Knatchbull.
Sr Roger Palmer.   Sr Wm Masham.   Mr Goodwin.
Mr Purefoy.   S^r Jo. Wray.   Mr Bodwell.
Mr Moore.   Mr Corbet.   Sr Rob. Harley.

HENRY BELL, a part of Luther's workes, which he calls "Luther's last divine discourses," whereof 20 m. were printed, as this is dated Francford, 1574. This book long obscured, the rest for aught is knowen all burned, was found eight or nine yeares since.

He translated itt; desired to have it printed. The Archbishop saw the translation, which he sent for per Mr Bernes; liked itt; confessed he had not scene of that worke before; kept itt one yeare and a quarter; desired the originall; had that three quarter of a yeare. After the last parliament noted (*sic*), in December last, he said the book should be printed; but one head left out. Dr Bray told Mr Bell he doubted whether this were Luther's; said that somewhat there was fitt to be expunged; but what part, no intimation.

PAUL AMARANT, late of Wolterton, and, before that, of Ermingland, in Norfolk, clerk, was cited to the Bishop Wren's Visitation, in May 1636. Item, 13 May, being casually and voluntary in the cathedrall, he was charged of Dr. Corbet to be att evening service there: but he excused himselfe, saying, he was to preach next Sabaoth; whereunto the Dr. replyed, saying, Are you a devill, to call itt the Sabaoth? He went with the Dr. to prayers: behaved himselfe reverently : but was suspended for not bowing att the name of Jesus.

HENRY WILKINSON presented articles exhibited to him, when he was denyed to be minister.

ORDERS.—1. Mr. Bell to bring in that volume of Luther, and his translation, upon Fryday next, *horâ consuetâ.*

2. Send for a book written per Mr. Ward, entituled "Theologicall quæstions, dogmaticall observations, and evangelicall essays upon St. Mathew."

3. Move for Mr Amarant's petition, to be transmitted hither; because of use of his language, and he verst in the presse.

4. Move Mr. Wheeler and two lawyers to be added.

5. Thomas Payne * to be summoned.

6. Send for ten yeares registers of High Commission Court, and of the bishoprick of Norwich and of London, to be forthwith brought.

7. Move for Mr. Bell's petition to be referred hither, itt not having been read.

The Committee adjourned to Fryday, 27 November, *horâ consuetâ.*

27 NOVEMBER.—IBIDEM.

Sr Edward Dering.	Sr William Bruerton.
Mr Purefoy.	Mr Corbet.
Lord Ruthen.	Mr Knatchbull.
Mr Moore.	Mr Goodwin.
Sr William Masham.	Mr Jephson.

THOMAS PAYNE, printer; three monthes since he was setting his presse for Bishop Andrews his Catechisticall Doctrine. But Richard Badger † (beadle to the Company of Stationers) did come and forbid

---

* It was originally written " Thomas Payne, the printer, to be summoned ;" but "the printer " is crossed out.

† In text it is Bageant, corrected to Badger.

him to proceed therewith; and this he did in the name of my Lord of Canterbury, by word of mouth, not shewing any authority; but yet gave this reason, that the printing of this book was against the King and state, because it was against the decree of the Starre Chamber to print it, unlesse he (the sayd Payne) had a new licence for it; and then the said Bageant (*sic*) took away four reame and a half of printed paper of it, beeing one sheete and a half.

ORDERS.—Mr. Corbet and Mr. Bagshaw, to peruse the High Commission registers, there to collect, and thence to present hither what they shall conceive suitable to the order of the Grand Committee.

Mr. Bell to attend on Tuesday next with his booke.

Dr. Bray to attend; the time, as the present distance of the place where he is; the cause, to answer upon what part of this last work of Luther he did deny itt to be published.

Mr. Ward, of Hogsden, to come and to shew what pointes of doctrine were blotted out of his work, licensed per Tho: Wykes.

Richard Badger to shew cause why, and authority whereby, he forbad the presse, and toke away Bishop Andrews' Catechisticall Doctrine.

This Committee adjourned to Tuesday next, *horâ et loco consuetis.*

1° DECEMBRIS.—16TO CAR.—IBIDEM.

DR. BRAY—convented—entered protestation of his convocation privilege—answered, he did deny the publication of Mr. Bell's translation, not for any point of doctrine there to be excepted against; but onely, as not acknowledging it as any peece of Luther.

Concerning Dr. Pocklington's two bookes, *Sunday no Sabath,* and *Altare Christianum,* he did license the MS. copy; and (if the print be as the copy) he doth professe them to be consonant to the doctrine and discipline of the Church of England.

Concerning the Sabath, he sayth, that there is a rest due, and a time to be allotted for the publick service of God; but not *virtute precepti quarti,* which doth not enjoyne a *quota pars* to us.

Mr. Corbet—that Dr. Featly's sermons were castrated.

Jo. Rothwell, stationer—Dr. Featly doth complayne that his sermons (in fol.), being sett out in the last Archbishop's time, this Archbishop sent for him since; quæstioned the authority of the issuing them; had the book surveyed per Dr. Bray; printed per Nico. Borne: seventeen sheetes of paper were denyed, to the printers detriment, &c.

Idem Rothwell affirmeth that Mr. Fenner's bookes were denyed the presse, *eo nomine* because they were his, as will be proved per Thomas Nicholls—and this was by Dr. Wykes.

Paul Amirant's petition and cause to be heard on Tuesday two monthes, viz. 23 January, and he desired, but not enjoyned, to certify his opinion of this last peece of Luther.

Richard Badger (bedle to the Stationers) being asked, why he did cease at Thomas Payn's booke then in presse, called " Bishop Andrews' Catechistical Doctrines," answered, itt was not entred among the bookes to be licenced, and therefore, by order of the wardens of the company, he did cease it, which was, afterward, liked or allowed per the Archbishop.

Henry Wilkinson presented a petition, that, for a sermon against lukewarmnes, he was suspended from reading a divinity lecture, being all the spirituall promotion he had.

John Vicars, intimation versus Dr Baker et Dr Wykes, for denying licence to his bookes.

Mr. Tate, that " The Compleate Justice" is forged.

Orders.—Mr. Wilkinson's sermon to be sent for from Oxford.

Richard Badger, printer of Pocklington's book, to be sent for.

Nicholas Borne, printer, to bring the sermons of Dr. Featley.

Peter Coale att the Exchange, stationer, to appeare about bowing to the name Jesus.

Robert Dormer, of Grub Street, Jo. Bartlet, of Paul's Church Yard, about inserting new sence, by the new licencers.

Mr. Vicars, and Ann Griffen, to be heere.

Thomas Nicolls, printer, to be heere.

. . . . Young, a printer in Bredstreet, concerning "The Complete Justice."

Adjourned to Thursday, 3° Decembris.

3 DECEMBER.—IBIDEM.

Memorandum. Michael Sparks, in Little Old Baily, is willing to testify concerning restraynt of the presse.

Memorandum. I am to write a letter to Dr. Featley.

PETER COLE. In a booke of Dr. Sibbes, upon the third chapter to the Philippians, there were wordes inserted for the bowing at the name of Jesus, per Dr. Wykes. The copy is with Richard Coles in Aldersgate St.

RICHARD CARPENTER, clarke, now parson of Polling in Sussex, having made a recantation sermon at Paules, was angerly denyed the publication of itt, per Dr. Baker. The reasons — Because the Church of Rome and we are in a peaceable way, and therefore not fitt to augment controversys. He farther advised him, saying, " Be patient, the time may come that you may be heartily glad that your sermon is not printed." In that sermon (he the said Baker by violent counsell overruling him) he put itt as a speciall motive of his conversion, the outward sight of order and decency in this church ; and advised him also to say as little as might be (something must be said) against the church of Rome. Mr. Carpenter urging for the presse, he the said Baker asked, " What, will you turne to Rome againe ? If you will, you may, the Church of England hath no need of you."

ORDERS.—A warrant for Mr. Amirant to search the Bishops of Norwich registers, and to summon wittnesses.

Mr. Vicars to make good his petition on Tuesday next.

This Committee adjourned to Tuesday, 8 December.

8° DECEMBRIS, 1640.

THOMAS ROSSE of St. Magnus, cheesemonger, doth informe, that, about May last, diverse crosses, meddalls, Agnus Dei's, and amulets, were landed att Somers key, directed to one Monsr. Romee.

Item, he informeth, that Robert Peak, neare to Holborn Conduit, hath printed many pictures for the New Testament, and so bound them up.

RICHARD MORE, Esq. did send to one Philemon Stephens, a stationer, to gett licensed, " A True Relation of Enock ap Evans his story;" but the relation was denyed to be printed, by Dr. Wykes.

Mr. CARPENTER sayth, that he, meeting with one father Price, a Benedictine monke, and, expostulating with him about some injury received, the said Price, the next day, procured and sent a messenger for him the said Carpenter to attend Secretary Windebank, att nine of the clock, where the Secretary did threaten the said Carpenter for molesting the said Price.

ANNE GRIFFEN, widow, doth affirme that one part of Mr. Vicars petition.

She further sayth, that she, having the copy of fower sermons made by Dr. King, Bishop of London, and delivered to her by Dr. King, his sonne, Deane of Rochester.*

ORDERS.—Robert Yong to be sent for, for printing the Scottish Liturgy and the Scottish Testament with pictures, and " The Compleate Justice."

Robert Peak, at Holborn Conduit, to shew cause why he doth print such pictures, and why he bindes them up together, the book and the pictures.

Philemon Stephens, of Paul's Church Yard, to be sent for to testify.

Mr. White, minister, to be sent to, as Mr. Knatchbull hath undertaken, concerning Dr. Clark's sermons.

---

* There is something incomplete in this sentence, as well as the preceding ; perhaps it should be pointed thus—" She further sayth that—she having, &c." And the meaning of the whole may be " Anne Griffen affirms to (*i.e.* confirms) that one part of Mr. Vicars petition—and does so, having the copy," &c.

Mr. Vicars to make good his petition on Thursday the 17th December; and to have warrant for wittnesses.

Committee adjourned to Thursday, 10 December—*hord et loco consuetis.*

10 DECEMBER, 1540.

It was unanimously resolved upon the quæstion, that Mr. Wilkinson is free and cleare from every charge by the Vice-Chancellor layd upon him for his sermon.

Memorandum. The Committee desireth that I would go and speake to my Lord Primate of Ireland,* to know whether that part of the Vice-Chancellor's intimation concerning his Grace were true or not.

Memorandum. So I did, and his Lordship sayth itt is false.

WILLIAM STAMPE informeth, that, when Mr. Henry Langly did present himselfe to receive orders, Mr. Fulham, chapleyn to the Bishop of Oxford, did propound these quæstions following, viz. :—

1. Whether the Booke of Sportes be allowable.

2. Whether bowing toward the altar be superstitious.

3. Whether the Church have power to determine matters of fayth.

Unto these Mr. Fulham required a peremptory answer. This informant desired Mr. Fulham to forbeare this way; but he answered, "No. These quæstions were as a shibboleth, to determine who were fitt for orders, and who unfitt." Mr. Langley refused, but, att same time, Mr. Besbeech and Mr. Anderton did subscribe to the first and third, affirmative—to the second, negative.

PHILEMON STEPHENS affirmeth, that about four yeare since, the Relation by Richard More, Esq., of Enoch ap Evans, was refused the presse by Mr. Wykes, because (as he said) he had licensed the former by Mr. Studley.

" Reeu's catechisme" delivered to Sir Robert Harley; " Epistle of Jesus" to Sir William Brereton.

* * i. e. Archbishop Usher.*

ORDERS.—A report to be made of Mr. Wilkinson's cause.*

Mr. Thomas Langley, to make good his petition on Thursday 26 January,† and to have warant for witnesses, and to searche recordes.

---

* At p. 43 of his Speeches, Sir Edward gives the following as his speech on bringing up the Report to the Grand Committee of Religion, 18 Dec. 1640. " Mr. White, this Grand Committee for Religion did authorise a Sub-Committee (among other things) to take into consideration the unjust sufferings of good ministers oppressed by the cruell-used authority of Hierarchicall rulers. In this (and in other points) we have entered upon many particulars; we have matured and perfected but one. If we had lesse worke, you should (before this time) have had more: but complaints crowd in so fast upon us, that the very plenty of them retards their issue. The present report which I am to make unto you is concerning Mr. Wilkinson, a Batchellor in Divinity, and a man in whose character do concur learning, piety, industry, modesty. Two hardships have been put upon him— one at the time when he presented himselfe to receive orders, and that was thus. The Bishop of Oxford's Chaplen, Mr. Fulham, being the Examiner (for Bishops now do scorne to do Bishops' work ; it belongs to himselfe), he propoundeth foure questions to Mr. Wilkinson, not taken out of the depth of Divinity, but fitly chosen to discover how affections do stand to be novellized by the mutability of the present times. The questions were these—1. Whether hath the Church authority in matters of faith ? 2. May the King's Booke of Sports (so some impious Bishops have abused our pious King, to call their contrivance his Majesties Book)—may this be read in the church without offence ? 3. Is bowing to or before the altar lawfull ? 4. Is bowing at the name of Jesus lawfull ? The doctrine of the first affirmed will bring a dangerous influence upon our beliefe, by subjecting our faith to humane resolutions. The other three are disciplinarian in the present way of novellisme. As soon as Mr. Wilkinson heard these questions—'lupum auribus'—he had a wolfe by the eares. And, because unto these captious interrogatories he could not make a peremptory answer, Mr. Fulham would not present your petitioner to the Bishop for ordination. Thus you see, Mr. White, a new way of simony. Imposition of hands is to be sold, if not for money, yet to make a side, a party, a faction. They will not confer orders but upon such as will come in and make party with them in their new practises, as is evident by these questions. Take this, in this kind, as a leading case, a first complaint ; more are coming. And Mr. Wilkinson shall have the poore common comforte, 'Solamen miseris socios habuisse.' I proceed to his second sufferance, which was by the Vice-Chancellor of Oxford, for a sermon preached in his course at St. Mary's

---

† This must be an error of Sir Edward's for " Tuesday."

Henry Moseley, at the Prince's armes in Paul's Church yard, to shew cause why the "imprimatur" is left out in Dodona's Grove, and why a leafe altered, and to bring one of each impression.

Philip Chetwin, mercer, att the bl. beare in Cheapside, to be sent for about Jones his worke on the Hebrewes, licensed and defaced per Mr. Baker;—intimated by Sir William Brereton.

This committee adjourned to Tuesday, 15 December.

1640.
16 Car. 1.

in Oxford. Short to make, he preached better then they were willing to heare. The sermon fell into the eares of a captious auditour. For this sermon he stands now suspended by the Vice-Chancellor from all the spirituall promotion that he had, which was only the reading of a divinity lecture in Magdalen Hall. The Committee required the Vice-Chancellor to send unto us the sermon, with his exceptions in writing. They were brought, and, being received, they are three in number; great, and weighty in the accusation; none at all in proof. Nay, Mr. White, there is nothing presented unto us wherein to finde a colour or a shadow, whereby to make the accusation semblable, and consequently, the suspension just.—' Eequis innocens erit si accusare suffecerit.' The particulars insisted upon, pickt and chosen out of that sermon, by the Vice-Chancellor, are three; every one a hainous charge, and the first sounding little lesse than treason. Give me leave to read them, as Mr. Vice-Chancellor hath sent them in writing. 1. 'Our religious Soveraigne and his pious government, is seditiously defamed, as if his majesty were little better then the old Pagan persecutors, or then Queen Mary.' 2. 'The Government of the Church and University is unjustly traduced.' 3. 'Men of learning and piety, conformable to the publicke government, are uncharitably slandered.' The least of these, being duly proved, will make him worthy of suspension; but if Mr. Wilkinson be guilty of the first, he is not worthy to live. The truth is, the Vice-Chancellor hath learned 'audacter criminare;' and, fayling in proofe, hath only fowled himselfe. Your sub-committee, upon due consideration of the cause and circumstance, have hereupon unanimously voted, that Mr. Wilkinson is free from all and every of these exceptions made against his sermon by the Vice-Chancellor. We are all of opinion, that there is nothing therein that deserves 'notam censoris, nedum lituram judicis.' If, Mr. White, there be in a sermon, as there ought to be, 'aliquid mordacis veritatis,' shall the preacher be for this suspended? His mouth shut up for preaching truth boldly. It is contrary to their commission; for, sir, they have a great charter to speak freely. It is warranted unto them 'jure divino.' St. Paul doth own it, in his instruction of Timothy. The words are ' I charge thee, before God and the Lord Jesus Christ, preach the word; be instant in season, out of season; reprove, rebuke, exhort. . . For the time will come, when they will not endure sound doctrine.' Here is our case exactly. Here was reproofe; here was exhortation; here was preaching out of season, to unwilling, or to unprepared hearers: and yet, in season, the theme was necessary, and fitted to their want of zeale;

2 Tim. iv.
1, 2, 3.

15º DECEMBRIS.

ORDER.—Joseph Hunscott is assigned to make good his petition on the first Thursday of our meeting after Christmas.

17º DECEMBRIS.

Per BRIGHT.—Robert Mason, Doctor of the Law, and Chancellor of the diocesse of Winchester, confesseth he did suspend Mr. Bright, then Vicar of Ebbesham, in Surrey, for not reading in the church the King's Declaration for Sportes. Being asked by what law a minister doth incurre suspension for not reading the said book of sportes, he saith, by both the lawes, canon and civill. Being asked, by what authority he did itt, he sayth, by the Bishop's, whom he ought to obey so farre, that even " injusta sententia" must ty him to obedience, and to execute the sentence ministerially, though injust, unles itt be notoriously injust. He sayth, the Bishop's letter for suspension of him and other is dated 8th June, 1634, to suspend *ab officio et beneficio.*

but the only fault was, that ' the time is come when sound doctrine will not be endured.' Thus the committee found it : thus have I faithfully, but imperfectly, reported it, and do now subjoyn the opinion and request of your trustees to this Grand Committee. Mr. Wilkinson is innocent and free from this accusation. He had just cause to petition. The Vice-Chancellor hath been without cause, nay, against cause, rigid and oppressive. The sermon deserved thanks ; the preacher received injuries. His suspension to be taken off. The retracting and dissolving whereof ought to be as publicke as was the inflicting thereof. One worde more I ask leave to adde, and I hope I shall not therein erre from the sence of the committee, though indeed I received it not in command to be joyned to the report. This businesse, Mr. White, is spread into a wide and ample notice. Two great Primats have appeared in it, and that with different, perhaps contrariant, sences, sences as distant as Lambeth and Armagh. The Vice-Chancellor sayth, that 'the preacher was censured by the Most Reverend Lord Primate of Ireland, who heard him, to be a bold or rash fellow for it.' Hereupon, I attended that learned, pious, and painefull Primate, and did read these words of the Vice-Chancellour unto him. His answer was, that he takes it as an aspersion upon him. He remembers the sermon, and commends it. This is an additionall to the Report ; and, with this, I leave Mr. Vice Chancellor, and the Bishop's Chaplen (Fulham) to the wisdome and consideration of this Grand Committee."— Speeches, p. 43, 48.

The language of the first letter being to suspend according to law, being demanded, by what law the not reading of that book is a crime to bring suspension, he answered, by both lawes, both canon and civill.

After diverse monitions, att last, 24 January, 1634, Dr. Stanton and Mr. Bright were, both of them, by him actually suspended *ab officio et beneficio.*

Per BRIGHT *versus* William Kingsley, D.D., Archdeacon of Canterbury; he confesseth as the petitioner hath layd itt downe. Being demanded, by what order or command he received that prayer against the Scotts, and distributed the same; he answered, that itt was sent downe to him by the King's printer, as is customary for bookes of fast and other things; so he received them and dispersed them through the Jurisdiction where he is Ordinary, and thought himselfe bound to do. Being demanded, what authority enjoyned him to enjoyne others to reade and publish that prayer, and by what authority he suspended Mr. Bright for not reading what was not commanded; he said that he received no such commandes, but did itt of that authority which he conceived he did hold himselfe as Ordinary. Onely, he sayth, there was a letter, he knowes not when, from an officer (he knowes not whom), but one in the Vicar-General's office, directed to one Mr. Somner, a Register in Canterbury, to some such effect as the publishing or dispersing of the said prayer.

Per SNELLING.—John Sedgeweek, clarke, was present in the High Commission Court, when Mr. Snelling's cause was heard. Dr. Wood came up, staring and chafing, halfe out of breath, saying, "For Jesus sake," "for God's sake," "for the King's sake," "somebody helpe me against this puritan Snelling," "I demand justice against this dunce." For this he was reprehended by Sir Nathaniel Brent, who told him well of the good character of Mr. Snelling. Wood's fury continuing, Bishop White asked "What's the matter?" Wood sayd that this Snelling would not reade the Booke for Sportes, *ergo* he had suspended him. The Bishop sayd he had not done so much, and going on in his discourse, Sir John Lambe interrupted, saying, " Hold, my Lord." Mr. Snelling presented two answers : a large one that was rejected, then a shorter one was exhibited, which was received; and Dr. Ryves said it was an answer for theire turne, but it was first defaced (as Mr. Snelling says) by Sir John Lambe or his appointment.

After the day of sentence of deprivation, the Archbishop asked Mr. Snelling, saying, " Are you conformable ?" Mr. Snelling. "Yes, as farre as is by law established." Archbishop. "Are you conformable to the new conformity ?" Then turning to the company, said, " There is no more beleeving this kind of men, then of a dogge." Then, Bishop Wren said, " You may know him by his band, that he has a wonderfull tender conscience," and so said Sir John Lambe.

THOMAS GELLYBRAND, of Bred-street, doth affirme that Pauls-cray is worth 100*l.* per annum for one to live upon, and avoweth the hand of Grenhell the notary to be originall.

SAMUEL GELLEBRAND, of Paule's Church Yard, doth affirme that Dr. Wood received, or disposed of the whole profitt of the benefice of Paul's Cray during the suspension, except the Glebe Land.

ORDERS.—Mr. Pemberton is assigned Tuesday 12 January, to make good his petition, and to have warant for search, and for witnesses.

The Archbishop's letter about the Book of Sportes to be sent for. Itt is in his Register in Mr. Wade's office neare Doctors' Commons.

Mr. Snelling, Mr. Vicars;—causes to be heard on Tuesday next.

22° DÉCEMBRIS, 1640.—DUTCHY COURT.

BASIL WOOD, Doctor of the Laws, and Chancellor of Rochester, confesseth he did, as is alleaged, suspend Mr. Snelling *ab officio et beneficio,* for not reading the Book of Sportes. The dispersing and publishing of that book was commanded to Dr. Wood by Jo. Bolles, the deceased Bishop of Rochester ; and he was commanded by letter from the Archbishop of Canterbury, both which letters are produced. He sayth, that, when the Bishop doth command him by letter, he hath no part but patience and obedience.

Being asked by what law and authority he did suspend and excommunicate Mr. Snelling; he sayth he relyeth upon the Bishop's commands, and upon the King's booke. Being demanded, what place of the booke (there present) doth warrant him &c., he sayth, that he doth not find in the booke any authority for suspension or excommunication of ministers refusing; yet he sayth, that upon a verball command of the dead Bishop, and upon another verball direction from the Archbishop in his garden att Croyden, he did suspend Mr. Snelling; for he sayth that my Lord of Canterbury expressing his pleasure to be such, he did take that pleasure soe expressed to be as a command, and accordingly performed itt.

He confesseth also the excommunicating Mr. Snelling, *ut petitur.* He denyeth the removing of the Communion Table.

During the time of Mr. Snelling's suspension, the Doctor sayth, that he did allow him a moiety of his benefice: whereupon, being demanded by what law he tooke away halfe his living from him, and gave him (as he sayd) halfe of itt, (beside the gleabe); he sayth, he did it by the Canon Law; being asked, what Canon Law, whether the Papall Canon Law? he said, "Yes, by the Papall Canon Law."

Mr. Snelling sayth, he had but 68*l.* for four yeare and above, whereby he is so depauperated, that he now payeth 30*l.* per annum use; and is never likely, by his living, to be redeemed out of his debtes.

Jo. Gellybrand sayth, he did offer 60*l.* per annum for the tithes the last yeare, aº 1639, but the Doctor refused to accept itt, and lett the tithes out att 56*l.* per annum.

Mr. Vicars fayled to produce proofe to his petition.

Jo. Bridall, Gent.—To the last clause of Mr. Vicars' petition, sayth, that about two yeares since, he was att the High Commission

Court, on a day called a Mitigation Day, where he heard, that one Jo. Vicars, upon a petition of his, had the grant of 5*l.* by the Court, in the way of a reward for service there done.

ORDERED.—Dr. Wood to appeare and answer Mr. Pemberton, the 12 January, and to have copy of Petition.

The Committee is adjourned to Tuesday, 5th January, att two of the clock, this place.

5° JANUARII, 1640[-1.]

IT IS ORDERED, that if any MS. be refused the presse by the usual Licencers, the refuser shall be sent for, to show cause unto the Committee.

WHEREAS Dr. Bray, Dr. Haywood, Dr. Oliver, Dr. Baker, Dr. Wykes, and others, have licenced some bookes thought to be different from, and repugnant unto, the established doctrine of the Church of England; and have denyed the presse unto some good, pious, and profitable books (as itt is suspected and informed) itt is thereupon ordered that they, and every of them, shall be sent for, to attend this committee, att such times as Sir Edward Dering shall think fitt. And also, that he shall, att his discretion, send for the MS. originall copy of any book (within the last ten yeares printed), and for the printers to be and appeare before this Committee.

Mr. Vicars is to prove his petition on Thursday next, 7° Januarii.

7° JANUARII, 1640[-1.]

JO. ROTHWELL, stationer, sayth, that about five weekes since, Dr. Wykes did refuse to licence the booke of Mr. Vicars, and gave this reason; because the Image of Christ was in churches as yett, and, untill they were pulled down there, he would not licence itt.

1640-1.
16 Car. I.

IDEM, Rothwell sayth, that Dr. Featley did tell him that Sancta Clara's booke was allowed by the Queene's preistes; and that the said Doctor did say, that he did conceive that the Archbishop did give permission to the printing of itt.

[DR. FEATLEY.—The censures of many preistes before the printed booke of Sancta Clara, viz. :—

Jacobus Dreux, Londini, ulto Julii, 1633.

Thomas Blacklow, 5 Julii, 1633.

William Tomson, 20 Aprilis, et 22 Julii, 1633.

T.P. Thomas Philipps, 16 Aprilis, et 11 Julii, 1633.

Ægidius Chaissy, 20 Junii, 1633.

Jo. Gennings, 20 Julii, 1633.

Petrus Martin, 24 Augusti, 1633.

D. David, Londoni, 3o Kal. Septris, 1633.

Idem Dr. Featley sayth, that Bishop Moreton (lib. 10, 21) did in a leafe refute Sancta Clara; but it was dispunged per Dr. Bray, sed quære, quia (10, 21) impress: fuit, 1631, sed Sancta Clara, anno 1634.]*

ORDERED.—That Sir Edward Dering do intimate to Dr. Featley to come, and to declare himselfe *de supradictis*, and also of Pocklington, page 108, etc.

Dr. Pocklington, to appeare, and answer the exorbitancys of his booke.

. . . . Calvert, of Distaffe Lane, bookbinder, to appeare and testify *inter* Vicars *et* Wykes.

Mr. Vicars, to bring in his several MSS., and Sr Edward Dering to have power to receive them.

---

* These clauses within the brackets do not stand in this place in the manuscript. They are there inserted at the end of the book, but with a reference to this place, as though intended to come in here. It appears also from the context that this is their proper place.

12º JANUARII, 1640-1.

Sr Edward Dering.	Sr Edward Boys.
Sr William Masham.	Mr Heyman.
Mr Jo. Moore.	Mr Ashton.
Mr Rich. Moore.	Mr Purefoy.
Mr Knatchbull.	Mr Searle.
Mr Bodwell.	Mr Shuttleworth.
	Mr Roos.

PEMBERTON *versus* DR. WOOD.

Ad 1.—Dr. Wood confesseth the suspension and the cause.

Report.—Itt was an undue, illegall proceedance, and a greate oppression; *v.* "Acta Cur." perducta per Drem.

DANIEL MERCER, of Southwark, draper, *testatur* Mr. Pemberton said, "He had a good rule to follow."

Dr. —" What rule?"

Pemberton.—" The Scripture."

Dr. —" I pray God itt be not a crooked rule."

Pemberton.—" God forbid."

This is denyed by Dr. Wood, who sayth it were a blasphemous saying.

WILLIAM HEYCOCKES, of Southwark, brewer, doth testify the same.

Ad 2.—" By what authority did you suspend a minister for not reading the Booke of Sports?"

Dr. —" By virtue of a statute t. II. 8. and for contumacy, in not obeying the Bishop's command." He voucheth the King's booke for his authority, shewing the place where a publication is required, which being unperformed, the punishment was arbitrary in the ecclesiasticall judges, according to the manner of theire censures.

Rep.—The booke gives no such authority; and he offendeth in pretending a defence of his fact by an arbitrary power.

Ad 3.—DANIEL MERCER, WILLIAM HEYCOCKS, } affirme. *Ideo* Rep.*

---

* *Ideo* Rep. *i. e.* " Report accordingly."

1640-1.
16 Car. I.

Ad 4.—WILLIAM HUBBERT, WILLIAM MUSGRAVE, affirme, and say, that, when Mr Pemberton sayd he would appeale to the King, D^r said, that appeale should do him no good. —*Ideo* Rep.

Ad 5.—D^r *fatetur. Sed de le* sequestration, he sayeth itt was ten weekes after before itt was sent to the churchwardens; and he beleeveth that a pursivant was sent: but itt was more suddain, for Mr Pemberton produced the warrant for attachment copyed, dated 23 November, viz. cleaven days after his suspension.

Quoad le 20*l.* which is estreated into the Exchequer; the D^r sayth, that itt was sett on him for not appearing in the High Commission Court, but not as a fine, but onely as *pœna contumaciæ*, which 20*l.* was the pœnalty as signed 26 January (two monthes after the former attachment), and is both attachment, intimation, and *subpœna ut patet.*—*Ideo* Rep.

Ad 6.—D^r presumeth the resignation was willing: *et quoad* suspension that yett holdes; onely the D^r sayeth, that, since the Parliament began, he hath, *quantum in se*, released the suspension, unknowen to Pemberton; and are of opinion* that these usages were forcive, to cause Mr Pemberton to resigne.—*Ideo* Report.

Ex parte Doctoris.—ABRAHAM SHERMAN, clerk, sayth, that in the chamber (whither the Court was adjourned), but *non sedente judice*, he thinkes Mr Pemberton did say, "Will you suspend me because I will not be perjured?" It being spoken *per* Pemberton (*ut putat*), but neare the doore, the Doctor then att the window.

12 January.

THOMAS WEBB, apparitor, affirmeth the word "figge," &c.

The Doctor referreth himself to the letters of the Bishop and Archbishop formerly delivered in, in Mr Snelling's cause, as to a sufficient command, both for publication and for suspending; and doth object *versus* Pemberton his shifting places in disguise of habit *et* colours.

* *i. e.* the Committee are of opinion.

The votes all consented.

1. Petition is proved.

2. D^r neyther hath justifyed nor well excused himselfe.

3. Pemberton is to be repayred.

4. Suspension to be taken of.

5. Doctor suspended; *et idem* Doctor brought him into the high commission.

6. The benefice is better than 80*l.* per annum, and is totally lost by this occasion and the pursuite of the Doctor, who said he would be his adversary, as is proved, and so hath been, to the neare undoing of the Petitioner and his sixe motherlesse children.

This Committee adjourned to Thursday, 28 January.

[At the end of the Note Book is the following tabular arrangement of Names, apparently representing the list of the Committee as first formed, and the alterations or additions subsequently made :—]

DIE LUNÆ, 23 NOVEMB. 1640.

Sr Edward Dering.	Sr Oliver Luke.
Sr Simonds Dewes.	Mr Upton.
Sr John Clotworthy.	Mr Cromwell.
Sr Roger Palmer.	Mr Arthur Goodwin.
Mr Purefoy.	Mr Bodwell.
Lo. Ruthen.	Mr Jephson.
M^r Jo. Moore.	Sr Robert Harley.
Sr Henry Mildmay.	Sr Anthony Ireby.
Sr William Masham.	DIE LUNÆ, 14º DECEMBRIS.
Sr William Brereton.	Sr Edward Boys.
Sr John Wray.	Mr Rouse.
Sr Edward Hungerford.	Sr Arthur Haselrigg.
Mr Corbet.	Mr Pelham.
Mr Knatchbull.	
Sr Gilbert Pickering.	DIE SABBATI, 19º DECEMBRIS.
Mr Bagshaw.	Sr Peter Wroth.

Mr Prideaux.

Mr Ash.

Mr Spurstow.

Mr Rolles.

Mr S. Ashton.

Mr Evelyn.

Mr Richard Moore.

Mr Hill.

Mr Searle.

Mr Shuttleworth.

Mr Roos.

Mr Buddon.

Mr Bond.

Mr Walton.

Mr Heyman.

Mr Pottes.

45.

[At the end of the Book is a classed Index, as follows. The references to the pages are omitted as useless here :—]

SUFFERERS.	OPPRESSORS.
Bell.	Fulham.
Amirant.	Bishop of Oxford.
Wilkinson.	Mason.
Ward.	Bishop of Winton.
Carpenter.	Kingsley.
Vicars.	Wood.
Henry Langly.	Wren.
Bright.	Lamb.
Stanton.	Archbishop.
Snelling.	Bolles, Bishop of Rochester.
Thomas Langley.*	Corbet.

WITNESSES.†	READY TO BE REPORTED.
Stampe.	Bright.
Sedgeweeke.	Snelling.
Gellybrand.	Carpenter.

* He has omitted Pemberton from this list.

† These lists do not contain the names of all the witnesses, authors, licensers, &c., but seem to have been as commencements of incomplete indices.

BOOKES.

AUTHORS.

Pocklington.
Featley.
Sibbes.
White.
Clarke.
Vicars.
Reeves.
Epistle of Jesus.
Bell.
Jones.

LICENCERS AND DENYERS OF LICENCES.

Bray.
Weekes.
Baker.

PRINTERS AND STATIONERS.

Payn.
Borne.
Badger.
Dormer.
Bartlet.
Yong.
Cotes.
Stevens.
Moseley.
Honscote.
Chetwin.

WITNESSES.

Rothwell.
Sparkes.
Dormer.
Bartlet.
Cole.
Rosse.
Peake.
More.
Griffen.
Stevens.

[The Book contains also some little other Index matter, which is omitted as unimportant.]

PETITIONS AGAINST THE CLERGY FROM PLACES IN THE COUNTY OF KENT,

WITH THEIR ANSWERS AND OTHER PAPERS RELATING THERETO.

I.

Defence of Dr SHELDEN, Vicar of Apledore *cum* Ebeney.

Certeine particulers concerning the present Vicar of Aple-doore *cum capella de* Ebeney.

First.—When Dr SHELDON, the present vicar, came to the sayd living, about twenty-eight yeares past, hee found placed there by Dr Walsall and Dr Neweman, his predecessours, Curate at Apldoore Mr John Hopton, and at Ebeney Mr Daniell Pickard, both men of sober and honest conversation, and yet neither of them allowed for preachers, but tollerated for expounders. These twoe (requiring him of Apledoore to preach) continued Curates till their deaths, giveing to him at Apledoore above twenty pounds per annum, and, after his death, to his Curates he hath given twenty-one, and eightene at least in money and profits to others, and to him that now is Curate, Mr Clement Barling, a licensed and dilligent preacher, and of honest and sober conversation, he hath given, and doth give, as much as he hath desired, twenty pounds per annum, quarterly payed, and besides the church dutyes, value nigh fifty shillings per annum.

Secondly.—To the Curate of Ebeney, Mr Daniell Pickard, whom he continued Curate with desire of his parishioners, though Ebeney had bin served by on Mr Adams and others for tenn pounds per annum; and although the first fruit office upon record requireth that the Vicar of Apledoore should give to him that serves at Ebeney (to—to small a stipend) under eight pounds per annum; yet the present Vicar, Dr Sheldon, increased the stipend of the said Curate Mr Daniell Pickard, for, whereas he had before about some twelve pounds per annum, he raised it to sixtene pounds per annum; and to the Curates that he had there since, with desire of his parishoners, he hath given either eightene or ninetene pounds by the yeare in money and profits; and now to his present Curate Mr Grifith Wood, a man of sober, peaceable, and honest conversation, and a licensed preacher, and sufficient for his learning (as shalbe proved), he hath given and doth give sixtene pounds per annum, quarterly payed, and in other profits three pounds per annum, and in all ninetene pounds.

Thirdly.—The utmost yerly valew of the vicaredge of Apledoore cum Capella de Ebeney is not above 170l. per annum, for the defraying of all charges, the payment of the Curate's stipend, paying of tenthes, subsidies, and procurations, and continuall nedfull repayring of ould houses, and for the better maintenance and provision of the sayd Dr Sheldon and his family, his wife and five children, who, besides what he hath from Apledore and Ebeney, hath only a small vicaridge called Bersted, and in utmost valew about some thirty-foure pounds per annum, where he resideth and constantly readeth the whole service apointed, catechiseth (with expownding) ech Lord's day in the yere.

These particulers are testified to be true, and shalbe readie to give testimony of the truth hereof.

[Endorsed by Sr Edward Dering, "1640—*ex parte* Sheldon."]

II.

PETITION to the House of Commons against the Granting of Marriage Licences by the Prerogative Court of Canterbury;—from the Parishioners of MARDEN.

To the honorable the house now assembled in Parlament.

The humble Peticion of the Inhabitants of MARDEN in Kent.

Sheweth and presenteth to this honorable house, the great inconveniences and greivances which, within six weeks now last past, have bin occasioned through licences for marriage granted by the Prerogative Courte of Canterbury, as namely—

1. Thus, one Robert Waterman, of the parish of Marden, by a licence thence obtained, was married to his former wives owne sister.

2. That one Alice Medhurst, of this parish also, having land of inheritance of the yeerely value of eighty-and-twenty pounds, by licence had, was married before she did come to the full age of nine yeeres, to one John Batherst, of Cranebrooke, a very poore man, and of no estate at all, either in goods or lands.

These things, and to omitt all other mischeifs formerly here insuing among us in this kinde, we whose names are here under written are bold humbly to informe this honorable house, and we leave thesame to the grave consideracion of this worthy assembly, and we shall humbly pray for the King's Matie long and prosperous raigne over us, and for the happy proceeding of this house of Parlament.

The mark × of ⎫	John Stephens.
Elisha Burch, ⎬Churchwardens.	John Osborn.
Thomas Danne, ⎭	John Walter, senior.
Walter Munn.	Richard Glover.
The marke × of Thomas Stear.	The marke × of Jo. Thurston.
Nicholas Parkes.	John Usburne.
Tho. Williams.	John Walter, junior.
Georg May.	Osman Cook.
Willyam Stevens.	Robert Drast.
William Juell.	Thomas Post.
The mark × of John Harenden.	John Cunny.

[Endorsed by Sr Edward Dering, "4 Dec. 1640, Petition, Marden."]

1640-1.
16 Car. I.

29 January.

III.

PETITION to the House of Commons against Dr MERIC CASAUBON, the Vicar;—from the Parish of MINSTER.

To the honourable House of Commons assembled in Parliament.

The humble peticion of the parishioners of the parish of MINSTER, in the Isle of Thanet, in the County of Kent.

In most humble wise showeing,

That MERIC CASAUBON, Doctor of Divinity, and one of the Prebends of Christ Churche, Canterbury, doth at present (besides his Prebend's place) hold and enjoy three severall liveings, namely, the Parsonage and Vicarage of Minster aforesaid, of the yearely vallue of 240*l.* per annum, or thereabouts (as he hath advanced it), the Vicarage of Mounckton, and the Vicarage of Birchington.

And may it please this honourable house to understand, that both the said Doctor and Mr John Picard, Clerke, his Curat at Minster aforesaid, are zealously observant of all innovacions, as bowing and cringeing to the Communion table; and the Doctor being demaunded why he bowed thereto, aunswered, bycause the Sacrament was there administrede.

And, bycause the said parish would not rayle in the Communion table, the said Doctor, at his owne charge, against the parishes consent, rayled it in, and removed the Communion table, and sett it close to the wall, at the east end of the Chancell, altarwise (as your peticioners conceive), and hath cutt and defaced the Chancell in many things; and for his actions gave this reason—that he was the Lord Archbishop of Canterburies cheife Chaplen, and therefore he would shew his Grace his forwardnes in it; and threatend your humble suppliants, that, if they would not come upp to the rayle to receive the Comunion, they should answere it before the Lord Archbishop and the Highe Comission; for feare whereof the greatest part of your peticioners, to the great griefe of their consciences, did goe 1640-1.
16 Car. I. upp to the rayle to receive. And his said Curat, no lesse zealous and earnest that way, refused to administer the sacrament of the Lord's supper to some of the said parish bycause they would not come upp to the rayle to receive it.

And, whereas the marshe and pasture lands in the said parish of Minster never heretofore paid above xijd. per acre for tythes, yet the said Doctor, since his comeing, hath exacted xviijd. per acre, and his said Curat reports that he will have ijs. vjd. per acre; and, more than this, he exacteth tythes of poore people that live by the almes of the Parish, and, for non-payment, cites them to the Court, and maketh poore servants pay vjd. a peece for their offerings at Easter, or putts them back, and will not lett them receive.

Therefore, your humble peticioners doe, in all humility, beseeche this honourable house, to take the premisses into their consideracion; and seeing that the said liveing at Minster will recompence the paines of an able and godly-minded minister, in your wisdomes (if soe it seeme good to you) be pleased to order, that such a one be setled there, and, for the continuance of love betwixt the minister and people, your peticioners doe most humbly beseech this honourable house, to sett downe a certaine rate, what every acre of marshe and pasture land and other things titheable shall pay; and that the minister may have power to recover the same at comon lawe, or as cesses for the poore are levyed, or otherwise, as to your wisedomes shall seeme good.

And your humble suppliants, as in duty bound, shall continually pray for his majesties long and happy reigne over us, and the prosperous successe of this highe and honourable Court of Parliament, &c.

Edw. Harnett, constable.	Edward Taddie.	Isaak Willor.
William Goldfinch.	Stephen Sayar.	William Gillse.
Marke Ambrose.	William Christian.	Edward Cuppage.
Thomas Jenkin.	William Ladd.	Robard Shumard.
Boys Ower ⎰ church-	John Hwet.	John Wotton.
Robart Welles ⎱ wardens.		

1640-1.
16 Car. I.

Thomas Cowell.	Edward Fuller.	John Twyman.
Mathew Dasonn.	Edward Wilbor.	William Gee.
Robert Hummerdine.	Richard Stears.	Henrie Dudarde.
Henry Tery.	Abell Terry.	
John Barber.	John Batho.	
Edward Newman.	John Ambros.	
Henry Huffam.	William Coffam.	

[Endorsed by Sr Edward Dering—"1640, 29 Jan. Petition. Minster v. Casaubon," and below this, in another hand, "Com. of Relig."]

IV.

Petition to the House of Commons, against Dr. MERIC CASAUBON, the Vicar, from the parish of MONCKTON.

29 January.

To the honourable House of Commons assembled in Parliament.

The humble peticion of the parishioners of the parish of MOUNCK-TON, in the Isle of Thannet, in the county of Kent.

Most humbly shewing,

That MERIC CASAUBON, Doctor of Divinity, and one of the Prebends of Christ Churche, Canterbury, doth (besides his Prebend's place) hold and enjoy three severall liveings; for he is Vicar of Mounckton aforesaid, of the vallue of 80*l*. per annum, or there-abouts; and Vicar of Birchington; and Parson and Vicar of Minster; all in the said Isle and County, soe that, beside his temporall estate, his spirituall livings are estimated at 640*l*. per annum, or thereabouts.

And may it please this honorable house to understand, that the said Dr Casaubon is zealously observant of all innovacions, for he hath inforced the parishioners of Mounckton aforesaid to rayle in and separate the Communion Table from the rest of the chancell, to their charge of 5*l*. When it was done, bycause it satisfyed not the

Doctor's phancy, he procured new processe against the Churche-wardens to alter it; and an excommunicacion against them, for not being soe speedy therein as he required, to the parishes charge of xls. And to shew his unbridled humour, he caused the Church-warden then under excommunication, before he could be absolved, to bind himselfe by oath given him ex officio, to performe within a limited tyme what was by him required to be done in the innovations.

And, although there is sufficient meanes in the said parish of Munckton, without the helpe of any other place, to maintaine a preaching Minister there, yet he himselfe seldome comes thither, but he keeps a Curat there, a weake and an unable man, unworthy of imitacion, eyther in life or doctrine.

And yet the Doctor, not herewith satisfied, hath exacted 4d. in every acre of marshe land more than formerly was paid to his pre-decessors, and to the great oppression of your poore petitioners.

Therefore, your humble suppliants doe, in all humility, beseeche this honourable house, to take the premisses into their consideracions, and in their wisdomes be pleased to order that there may be an able and godly preaching Minister setled in the said parish of Mounckton, distinctly by itselfe, seeing there is sufficient meanes to maintaine a preaching Minister, and a moderacion in tythes; and (if it please this honourable house) a certaine rate sett downe, what every acre of marshe or pasture land, and other things titheable, shall pay: and also, that the said Doctor may give your petitioners satisfac-tion for the charge they have beene putt to in the said innovacions.

And your poore and humble suppliants, as in duety bound, shall continually pray for his Majesties long and prosperous reigne over us, and the prosperous successe of this highe and honourable Court of Parliament, &c.

Thomas Foche.	Fran. Saunders.
Henry Paramor.	Jefferie Sandwell.

[Endorsed by Sr Edward Dering—" 1640. 29 Jan. Petition. Monkton v. Casaubon," and, under this, in another hand, "Com. of Relig."]

1640-1.
16 Car. I.

V.

Reply of Dr. MERIC CASAUBON to the charges against him, made by the Parishes of MINSTER and MONCKTON.

12 March.

To the petitions of Minster and Mounckton, in the Ile of Tanet, to the Honorable House of Comons, &c.   The humble and true answer of MERIC CAUSABON, D.D., Vicar of both those parishes.

First.—Whereas both petitions make Minster, and Mounckton, and Birchington three severall livinges; I answer, that Birchington is but a chapell of ease to the Vicaridge of Mounckton, nor ever was otherwise accounted; both which (Mounckton and Birchington) together, besides what I pay to the King and twoe Curates yearly, have not beene worth to mee, one yeare with another, above 50*l.* per annum.   These twoe parishes of Minster and Mounckton stand close together, and I succeeded in both Dr. Clerck (a man of worthy memorie), who held them as I doe.

Secondly.—Innovations are laid to my charge, remooving of the Communion Table, rayling of it, and bowing.   The twoe first I did not, nor was present when they were done.   In Mounckton, they were compelled by the Court, without any intermeddling of mine, as will appeare by the Records of the Court, and expresse testification of those (if need be) who had a hand in that business.   At Minster, I acknowledge, I did more than once perswade them quietly to submit to the Order of the Court in that behalfe, fearing they would be compelled and punished (as in other things commanded hath beene observed) if they refused.   Other threatning than this, I never used.   My Curat, Mr. Pickard (an honest pious man) ignorantly refused (fearing the Order of the Court) to administer the Communion to twoe that would not come up to the rayles; which, when I heard, I disliked, and he did it noe more after that; and not long after (viz. at Christmas 1639) I was there myselfe, and administered unto all those that did not, as well as those that came up to the

1640-1.
16 Car. I.

rayles. I was att the charge of decent rayles, because the Parishioners had bene att a great deale of charge about the reparations of the Church, casting of the bells, with the addition of one, and expected that I alsoe would doe somewhat. As for bowing, I never used it till we were commanded it in our Cathedral of Christ Church, and that I saw it generally practised by others. However, I never required it of others, neyther was I ever told by any of eyther Parishes that it was offensive; and certainly by my preaching in that verie point of the Sacrament, they could not but know that I am noe wayes inclinable to Poperie, which I hope they will acknowledge.

Thirdly.—I have allwayes resided upon one of the twoe Vicaridges most part of the summer, except when I have beene hindred (as once by the plague) unavoidably. I would willingly reside longer, but for the unhealthines of the place. However, att all tymes of the yeare I frequently repaire thither and preache. The Curate that I have in Mounckton is approved by the greater part of the Parish, and was soe well liked for a while by some that have now testyfyed against him, that they offered him a good reward (whereas I require but once) to preach twice every Sunday, forenoone and afternoone.

Fourthly.—I never required any more, neither in Mounckton nor Minster, as due, but onely my tythes in kind, as out of all question they are due in both places. To give them the better content, I received for a while, in liew of tythes in kind, after the rate of 14d. by the acre for marsh land; and afterwards 18d. which they cannot but acknowledge to be a verie easie composition, whereas in Minster, above 40 yeares agoe, they compounded with Dr Clerck (my predecessor) for 1s.; and in Mounckton, above 30 yeares agoe, for 14d. by the acre, when lands were lett (as I conceive) for little more than halfe of what they now are in both places.

Lastly.—I doe not remember, neyther doe I beleeve, that I ever sued for tythes any that receyved almes of the parish; but that I have releeved many poore there, and pay for the schooling of sixe poore children of the Parish 4*l.* yearly, is not, I am sure, unknowen unto them.   Neyther doth my Curat Mr Pickard (as he tels me) require any more of any for his Easter duties then hath allwayes beene paid unto him in my predecessors tyme, for many yeares before I had to doe with it; nor more than is paid in some other Churches of the Isle of Thanet at the present.

[Endorsed by Sir Edward Dering, "1640, 12 March, Dr Casaubon."]*

VI.

Letter from Mr NICOLS, Incumbent of NORBORNE cum SHOLDEN, soliciting the support of Sr EDWARD DERING, under charges made against him by some of his Parishioners, to the House of Commons.

HONORABLE SIR,

My best respects and service presented unto you, and I pray be pleased to pardon my presumption in pressing into your presence by my letters.   Necessitie compells me, and putts me on. This day, 2 or 3 of my Parish are gone to London to put up a Bill against me in the Parliament, which I heare consists of 2 parts: First, to take away my Chappell of Sholden from Norborne, and to have it enacted that it may be an intire Church of itselfe, whereas it has beene a Chappell annexed unto Norborne Church almost 400 yeares.   2. To complaine of me for some fault &c. comitted by me at some times abroad in companie.   For the first, if I loose Sholden,

---

* Dr. Casaubon, the son of the learned Isaac, was dispossessed of his livings, but was reinstated at the Restoration.   Shortly afterwards he exchanged Minster and Monckton for the rectory of Ickham in the same county.   He died in 1671, in the 72nd year of his age.

1540-1.
16 Car. I.

perii, I am undone, and my wife and children. For the second, *humanum est errare;* pardon humane frailties and personall infirmities; and where proofes against me are not certaine, I pray judge charitablie; *nam, ampliandi sunt favores,* as the Sicilian speakes. I can excuse my selfe *a tanto,* though *non a toto.* I have the hearts of all my Parishioners, and their hands to (except it be of 3 or 4 of the combiners against me), as I shall shew when occasion is offer'd. Those that complaine of me doe it not for God's glorie and the good of his Church (for then I could have borne with it), but they violentlie proceed against me out of revenge, envie, hatred, malice, and all uncharytableness, as I shall make it plainelie to appeare heereafter. Noble Sir, you know me, *intus et in cute;* and you have allwaies loved me, and I have beene your honorer, admirer, and servant, and ever will be. I pray, Sir, imbarke yourselfe into my quarrell at this present, and stand up in my defence, and I shall be bound to pray for you all the daies of my life. I have written to Sᵣ Edward Masters, Sᵣ Peter Hayman and to Sᵣ Thomas Peyton, to joine themselves and their freinds and forces for me. I heare Sir Edward Boys is made against me. I beseech you, Sir, stave hym of from hurting me, and winne his love to helpe me. Thus, concreditting my selfe and all that I have to your custodie and protection, I rest

At your honors cõmand,

EDWARD NICOLS.

Norborne, Janua. 25ᵗʰ 1640.

[Superscription.]
To the Honorable Sᵣ Edward Dering, Knight
and Baronett, present these I pray.

[Endorsed by Sᵣ Edward Dering—" 1640. Jan. —. Mᵣ Nicolls."]

1640-1.
16 Car. I. Mr EDWARD NICOLS, Incumbent of NORBORNE, his 2nd Letter to Sr
EDWARD DERING, requesting further time, and that he may be
spared the charges of a Summons by the Pursuivant-at-Arms.

NOBLE SIR EDWARD DERING.

1 February.   My best respect and service allwaies attend you.   Sir, I
made bold to write unto you the last weeke ; and Sr Edward Master
writes, he delivered it unto you on Thursday last. (I am much
bound unto him for it.)   I pray give me leave to second my first
enterprise.   I understand that Sampson and Rogers, on Tuseday
last, delivered their Bills or Petitions unto you against me.   I pray,
Sir, be pleased, that in regard I am not well, you will be pleased
to differ, and put of the calling upon me to appeare in the Parliament
for a month or 6 weeks, or longer, if you may ; I shall be much
ingaged unto you for it; for trulie I have such a paine on my heart
and stopping in my stomacke that I am scarce able to walke up and
downe (though blessed be God) I preach twise everie Lord's day, as
I ever did.   Eminent Sir, I beseech you let me have your answer
this weeke, if it may be, that soe my mind may be setled and disposed for studie.   I desire to be sent for by ordinarie summons,
your letters, and not by a Pursevant of Armes, to prevent charges
and the clamor of the common people, who thinke a man must
streight be hang'd when he is soe sent for.   Learned Sir, *Omnis in
te spes sita est.*   Deale with me as you please.   Thus presuming
upon the constancie of your love towards me, my consccience
assuring me that I have allwaies beene God's faithfull servant and
his Majesties loiall subject, and painefull in my calling, and praying
for the prosperitie of the Parliament, and for your health and happines, I rest

Your honors servant in the Lord,

EDWARD NICOLS.

Norborne, Feb. 1, 1640.

My brother, Mr Thomas Nicols lives in St Andrew's Court in Holborne. How happie should I be if you would stoope soe low as to send a letter thither for me; he will speedilie convey it hither.

1640-1.
16 Car. I.

[Superscription.]
To the honorable Sir Edward Dering, Knight
    and Baronett, present these.   I pray with
    speed.

[Endorsed by Sir Edward Dering—"1640, 4 Feb.   Mr Nicolls."]

VIII.

COMPLAINT against their Rector SAMUEL KEAME, by the Parish of LITTLE CHART.

NOBLE SIR,

4 January.

     Your vicinity of dwelling to the parish of Little Charte, in the County of Kent, cannot but give you to understand how ill our aforesaid parish hath beene served by our minister SAMUEL KEAME, Rector of the said parish for theis three yeares space last past, where he hath not performed his service above sixe tymes within the said three yeares; in which tyme, the Cure thereof hath beene divers tymes unserved, and sometymes discharged by drunken ministers, notwithstanding divers complaints thereof made (not onely by my selfe, but alsoe by the officers of the said parish) both to the Court Christian, and to the Comissary, without any redresse.   Yet the place where he now inhabiteth, called Lower Layton, being but (as we understand) a Curateshipp, is estimated at lesse then thirty pounds per annum, and the aforesaid parish of Little Charte, being a Parsonage, is worth a hundred pounds per annum.   Our earnest desires therefore are, that you would be pleased to take some course that he may be enforced to returne unto this place, being the proper place of his abode, both by lawe and conscience ; and so, comending the further prosecution hereof to yourselfe, We committ you to God, and rest,

Your assured loveing Freinds,

Rob. DARELL.
JOHN DARELL.

Calehill, January 4to, 1640.

Calehill, January 4to, 1640.

The Certificate of the parishioners of Little Charte to the conteints aforesaid.

Henry Duke	} Churchwardens.	Walter Pemble.
Isake Sariman		Henry Swyft.
John King × his marke, constable.		Richard Fild.
Bengabin (*sic*) Broune × his marke.		Robert Rutting.
Richard Masten × his marke.		Walter Buchar, × his marke.

[The Superscription is gone.]

IX.

PETITION to the House of Commons against ROBERT ELYE the Incumbent, for Non-residence ; and against JOHN TERRY the Curate, for Drunkenness, &c., by the parish of SMARDEN.

To the Right Honourable the Commons House, now by God's devine providence assembled this present Parliament.

The humble Petition of the Housholders and Parishioners of the Towne and parish of SMARDEN, in the County of Kent, declaringe also their lamentable greavances occassioned by the non-residence of their minister, and his nott providing an able Curate,

In submissive manner sheweth,

That, whereas the Benefice of SMARDEN abovesaid (beinge farmed to one John Armestronge, of Betresden, att 120*l*. per annum) is in the handes of one Mr. Robert Elye, a double beneficed man, who resideth att his Benefice of Charinge, distant by estimacion about six myles ffrom Smarden, yett hath nott bene with us these six yeares past, but placeth Curates with us, from time to time, soe negligent in their callings, and vitious in their lives and conversacions, as are very offensive and greaveous unto us. And, although, upon the change of our last Curate, wee importund him the said Mr. Elye, by a generall peticion from the most part of us the said parishioners, that he would graunt us that favour to make choise of our Curate, wee beinge then in possibility of obtaining a very able and sufficient man, diligent in his callinge, and of blamelesse life and conversacion, upon consideracion wee should make up the 20*l*. per annum hee would allow a Curate (and noe more) a competent meanes, which wee were willinge and should have concluded to have done, but this prevailed nott, but hee put over us (*colens nolens*) one Mr. John Terry, a man, both for his negligence in his cure, and scandelous life and conversacion, equivalent to the former, as may appeare by these instances followinge.

First.—The said Mr. Terry hath bene negligent in the dutyes of his callinge; soe that, when the congregacion have been come together one the Lord's day, hee hath bene absent, none knowinge where, or one what occasion: when corpse have bene to be buried, he hath bene soe distempered with beere that he could not read the buriall.

Secondly.—The said Mr. Terry (being a man much inclined to the horrid vice of drunckenes) doeth often frequent blind and unlycensed alehouses, wherein he hath bene soe overtaken in the said vice, thatt hee hath bene found lyinge in the streete and dirt, nott able to helpe himselfe, but two men have lead him to his house.

1640-1.
16 Car. I.

Thirdly.—The said Mr. Terry is a flighter, and that nott only in his owne house *(nocens plus exemplo quam peccato)* but a breaker of the King's peace, in strikinge others, both men and women; and that even att the church doore. All which particulars wee can prove by oath, by divers wittnesses of sufficient creditt in our parish.

And although for these and the like enormityes, wee have nott only complained to Mr. Elye, to have him removed, but also have presented him two severall times unto the Court of Canterbury; but noe way could wee finde any redresse; neither could wee ever heare that any thinge was said or done to him by the said Court, for his amendment (unless itt were by a purse potion that workes nott) but he proceedeth *(a malo ad pejor)* to our great griefe and disquiett.

Wherefore, wee humbly beseech this honourable assembly, to take some order (as in their wisdomes shall be thought meete). If nott that wee may make our owne choice of a more able minister, that may reside with us (non-residency beinge soe generally pernitious), yett that wee may have a man of more reformed life and conversacion; and competent meanes may be allowed out of the said Benefice for the meintenance of such an able minestery.

And wee shall (as duty bindes) pray daily for the prosperous success of this honourable assembly, in through remormation *(sic)* of the Church, &c.

Richard Barrowe.	Jacob Turner.
Samuell Bottinge.	John Draner × his marke.
William Wickham.	Richard Petter.
John Hincksell.	Thomas Colly.
Thomas Cheseman.	The mark × of John Humfary.
Thomas Hopper.	Thomas Winter.
John Ball.	Thomas Igldene.
Thomas Claget.	Jonas Masters.
John Gottly.	Richard Villes.
The marke × of John Tornor.	The mark × of George Poost.

John Tarpe.
Anthony Watts.
Thomas Mofor.
The marke of Nicholas ✕ Tailor.
The marke of Thomas ✕ Turnor.
The marke of William ✕ Euens.
Henry Sharpe his marke HS.
William Crutenden.
Joseph Smyght.
John Anduill.
The marke ✕ of Joseph Acrise.
Thomas Grenell.
The mark of Robert Turner.
Robert Wekes.
Robert Canton.

John Cooke.
John Mungum.
James Weecks.
John Gouldwell.
John Richison.
Henery Kinken.
Richard Longly.
Josias Mawle?
Robert Greene.
William Cooke.
Walltar Gilliam.
John Gould.
John King.
John Bige.
Robert Pett.
Henery Biame.
Thomas Muncke.

1640-1.
16 Car. I.

[Endorsed by Sir Edward Dering, " 1640, 5 Jan.   Smarden.—Se."]

X.

PETITION to the House of Commons against DOCTOR VANE, Minister of CRAYFORD, for unsound doctrine—from the parishioners of DARTFORD.

    To the honourable House of Commons at this present assembled.   9 January.

    The humble Petition of divers of the Parishioners of the Parish of DARTFORD, in the County of Kent, and others whose names are hereunder written,

    Humbly sheweth,

    That THOMAS VANE, Doctor in Divinity, and Minister of the

parish of CRAYFORD, in the said County of Kent, did preach at Dartford aforesayd, on the second daye of Aprill, anno domini 1637, and delivered these poynts following: viz., that it was necessary for every man to confesse his sinnes to the Preist, and shewed many reasons for it, amongst which one was, because the Preist had power to forgive him his sinnes, which he prooved by that place, " whose sinnes you remitte they are remitted, and whose sinnes you reteyne they are reteyned." He did then alsoe preache against predestinacion, and for free will, to the great discomforte, trouble, and greife of many of the auditors.

That, about five yeare since, the sayd doctor did preach at Stone, in the sayd County of Kent, within two myles of Dartford aforesayd, at the baptisinge of one John Wares childe, and did deliver this for positive doctrine, that those children which dyed before they were baptised could not be saved, and therefore, in case of necessity, laycmen or midwyfes might baptise, the minister or preist being absent.

That, about a yeare since, the sayd Doctor preached at Horton in the sayd County, within three myles of Dartford aforesayd, and in that sermon delivered these doctrines:—That almesdeeds were more acceptable sacrifices to God than prayers or prayses, because (sayd he) if I offer a sacrifice of prayer or prayse I offer that to God which cost me nothing: and that all sinnes were spotts that defile the soule, but some were greater, some lesser, and some like fethers or dust, that vanished and defiled not the soule.

That, drincking with certeyne gentlemen at the Bull in Dartford, did confidently affirme and saye, he was perswaded that the first motion and inclination of the hart to any sinne without consent was not sinne.

And your Petitioners doe further complayne, that the sayd Doctor, after he had preached the sayd sermon at Dartford, went into the Chaunsell, and bowed himself towards the Comunion table, and then went up to administer the sacrament: and, when he consecrateth the bread and wyne, he lifteth them up, and boweth three severall tymes; and, although it was none of his parish, yet he forced the people to come up to the Raile, which was the first tyme that they were brought to receive kneeling at the Raile.

May it therefore please this honourable assemblie to take these severall complaints into their serious consideration, and for redresse thereof, and to prevent the spreading and publishing of such like pernicious and popish doctrine, to doe herein as to your great wisdome and godlie disposition shall seeme most meet. And your petitioners shall ever pray, &c.

Thomas Rogers.	William Baines.
Ro. Heath.	Barnard Ellis.
Robert Watts.	John Phipps.
Willm Motley × his mark.	Thomas Andrews.
John Smith.	William Fellow × his mark.
Raphe Gouldsmith.	William Lee × his mark.
Thomas Smarte.	John Lambe.
Thomas Rownd.	William Best.
Richard Saxbey × his mark.	

[Endorsed by Sir Edward Dering, "1640, 9 Jan. Petition, Dartford v. Dr Vane.—Sc."]

XI.

Letter from Mr CULMER * to Sr EDWARD DERING, announcing that a Petition against the Archbishop is coming from Canterbury.

NOBLE SIR,   8 January.

There are some of Canterburie who intend to waite upon you with a peticion which they have to preferre, touching the greev-

----

* Nicknamed "Blue Dick of Thanet," v. Wood's Fasti, ii. 447.

ances which that great Cittie hath and doth susteyne under the tyranny of Prelacie and Cathedrall there, which darkneth the wholl Cittie. They moved me to write to you, which I have done to satisfie them, not doubting (as I tould them) but you would take their cause into harty consideration without a preface. Sir, all that wish well to Sion heer give you many thanks for your zeale and labours for Christ against Antichrist. I am emboldened thus to trouble you, considering your ancient favours towards me, and your kinde offer (when I saw you in London last tearme), to sett your hand to my petition. I shall ere long clayme your promise, for the present preferring the common cause. I have had very ungracious dealeing from the Lambeth Patriarch, by whom I have bene deprived of my ministry, and all the profitts of my Liveing three yeares and seaven monthes, haveing my selfe, my wife, and seven children to provide for; such is the Prelates tyranny for not consenting to morris daunceing uppon the Lords day. Heer ar some priests who have played their parts in advanceyng the Romish project, whose parishioners ar silent: the honest men that will wayt upon you can acquaint you with some particulars: soe, ceasing to trouble you in your most weighty imployments, I crave pardon for my boldnes, and, committing you to the protection of the Lord,

> I remayne,
>> Your obleiged freind and servant in the Lord,
>>> RICHARD CULMER.

Harbledowne, neer Canterburie,
   8 Jan. 1640.

      [Superscription.]
To the Right Worshipfull, and my worthy
  freind, Sir Edward Deering, at his house
  in St Martins lane, neer the Church, present these.

[Endorsed by Sir Edward, "1640, 11 Jan. Mr Culmer."]

1640-1.
16 Car. I.

XII.

PETITION to the Knights of the Shire for Kent against EDWARD HENSHAW, the Vicar, for non-residence and neglect of duty, by the parishioners of SUTTON VALENCE.

To the right worshipfull Sir EDWARD DERING, Knight and Baronett, and Sir John COLEPEPER, Knight, Knights of the Sheire for the county of Kent.

12 January.

The humble Peticion of the Inhabitants of the parish of SUTTON VALENCE, in the said Countie.

Humblie shewing unto your worshipps, that Edmund Henshaw, Clerke, is Vicar of that parish, as alsoe of the parish of BRENCHLEY, where he now dwelleth, both vicarages being worth, by credible report, 200*l.* per annum, of which parish of Sutton his brother was last of all Curatt under him, whoe dyed about three monthes sithens: before whose death (by reason of his sicknes) wee were not only much neglected, both in devine prayers and preaching, at least three monthes together, but alsoe since his decease verry uncertainly supplied in both. Soe that on the nativity of our Saviour Christ last wee had neither devine service nor preaching; and on the last fast appointed by His Majesty, some fewe prayers by a neighbour minister, which begann not until past twelve at noone, and ended within halfe an houre; and, at other times soe neglected or uncertainly supplied, that wee are, for the most part, forced to repayre to neighbour churches, the said Vicar himselfe not comeing at us at all, nor any other minister that hath administered the Sacrament to us, since August last.

In tender consideracion whereof, humblie desire your worshipps wilbe pleased to take such speedie course for redresse hereof as to your grave wisdoms shall seeme best. And wee shalbe for ever bound to pray, &c.

1610-1.
16 Car. I.

Ja: Buckhurst.	Thomas Lucas.
James Swyft.	John × Usher his marke.
Tho. Tyndall.	Thomas × Homden his mark.
William Wood.	Samuell Huet.
Richard Wood.	Henry Christian.
John Simcotte.	Henry Cultburts × mark.
Giles Bishopp.	Walter Walton.
Robert Lake.	

[Endorsed by Sir Edward Dering, " 1640.   Petition.   Sutton Valence *v.* Heinshaw, 12 Jan."]

XIII.

Letter from Mr WILLIAM FINCH, to Sr EDWARD DERING, complaining of the Popish practices of Mr Edward Boughen, minister of WOODCHURCH.

13 January.

RIGHT WORSHIPFULL SIR,

  Praysing God who hath enabled you for his service in his church, I an unworthy member therof having prayed, and so continuing, for the reformation of what is therein amisse, doe now toward that great marke adde my poore and weake endevour, by informing you of the estate of the ministry at Woodchurch, performed by Mr. Edward Boughen,* with single sermons on the Lord's dayes, and oftentimes with the onely reading of an homely, and, in his absence, without either. He is a man (as I conceave) superstitiously affected, by his actions manifested,—in his exalting the Communion Table, and violent compelling the Churchwardens to rayle in the same, refusing to administer to such as came not thereunto, his seldome warning of Communions, viz., once a quarter, or thereabouts; besyde, att Easter time, his walking the parish round in his surplasse and hood,

---

* *Vide* Wood's Athenæ, iii. 388, and Walker's Sufferings of the Clergy.

1640-1.
16 Car. 1.

reading prayers and psalmes at divers crosse wayes, and digging crosses in the earth at divers places of the outbounds of the same: by his gesture—bowing att, to, or before the Communion Table, att the naming of Jesus, and when he prayes that petition, " Thy will be done in earth as it is in Heaven:" by his words—bidding some of the last communicants to " drink agen, more, better, it will doe you noe hurt," *et alia hujusmodi*. Hee is allso, as I judge, unsound in doctrine, declared by his preaching that Bishops are the head of the church next under God and Christ; that the edicts of princes and lawes of Bishops are equally to be obeyed for conscience' sake; by his obscure handling of such places of scripture as seeme to implye generall salvation, the doctrine of beleevers' assurance of salvation, and of the sacrament: viz., " Will yee beleeve St. Paul, when he sayeth, *In the night*, &c.—and will yee not beleeve our Saviour, who sayth, *This is my body*?" I verily beleeve he will not deny any of theise his actions, words, or gestures : If he should, there are sufficient wittnesses to prove every perticuler, whose names I shall readily give you, if parishioners doe not shortly joine in an information concerning the premisses; theise I have privately certifyed, fearing lest that the parishioners may too long delay; and, having finished my information, I pray to God our Heavenly father in Jesus for reformation to blesse the whole Court of Parliament with hevenly wisdome and understanding, that they may rightly settle and determine all the weighty affaires both now in and yett to come into their hands, and that he would blesse your worship with hapynes external, internall, and eternall, whereunto he sayth Amen who is your worship's in the Lord to commaund,

WILLIAM FINCH.

Woodchurch, this 7th of January, 1640.

[Superscription.]

To the right Worshipfull Sr Edward Deering at his
chamber, London, theise present, I pray you.

[Endorsed by Sir Edward Dering—" 1640, 13th Jan. Mr Finch."]

1640-1.
16 Car. I.

XIV.

PETITION to the House of Commons, against their impropriate Rector, BANCROFT, Bishop of Oxford, and Mr MOUNTEYN, their Vicar, from the parish of ST. MARY CRAY.

16 January.

To the Right Honourable the Knights, Citizens, and Burgesses of the House of Comons, now assembled in Parliament.

The humble Petition of the Inhabitants of the Parish of St. MARY CRAYE, in the County of Kent.

In all humblenes, your Petitioners shew—

That the Tythes which your Petitioners do yerely pay unto the Parson of St. Mary Craye aforesaid doth amount to the some or value of 120*l*. per annum, and to the Vickar of the said parish to the value of 30*l*. per annum and upwards.   But so it is, may it please this honourable assembly, that, notwithstanding wee pay tythes to the Parson to the value aforesaid, yet your Peticioners have not any allowance from him towards the maintenance of a Preacher, nor for the releife of the poore, nor any other parish charge whatsoever.

That the said Vickar, once in a moneth, or two monethes, makes a Sermon to your Peticioners, and putts in a reader to reade service, to whom he payeth some ffive or six pownds per annum.

This being a very great greivance and lying very heavy upon your Petitioners, they being very poore, and not knowing how to helpe themselves, but by appealing to this honourable howse, are become humble sutors that you will be pleased to take the deplorable condicion of your Peticioners into your consideracion; so as they may have redresse of this great greivance, to the glory of God, and the great comfort of your Peticioners; which they humbly leave to this grave and honourable assembly.

And the Petitioners (as in duty bound) shall ever pray for the good successe of this Parlyament.

Mathew Draper.
Margaret Frith.
William Haman. ×
Jhon Leues. ×
George Peartch.
Henry Boumer. ×
George Wiburne.
William Partredge.
William Steevens. ×
Jeramie Manige. ×
John Starte. ×
Robarte ?
William Bebside.

Edward Manynge.
Thomas Trenchfielld.
Tobie Manning.
James Jemett.
Edward Spurling ?
Thomas Borman.
Mathew Maning.
Thomas Bagffield. ×
Henerie Rumneye. ×
William Cod ?
Edward Hodgson.

1610-1.
17 Car. I.

[Endorsed in the handwriting of Sir Edward Dering. " Mem. The parsonage is impropriated to Dr. Bancroft, Bp. of Oxford. Richard Spencer, Esq. is tenant to him. Mr. Mounteyn is Vicar. 1640. 16 Jan. Petition. St. Mary Cray *v.* Bp. Oxford."]

XV.

PETITION to the House of Commons for a Resident Minister in each of their Parishes, from the Parishioners of SHOREHAM and OTFORD.

To the right honourable the Knights, Citizens, and Burgesses of 19 January. the Commons house of Parliament.

The humble Peticion as well of the Inhabitants of the parish of SHORHAM, in the County of Kent, as alsoe of the Inhabitants of OTFORD, in the same County,

Humbly shew,

That the Impropriations of the Personages of theis two parrishes doe belong and apperteyne to the Deane and Chapter of Westminster, and that theis two Parrish Churches have noe Vicaridges endowed;

1610-1.
16 Car. I.
but are about a mile and a halfe distant, th'one from th'other, and
they are of good Value; vizt. Shorham, worth 160*l.* per ann., and
Otford worth 200 marks per ann.   And which Parsonags, being of
soe good value, yet the sayd Deane and Chapter allow the presente
Incumbent, Mr. Emerson, onely xx^li per ann. and his dwelling, to
mayntayne himselfe, his Wife, and Children, and noe more, for the
serving of both Cures (he being a honest and laborious minister, and a
preacher of God's word, and one that liveth peaceably and quietly
amongst his Parishioners), which service is too heavy for him, for
when he is doeing his service at one Parrish, th'other is neglected;
and the meanes being so small, the parishioners, by the assistance of
Sir Robert Heathes benevolence (of late years) and the Contribucion
of parishioners of each parish, have beene forced to hire an assistant
to the present curatte.

Most humbly therefore beseech your honors to be pleased that each
Parish may have an honest preaching Minister, and alsoe Competent
and sufficient maintenance for each Minister, as this honourable house
shall thinke meete.   And, &c.

[No signatures.   Endorsed by Sir Edward Dering, " 1640, 19 Jan.   Petition
Shorham et Otford."]

XVI.

PETITION to the House of Commons for a Resident Minister in each of
their Parishes, from the Parishioners of SHOREHAM and OTFORD.

19 January.
To the most honourable and high Court of Parliament now
assembled,

The inhabitants of SHORHAM and OTFORD, in the Countie of Kent,
doe humbly shewe and petition as followeth:—

First.   That the sayd Shorham and Otford are distinct parishes, each
havinge a faire and large Church, the one distant above a mile from

the other; the parish of Shorham consistinge of eyghtie families, at the least, and Otford of sixtie.

Secondly, That the tithes and gleabe of Shorham are worth one hundred and sixtie poundes by the yeare ; and the tithes and gleabe of Otford worth two hundred markes yearely. Both which spirituall livinges are annexed to the Colledge of Westminster, and yet the sayd parishes provided by them but of one minister onely, whose whole maintenance by the Church doth not amount yearely to twenty-foure lib.   Soe that we the inhabitants of both parishes have bene necessitated, from time to time, to contribute (besides the small benevolence given to Mr. Emerson, our present minister,) to the maintenance of another minister, to assist the sayd Mr. Emerson, in the worke of the ministery.

We doe therefore most humbly beseech the most honourable Court of Parliament to provide that the sayde Mr. Emerson our Minister (who hath remained with us twenty-five yeares at the leest, preachinge in one of the Churches aforesayd every Sabbath day (except when he hath bene let by sicknesse, or other extraordinary occasion), sounde and orthodoxe doctrine, and further gained our love by his honest and peaceable life and conversation) may have such competent maintenance setled upon him, for the present, and his successors after him, as shall be found meete accordinge to the wisdome of this honorable assembly, and that for the worke of the ministery in Shorham only.   And that the parish of Otford may also have competent maintenance allowed for an honest and able minister to undertake the charge of the ministery for Otford only. So that we the parishioners of both may be disburdened of the charge we have a longe time voluntarily undergone, over and above the payinge of our tithes by lawe injoyned.   And wee your humble suppliants shall be further bounde to give thankes to Almighty God for his goodnesse, and also to pray for the prosperity and happinesse of this most honorable assembly, so well affected to such pious workes.

1640-1.
16 Car. I.

David Polhill.
John Polhill.
George Dennis.
Edward Everest.
John Rogers.
Thomas Ebbott.
Rob. Petty.
Thomas Dennys.
Edward Smale.
Henry Stileman.
John Stileman.
Thomas Baker.

George Burtton.
Nicholas Wigsill.
Walter Harman.
William Edwards.
William Rogers.

John Round.
Robart Olliver.
Edward Durling.
Alexander Lewin.
James Goldsmyth.
William Hartnupp.
David Perritt.
Daniel Mallin.
John Hills.
Thomas Lushe.
Miles Darker.
Samuel Walker.

[Endorsed by Sir Edward Dering," 1640, 19 Jan.   Petition.   Shorham et Otford."]

XVII.

PETITION to the House of Commons for a Resident Minister in each of their Parishes, from the Parishioners of SHOREHAM and OTFORD.

9 March.

To the most honourable and high Court of Parliament now assembled,

The humble Petition of the Inhabitants of SHOREHAM and OT-FORD in Kent, who doe humbly shew, as followeth :—

That whereas Shoreham and Otford are two distinct parishes, about a mile distant each from other; the parish of Shoreham, consisting of 80 families, and the parsonage valued at 160*l.* per annum ; the parish of Otford of 60 families, and the parsonage valued at 200 markes per annum, both which are annexed to the Colledge of Westminster, and yet the parishes are provided (at the charge of the said colledge) of one minister onely,—namely, Mr. Emerson, whose maintenance is not worth above 24*l.* per annum ; so that wee the Inhabitants of either parish (over and above our tythes

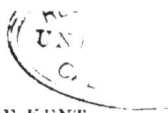

duly payed) have beene moved, by way of benevolence, from time to time, to contribute towards the maintenance of another minister, to assist the said Mr. Emerson in the worke of the ministerie, that soe we might have the word of God preached, and the holy Sacraments administered in due time and order; the which assistant hath had no other allowance beside our contribution, except ten pounds per annum which Sir Robert Heath, one of the Justices of the King's Bench, Leassee to the Church of Westminster, for the Parsonage of Otford, hath voluntarily given him.

Wherefore, as we have petitioned that Mr. Emerson may have competent maintenance, for the present, and his successors after him, for the worke of the ministerie at Shorham only, so wee likewise humbly petition that Mr. Browne, our present assistant to the said Mr. Emerson, who hath beene resident with us theise foure yeares, and hath painefully preached the word of God, may have such competent maintenance as to your wisdomes shall seeme fit, for the present, and his successors after him, for the worke of the ministerie at Otford only; so that wee the Inhabitants of either parish may bee eased of the said contribution. And wee, as in duty bound, shall ever pray for your present and eternall happinesse.

1640-1.
16 Car. I.

Shoreham.*	Otford.*
Edw. Gilbourne.	David Polhill.
John Polhill.	Rob. Petty.
George Stace.	The marke of Christopher
Edward Reeve.	Lush.
The marke of Alexander	John Stileman.
Lewine.	The marke of Thomas Dennys.
George Carsting.	William Children.
The marke of John Rowne.	Thomas Lushe.

* The framers of the petition put headings, "Shoreham" and "Otford," as if to keep the signatures of the two parishes distinct; but the scrablblings of the subscribers make the distinction very difficult, if indeed possible. I think it was originally intended that there should be a double column of signatures to each parish. As nearly as I can guess, the first column viz. from "Gilbourne" to "Dab" are for Shoreham; and the second column, from "Polhill" to "Sharke" are for Otford.

Ezekias Brian.
Edward Euere.
Henry Stileman.
John Rogers.
The marke of William Gibson.
The marke of Thomas Powser.
The marke of Thomas Perone?
The marke of Edward Ffuller.
The marke of Arthur Durling.
George Dennis.
The marke of Mathew Garner.
The marke of William
    Hartnupp.
The marke of Robert Hills.
The marke of Thomas Ffielder.
The marke of Edward Polhill.
Sa. Spenett.
Thomas Pearch.
Thomas Dalton.
John Dab.

Samuell Walker.
The marke of John Hollans.
The marke of Robert Weary.
The marke of Thos. Durker.
The marke of William
    Edwards.
The marke of William
    Christian.
The marke of Walter Herman.
The marke of William Glover.
The marke of George Sone.
The marke of John Sharke.

[Endorsed by Sir Edward Dering, "1640, 9 March. Petition pro Browne per Sr Edw. Gelborn."]

XVIII.

PETITION to the Knights of the Shire for Kent, that the Vicarial tythes of FAIRFIELD, in the hands of the church of Canterbury, may be restored to the services of their church, from the Parishioners of FAIRFIELD.

To the Right Worshipfull Sr Edward Deering, Knight, and Sr John Culpeper, Knight, Knights of the Sheire for the County of Kent, assembled in the most honourable Courte of Parliament.

The humble Peticion of the Inhabitants of the Parish of Ffairefeild, in the County of Kent, aforesayd.

Your humble Peticioners shewe unto your good worships, that, albeit we have a Parsonadge and a Vicaradge, within our parish, of the yearely valewe of threescore pounds per ann., yet, soe it is, may it please your worships, that both our Parsonadg and Vicaradg (which was set out for a Vicar to doe the service of the Church) is leased out by the Church of Canterbary, and a smale stipend reserved for the maintenance of a Minister, which is soe meane that noe well deserveing man will accept of it, to wayte and attend uppon it, to read and preach the worde of God unto us, every Sunday and Holliday constantly, for the advancement of God's glory, and the comforte of our soules; soe that wee are in a manner left utterly destitute of the good meanes of our salvation; haveing a sermon but once in a moneth, and Common Prayer read unto us by one that serves annother cure, but seldome in due season; which is a great greefe unto us all whoe desire to be better taught and instructed in matters of our salvation.

In tender consideration whereof, your humble Petitioners earnestly desire your worships, being you are elected and called to that high place, to be gracious instruments for the good of God's Church, and your Country, to use your pious endeavours that the tythes belonging to our Vicaridg may againe be restored to the Church, for the maintenance of a preaching Minister, that, in time to come, wee may be better taught and instructed; and wee, and our children which are yet unborne, shall ever be bound to pray for your worships, in much happines long to continue; and rest in all humble service by you ever to be commanded.

William Gilbarte.
The marke of Steuen Hicksted.
Richard Halle.
Peter Mapleden.

John Barlinge.
Thomas Coly.
Willame Harden.

[Endorsed by Sir Edward Dering—" 1640, 21 Jan. Petition. Fayrfield v. . . . . ."]

*

1640-1.
16 Car. I.

XIX.

PETITION to the House of Commons against their Vicar, FFRANCIS WORRALL, from the Parishioners of EAST PECKHAM.

23 January.

To the Honourable the Knights, Burgesses, and Commons assembled in the High Court of Parliament.

The humble Peticion of the Inhabitants of EAST PECKHAM, in the County of Kent,

Sheweth,

• These ensewing greivancs in our said parish.

Ffirst.—That FFRANCIS WORRALL, Clerke, who is our Minister, is not only Viccar of our parish, but is also Viccar of Watringbury, a myle distante from the same.

2. That the said Mr Worrall doth many tymes serve the Cure John Hugin. himselfe of both these Parishes, and is soe uncertaine at such tymes in officiating his Cure, that, our Parish being spacious, the Pa-William Ffleete. rishioners cannot come to Church with any convenience in the morning, and at other tymes coming (at tymes accustomed in other parishes) loste theire labour, he being dispatcht and gone to his Cure at Watringbury.

3. He is very negligent in preaching, insomuch that we have not a Sermon at our parish above once in a fortnight (except it be a funerall Sermon, which is very seldome).

4. Our Communion Table is sett upp to the East end of the Chancell, close to the wall, alterwise, the said table there rayled in, Henry Denny. and a new wainscott at the East side of the said Table made with the picture of angells therein carved.

5. He did refuse to administer the Sacrament of the Lords Supper to one of the Inhabitants of the said parish, although in decent

manner he did desire the same, and offered himselfe in the Chancell, and all because the said Inhabitant would not come upp to the rayle to receive the same.

1640-1.
16 Car. I.

JOHN JUDD.*

[Endorsed by Sir Edward Dering—"23 Jan., 1640. Petition. East Peckham v. Worrall." "Pet. Se."]

XX.

PETITION to the House of Commons from the parishioners of HOATH to be separated from RECULVER, and to have a distinct minister for the Chapelry of Hoath.

To the honourable House of Commons nowe assembled in Parliament.

25 January.

The humble Peticion of the Inhabitants of the Burrough of HOATH, in the county of Kent,

Sheuinge,

That, whereas the parish Church of RECULVER in the said County was antiently impropriate to the Archbishops of Canterbury, and a Vicar endowed to serve the Cure there; to which Church the Burrough of Hoath was supposed to bee belonginge; and the Vicars of Reculver, for the time beeinge, have used to find a Curate to saie divine service in the Chappell of the said Burrough, there beeinge a faire Chappell or Church within the same Burrough: and Mr. BARNABY KNELL beeinge nowe Vicar of Reculver, and endeavouringe to compell the Inhabitants of the said Burrough to come to the said Church of Reculver, to heare divine service; and to save himselfe from the charge of maynteyninge a Curat to saie divine service in the said Chappell of Hoath, did, for three yeeres together, forbeare to saie divine service, either by himselfe, or by any Curate of his,

---

* The other signatures are in the margin, as if the parties signed to the particular clauses opposite their names, and not to the whole petition.

1640-1.
16 Car. I.

duringe all that tyme, whereby your Petitioners have beene inforced, at their owne charge, to hire a Curat to saie divine service in the said Chappell, or else the same would have hitherto remained unserved. And, fforasmuch as the said Chappell is very convenient for a parish Church, and the Inhabitants of the same Burrough maynteine and repaire the said Chappell at their owne charges, and alsoe the poore of the same Burrough, and usually goe the perambulacion of the lands within the same Burrough, as though it were a parish of itselfe, and have Churchwardens and Overseers for the poore there, and other officers as the neighbouringe parishes have; and the same Chappell is fower miles distant from the Church of Reculver, and hath noe way thither but the Common high waye, where horses goe, which in winter time is very fowle, and almost impassable for footemen; and many of the Inhabitants of the said Burrough are aged men, and not able to goe soe farre to Church: neither is it fit for the Inhabitants to carry their children soe farre to bee baptized.

For which causes, and divers others, your peticioners humbly desire that the Vicar of Reculver maye be compelled to find an able Curat, to serve the Cure in the said Burrough; or that the Vicaridge tithes and other profitts of the said Burrough maye be imploied for the mayntenance of such an able minister to serve the Cure there, as your Peticioners shall provide for that purpose; and that you wilbee pleased to take such course theirin as in your wisdomes you shall thinke fit, for the redresse and ease of your Peticioners.

William Joy.   } Churchwardens.
John Christian × his marke. }

Nicholas Hamman.   William Sinnock × his marke.
James Rose.   William Freind × his marke.
Thomas Rose × his marke.   William Pacy × his marke.
Valentine Ewell × his marke.   Nicholas Hooker × his marke.
John Austin × his marke.   } Overseers.
Robert Ferman × his marke. }
Thomas Hamon × his marke.   Robert Wilckes.

Richard Staynes × his marke.   Salomon Plumer × his marke.

John Christian the younger ×   John Browne × his marke.
   his marke.   Richard Clarke × his marke.

John Morris × his marke.   Robert Whetnall × his marke.

1640-1.
16 Car. 1.

[Endorsed by Sir Edward Dering—"1640, 25 Jan. Petition. Hoath, *n.* Knell."]

XXI.

PETITION of BARNABAS KNELL, Vicar of RECULVER, to S^r ED-
WARD DEERING, to have 18*l.* restored to him, which had been
kept back from him by the Petitioners against him at HOATH.

> To the honourable Sr Edward Deering, Kt. and Baronet,
> and one of the Oracles of the honnorable House of Parliament.

    20 July

The humble Peticion of Barnabas Knell, Clerke, the distressed
Vicar of RECULVER, in Kent.

Sheweth and seweth,

That whereas your Petitioner, aged 67 yeares, whereof he hath
spent neare 39 peicably, honestly, and painfully, in his well approved
Minestry at Reculver and Hoth, hath now at last by a defective
order made by Sr Nathaniell Brent, Commissary of Canterbury, by
direction (as he saith) of the Lord Archbishop, 18*l.* per annum
ordered to be paid to your said Petitioner, by certen of the Inhabitants of Hoth aforesaid, for the Tithes, &c. thence arising, deteyned
from him by William Joy, John Austin, and Thomas Hamon,
against law and concience, upon pretence of a peticion exhibited by
them to the house of Parliament, for a Minister to serve the cure
of the said Chappell, where never was any; the said Chappell being
erected only for Mass, and other superstitious ceremonies, at the
buriall of the dead; whereby your Petitioner, making scarce 24*l.*
per annum of all the Tithes of Reculver beside, is not only destitute
of meanes to susteyne himself, his wife of neere 60 yeeres of age, 2

sickly daughters, a poore sister aged 74 yeares, and an Orphan grandchild of 9 yeares (all which depend either wholy or for the most part upon your Peticioner) ; but is daly in danger of imprisonment for debt, whereby he wilbe hindred from his cure.

It would be your honors good pleasure, to take present order with the said Joy, Austin, and Hamon, for the payment of the said 18*l.* already due to your Petitioner; and what shall futurly be determined by the house of Parliament touching the service of the said Chappell your Petitioner shall most humbly submitt himself unto.

And be bound to pray for your honors long prosperity.

[Endorsed by Sir Edward Dering—"1641, 20 July. Petition. Mr Knell."]

XXII.

Statement of the disputes about HOATH.

The cause of HOATH stands thus:—

We find by antient records, that originally the church of RECULVER hath had these chappells belonging to it; viz., HOATH, ST. NICHOLAS in THANETT, ALL SAINTS, and HEARNE; the which chapell of All Saints, being fallen to decay, has of longe tyme and doth to this day belonge to the parish of St. Nicholas; the which chapells has all of them bin under the cure and charge of the Vicker of Reculver, not supplying all of them him selfe, but he finding a suffitient curat in each chapell; and, in the year 1310, Archbishop WINCHELSEY granted to the Vicker of Reculver all such small Tythes as were in RECULVER and HOATH, and sertaine yeerely pentions out of St. Nicholas and Hearne, as till this day is performed; as that the Vicker of St. Nicholas should have all such small tythes as were in St. Nicholas, paying to the Vicker of Reculver 3*l.* per annum ; and the Vicker of Hearne should have all such small tythes as were in Hearne, onely

1611.
17 Car. I.

paying to the Vicker of Reculver 40s. per annum ; and soe, by reason that Reculver and Hoath were lesse than either of the other two, and alsoe that the yeerely tythes of Reculver and Hoath did not amount to soe much as the tythes of either St Nicholas or Hearne, left the Church of Reculver with the Chapell of Hoath to the cure and charge of the Vicker of Reculver, the inhabitance of Hoath being no wayes bound to goe to the church of Reculver, to heare divine service, or receive the Sacrament, having within the said parish or chapelry of Hoath a fayer Church or Chapell, and Church-yard thereto belonging, of their owne, wherein they have bin alwayes used to heare divine service, receive the sacraments, baptize and burye, with all other writes and serimonies comanded by the Church of England, administered by the Vicker of Reculver; and sume yett living which can remember ever since Queene Maryes dayes, will testifie upone their othes that the Vicker of Reculver has bin used to come, once in every moneth, to serve the cure in Hoath Chapell and the other three Sundayes it has bin served by a reader: and that the Vicker of Reculver has bin used att all tymes to come to baptize, burye, and Church women within the Chapell of Hoath, soe oft as neede did require ; and thus stood the cause till Mr. Knell's dayes; but then Mr. Knell, that now is, cha[ng]ing Liuings with one Mr. Hunt that then was, the said Mr. Knell being setled vicker of Reculver and Hoath, tooke upone him, without all order, to com-pell the Inhabitants of Hoath to goe to Reculver, to have divine service and soe to alett their owne Chapell stand unserved ; but Com-plaint being made to the Lord Archbishop of Canterbury, his grace, in the yeare 1606, being then at Ffoord, one of his graces Manner houses within the said parish or chapelry of Hoath, compelled the said Mr. Knell to come before him, to answere what was complained against him, the which he did; but, when his grace had heard what the inhabitance could say for them selves, and what to them did belong from the sayd Mr. Knell; and alsoe what Mr. Knell could say for himselfe, did there threten Mr. Knell, that if he did not see the cure in Hoath Chapell better served, he would take it quite away from him ; but Mr. Knell then pleaded povertie, and that he had a wife and maney small children, and that he was not able to mayntayne them upone soe small a rate, did then intreat his grace, that he would be pleased to tollerate him to be absent from his cure in Reculver, one Sunday in every moneth, soe that the Clarke myght be tollerated to read divine service the other three Sundayes, according to the former custome; the which being considered of by his grace, made it, or caysed it to be made, by his ordinary, an order under his hand and seale, the which order was well and dulye performed all that Bishop's dayes, untill the yeere of our Lord 1636; but then, at the visitatione at Easter, houlden at Canterbury, by Sir Nathaniell Brent, the Clarke was sited in, and there forbidden by him to read divine service, alleaging that my Lord would not allow of a Layman to read divine service; soe that for one whole yeere we had divine service but once in every moneth, when the vicker of Reculver his turne came; but then, at the visitatione houlden at Canterbury by Sir Nathaniell Brent at Easter, in the yeere 1637, wheither by complaint made by the parishioners of Reculver, for want of their minister the moneth Sunday, or by Mr. Knell's owne meanes, we knowe not, but the sayd Mr. Knell was there forbidden by the sayd Sr Nathaniell Brent, not to leave his mother Church unserved the moneth Sunday that he came to serve his Cure in Hoath, alleaging that my Lord would not have his mother Church stand unserved, to goe to say divine service in a chappell or hamlett, and not forbidding the said Mr. Knell all together to leave his cure in Hoath unserved; but he, to save him selfe the charge of a Curat, tooke upone him of him selfe all together to neglect his cure in Hoath, for the space of three yeeres and upwards, except the administering of the sacrament once or twise in a yeere, and besides, to compell us to goe to Reculver to heare divine service; but the inhabitants of Hoath, finding themselves destitute of all heavenly comfort, made their petitione to my Lord of Canterbury his grace that now is for releife, who presently did referr it to one Mr. Sumner of Canterbury, to informe him how the Cause stood with Hoath Chappell, and what did belonge from the Vicker of Reculver therein; whome, upone receit of that referrence made

1641.
17 Car. I.

report in writing what he found in record; but there the matter dyed, and we heard noe more of it ; then we made a second peticione, and then his grace gave us this answere; that, if we would have a chapell of ease, we must pay for our ease ; but then, petitione being made againe by an other, the which when he had redd, referred the Cause to one Mr. Hart, his graces then solissiter, to make report unto him, how the Cause stood conserning Hoath Chappell, the which he did alsoe; but there, as the other, that dyed alsoe ; but then, a third Churchwarden being chosen, through the perswations of others, how that it was a shame that our Chapell should stand soe, and we goe to other Churches, and how that if my Lord had but a right informatione of our Cause, we should have a remedye, made a fourth petitione to his grace, the which when he had perused, referred the Cause to Sr Nathaniell Brent, to settle the matter that he heard noe more of it, to whome he did presently repaire, being then in London, whoe, when he had read my Lord's reference, appoynted us a day of hearing in Canterbury, the weeke after, which was about Whitsun-tide 1640, and did bid us to speake to Mr. Knell, to appeere before him the same day with us, the which, soe soone as we came home, wee did; but, before the day of hearing came, Mr. Knell went to Sr Nathaniell Brent, and did their make way for him selfe, that we should take the tythes unto our owne hands, and soe to give him 18l. a yeere; soe that when the day of hearing came, without we would take the tythes into our owne hands, and soe give Mr Knell 18l. a yeere, we were like to speede as before, and alsoe, being thretned by Sr Nathaniell Brent, that, if we would not agree to that order, we should stand to the Lawe ; and alsoe, that if ever we came before my Lord againe, to trouble him with this matter, we should be layd by the heeles, and being alsoe before thretned by other parishes for comming to their Churches, to be sited to the Court, for taking up of their places in there Pues, we were forced to condesend to an order which was against lawe, and to our great henderance.

[Endorsed by Sr Edward Dering—"1641. 6 October. Certificate, Hoath v. Mr Knell."

And enclosed in it is the paper subjoined.]

1611.
17 Car. 1.

Reasons shewed by the Inhabitants of the Borrough or Chapellric of Hoath, why they doe denye to goe to the parish church of Reculver to heare divine service, receive the sacrament, baptise, and burie their dead, &c.

First. For that we have within our borrough or chapellric a very fayer church or chapell, sittuat with in the midst of a church-yard, very convenient to bury the dead in; and alsoe we have within our chapell all ornaments dessent and fitting the service of God, as all neighbouring churches have.

2. Secondly. We are not fett in by perambulation by aney other parish, but have aways bin used to goe the bounds with in our sayd burrough, of ourselves, with out aney other.

3. Thirdly. We doe beare all offices within our Burrough, of our-selves, noe officer of aney parish medling with it, nor we with them; and we doe repaire our Church, of ourselves; and alsoe mayntaine our poore with out the helpe of any.

4. Fourthly. We have within our Borough or Chapelrye 40 poore famelyes, and most of theme be exceedying poore, the which doe contayne to 150 soules, and upwards, whereof are 100 and odd of them Communicants.

5. Fifthly. Our Chapell stands full fower myles from Reculver, and maney of our people are very aged people, not able to goe soe far; and maney children whoe are ill brought up for want of in-struction.

6. Sixthly. We have noe way to Reculver, but by the King's high way, the which in winter tyme is soe fowle that it is allmost un-passible.

7. Seventhly. If there be aney neglect by aney of the officers of our parish, or aney fault to be found in our Chapell, the Court takes hould of us as well as of aney other parish.

8. Eightthly. We doe carrie in bills of presentment at all visita-tions, and alsoe of all marriages, burialls, and christenings, dun within our borrow or Chapelry, by ourselves.

XXIII.

1641.
17 Car. I.

Petition to the House of Commons (that the Archbishop of Canterbury, as Impropriator, may be made to increase the income of the Vicar) from the Parishioners of WALMER.

The humble Informacion and Peticion of the Inhabitants of WALMER, in the county of Kent, and diocese of Canterburie. 25 January.

Sheweth and certyfieth

That, whereas our minister Mr ANTHONY BROMSTON is neither a persecutor nor innovator, nor a scandalous person ; but a diligent preacher, and of honest life and conversacion, having lived many yeeres amongst us : and, whereas the allowance for the maintenance of the minister there is not above xvj^{li} per annum, wherewith it had not been possible for him to susteine himselfe, his wife and many children, had it not been for the free contribucion of some few well disposed people well knowing his merit and integrity, and pitttying his small allowance. And, whereas the Rectorie or Parsonage there is worth 100l. by the yere, whereof he receiveth no part. And, where also a pension of viij^{li} per annum ought to issue out of the said parsonage, and of right to belong unto him as Vicar (as may appeare by Record in the Court of Augmentacion) whereof he yet never received part, notwithstanding peticion made for the same to the Archbishop of Canterbury, to whome the said parsonage doth belonge.

May it therefore please you (in tender care for the good of our soules) to take some course that a competent allowance may be provided for the maintenance of a preaching minister amongst us ; and if it shall seeme fitt unto your wisedomes that the arreares also of the said pension may be restored unto him, for the present releife of him (being a sickly weake man) and for the good of his wife and children.

And we the parishioners (together with him and his) shall be bound to pray both for your pious endeavours, and for the whole assembly of the high Court of Parliment.

Ni. L'isle.
Thomas Gillowe.
Will. Hugesson.
Richard Sladden.

John Samson.
John Gillowe.
Winter Gillowe.
Thomas Philpot.
William Lambert.
Henry Chandeler.) Church-
Richard Solmes.) wardens.
John Bowle.
Davyd Sayer.
Tho. Willington.
John Sladden.

John Adams.
Isake Samson.
William Gillowe.
Alexander Castle.
William Hamon.
Henry Hamon.
John Watson.
Anthony Ffoxe.
George Lull.
George Leake.

[Endorsed by Sr Edward Dering—"1640. 25 January. Petition, Walmer pro Bromston."]

XXIV.

Return to an Order of the House of Commons with Information as to the Rectory, Vicarage, &c. of GOUDHURST.

26 January.

The Information of the Parish of GOODHIRST according to that Order injoyned by the Honorable House of Commons December 19th, 1640.

Lett the Honorable Committee be pleased to understand, that our Parsonage of Goodhirst in Kent, in the hundred of Marden, is impropriated to the Deane and Chapter of Rochester, being in valew, as far as wee can understand, 100*l.* per annum.

The Vicaridge, estimated per annum att 100*l.*, or upwards, is possesed by Dr. Horsmanden, non-Resident, being also parson of Ulcombe in Kent, estimated per annum 200*l.* and upwards.

Our Cure in Goodhirst, in which is about 1,400 Communicants, hath bin faithfully and solely dischardge, for some yeares, by Mr. Edw. Bright, upon allowance from the Dr., on his part, but 24*l.* per annum, who standing now unjustly suspended, as his already heard cause in the Honorable House of Parliament testifieth, being a sufferer, formerly in Surrey, in the losse of a Living, and now in Kent, in the losse of his Ministry and meanes, is a well deserving Minister, faithfull and painefull in preaching, pious and peaceable in conversation, much desired by us, to be our Restored and Absolute Instructor, according to the tenour of our past petition in his behalfe.

John Austen.	James Besbeech.
Richard Besbeech.	John Morgan.
Robart Remington.	Robert Bathurst.
Samuell Austen.	William Perren.
George Besbeech.	

Inhabitants in the Parish of Goudhirst.

XXV.

Letter to Sr EDWARD DERING, enclosing the above Return and Information from the Inhabitants of GOUDHURST.

WORTHY SIR.

Our Services premised, wee are bold to present unto you the Information of our parish, draughted, as neare as we could, in all particulars, according to the order of your Honorable House, about the Impropriation and Valew of our Parsonage, worth and estimate of our Vicaridge, non-Residencie, and noe more, of our Dr and Vicar, true worth and condition of our late, yett now for a season lost, Minister, upon the hope of whose restoring and establishing our soules depend, and towards whom our desires are very hartie, sincere, and free ; may it be your pleasure but to further us what you may in our assured injoyment of him, and you shall oblige us and ours for ever, in most strong bands of all dutiful respect.

Mr. Bright desires us to present his service to you with all thankfulnesse, remembering your care and free furtherance in his Parla-

mentarie cause. Our hopes, yea our soules hopes, lye in your helpe.
Wee besech the Lord to prosper you, and that honorable parla-
mentaric assembly; to the great reformation of the land in generall,
and the soule saving good of our place in speciall. Thus being bold
to desire that to which wee know your owne true worth and willingnesse will freely leade you, wee now cease your farther trouble,
and will for ever rest,

Yours to command

John Austen.
Richard Besbeech.
John Morgan.
George Besbeech.
Robert Remington.
James Besbeech.
William Perren.

Goodhirst, 26th January, 1640.
Inhabitants of the Parish of Goodhirst.

[Superscription.]
"To the right worshipful Sir Edward Dering, Knight and
Barronett, at his lodging in Sr Henry Gibbs his house, in
St. Martin's Lane, these present." And endorsed by S^r
Edward, "27 January 1640, certificate Goudherst."]

XXVI.

Petition to the House of Commons for the restoration of their Curate M^r
BRIGHT, who had been suspended by the Archdeacon of Canterbury.
From the parishioners of GOUDHURST.

To the honorable the Knights, Citizens, and Burgesses
assembled in the Commons howse of Parliament.

The humble peticion of the Parishioners and Inhabitants of GOUD-
HURST in the County of Kent.
Humbly sheweth,
That your petitioners have, for a long time past, had the comfort

of a faithfull and able preacher, one Mr. Bright, as Curate and Lecturer of the said Parish, who, in his place, tooke much paines and care for the saveing of soules, till, about Michaelmas last, he was suspended by the Archdeacon of Canterbury; but for what cause your petitioners know not.

1640.1.
16 Car. I.

That Dr Horsmonden, being Vicar of the said Parish, but non-resident, hath lately, to cross your Petitioners' intencions of haveing the said Mr Bright settled as formerly, resigned up the said Vicaridge to one Mr Wilcocks, a man unfitt, and very unable to execute the great cure of the said Parish consistinge of many thousand soules, as will be sufficiently proved by good testimony.

Your Peticioners therefore humbly pray that this honorable assemblie wilbe pleased to take the premises into your grave consideracions ; and that your Peticioners may not be frustrate of a painfull minister ; and, if it be possible, that they may enjoy the said Mr Bright, whose ability, industry, and good conversation wee have had exceeding good tryall of.

And they shall ever pray &c.

John Morgan.
John Hartredge.

[Endorsed by Sr Edward Dering—" 1640. 12 March. Petition. Goudherst pro Bright."]

XXVII.

PETITION to the House of Commons, about the neglected state of their Parishes, from the Parishioners of LEEDS and BROOMFIELD.

To the Honorable the Knights, Burgesses, and Commons assembled in Parliament.

January.

The humble Peticion of the Inhabitants of the Parishes of LEEDS and BROMFIELD in the County of Kent.

Humbly shewing

That the Archbishopp of Canterbury is Parson of both our

1640-1.
16 Car. 1.
Parishes, and receiveth the proffitts thereof: and hath placed but one
Curate to serve in both our said Parishes, whose name is Mr. Richard
Marsh, allowing unto his said Curate, by common report, but
12*l.* 6*s.* 8*d.* per annum, for serving of both the Cures; so that wee
have not that preaching amongst us as we could desire, and might
be expected, if we had severall Curates over our Parishes.   And,
moreover, according to direccions from this honorable house, wee
humbly certifie that the aforesaid Mr. Marsh, the Curate aforesaid,
is Parson of Ruckinge, in the Countie aforesaid, where he is not resident, and the said Parsonage of Ruckinge is reputed to be worth
cxx^{li} per annum, at the least.

Wherefore, wee doe humbly desire, that you would be pleased to
weigh our condicion, and to doe for us therein as in your discreecions
shall seeme fitt.   And the rather for that some of us have beene
constrayned to goe to other parishes, for want of preaching at our
owne parishes.   And have beene cited, troubled, and molested for soe
doing, to the saddning of our hearts, and wasting of our estates.

John Saxby.	George Day.	The marke × of
Gregory Wattes.	George Jenings.	Thomas Wilmot.
John Startup.	Alexander Wattell.	Thomas × Yrige ?
Gregory Odierne.	Thomas Robens.	James × Dennes.
		Henry Colyson.

[Endorsed by Sr Edward Dering—" 1640. January. Petition.   Leedes and
Bromfeild *v.* Marsh.

"Principall witnesses   John Saxby.
Gregory Watts."]

XXVIII.

PETITION to the House of Commons that they may have a resident Vicar,
from the Parishioners of YALDING.

28 January.
To the honourable the Knights, Burgesses, and Commons now
assembled in the High Court of Parliament.

The humble Petition of the Inhabitants of YALDINGE in the County of Kent,

1640-1.
16 Car. I.

Shewing,

That the Parish of Yaldinge in the hundred of Twiford in the County of Kent is impropriated unto Bennett Ward, widdowe; and that the Parsonage tithes there, are of the yearlie value of clx^{li} at the least.

That the Viccaridge there is of the yearlie value of lxxx^{li}, besides the Viccaridge house and 30 acres of Glebe land, which is lett at xxx^{li} per annum.

That Mr. Ffrancis Taylor is our Viccar, who is also Rector of Clapham in the County of Surrey, and there residing, and non-resident with us, havinge not beene with us himselfe by the space of one quarter of a yeare now last past, and upwards, and not having sett over us any setled Curate in his absence, by the space of sixe monethes last past, and upwards.

Wee have had noe preaching Pastor that hath beene conscionable to performe his office faithfully amongst us by the space of thirtie yeares and upwards, whereby honest hearts are sadded, and others are very ignorant and lewd.

Our Communion table is sett upp close to the wall, at the east end of the chancell, alterwise; the east end of the said chancell (to which the said Table is ioyned) is new wainscotted, with Cherubyms carved in the said wainscott, and a rayle with two ascents thereto lately made. Mr. Thomas Tourney, who was our late Viccar, and is now Viccar of Wittersham, in the Isle of Oxney, in the said county, did usually bowe to the said Table, and adore it: soe that wee not knowing what the end and meaning of such things are, are thereat much troubled, and our consciences offended.

Wherefore, wee doe earnestly and humbly desire this honourable house to take consideracion of our condicions, and to remove our grievances; and so to provide that we may have faythfull pastors. Wee humbly make bold to mencion Mr. Ffrancis Cornewell, a painfull preacher of good report, which wee nevertheless recomend to your godly wisdome.

George Penhurst.

Ezekiell × Ffleet, his marke.

[Endorsed by Sr Edward Dering—" 1640, 28 January. Petition. Yalding v. Tailer."]

XXIX.

PETITION to the House of Commons against their Minister, for neglect and Popish practices, from the Parishioners of CAPEL.

February.

The humble Petitione of the Parishioners of CAPEL in the County of Kent, to the wright honerable Howse of Commons, against Mr. EDWARDE WALLIS, minister of Tudely and Caple.

First. He is not resident amongst us.

Secondly. Wee are served every other Saboth by a laieman, and sometimes we have a sermon but once a monyth, and now and then we have neyther praiers nor sermon. Wee hold Tudley to be worth 40*l*. a yeare and better; and for Caple, it is worth 40 markes a yeare; but we are willinge to mend that, soe we maie have a preachinge minister to our selfes, which we hope the honerable howse will afforde ous to have.

Thirdly. He is soe cerimoniall, that if he come out of the railes, he saith he should offend God; and said that, when he did aske God forgivenesse for his sinns, he must aske him forgivnes for that.

Ffourthly. He did dismise some five or sixe of us, when we presented our selfes one our knees in the chansell, to receive the sachrament, because we did not come to the raiels wheare he doth cringe and bowe.

Fifthly. He saies that if he be ever soe fare from his text, yet if he keepe but talkinge one, it will serve our turne.

Sixthly. He said that, after the Parlament was ended, he would come out of his railes to none of ous.

1640-1.
16 Car. I.

Seaventhly. He doth raile against the Scots in his pulpit, and out of his pulpit, callinge them dogs and divells; and saies he knowes not how to call them bade enough.

Eighthly. He saies, that if ever Scote goe to heaven, the divell will goe too.

Lastly. He saies there is more hope of a Papist then there is of a Puritant.

James Hunt.
Thomas Wood.
Robart Remington.

[Endorsed by Sr Edward Dering—"1640, Febr.—Petition, Capell *v.* Wallys.—Sc. m."]

XXX.

PETITION to the House of Commons, to increase the Income of their Incumbent, from the Parishioners of BRABORNE.

February.

To the Honourable House of Commons in the High Court of Parliament assembled.

The Information and Peticion of the Inhabitants of BRABORNE in Kent.

Most humbly sheweth,

That (according to your pious order concerning ministers and theire mayntenance) we doe certifie the Vicarage of Braborne to be a very small Liveing, by reason the Rectorie is impropriate, not only in the corne, but in all the hay, and all the Glebe lands, insoemuch that there remaynes to the Incumbent soe small a proportion as will not extend to 30*l.* per annum all manner of wayes.

That this small liveing is high in value in his Majesty's book, insoemuch, that, in time of subsidies at iiij^s. in the pounde, with the annuall tenthes and procuracions, the Incombent affirmeth that there is iij^{li} xij^s. yearely to be paide out of it, which deducted from the former portion leaves a remaynder too little (as we conceive) to mayntayne a preaching minister.

That this present Incumbent hath alsoe the ruines of much old houseing left unto him by his decayed predicessor, which he could never yet be able sufficiently to repayre; he hath also a wife and five children to sustayne upon this small meanes.

May it, therefore, please this honourable House to take into consideracion the smallnesse of this Liveing, with the charges that lye upon it, and the necessities of this present Incomebent John Rosse, clerke, whoe hath lived amongst us now xvi. yeares, and in a lawdable manner, both for his life and doctrine: and soe to provide that his mayntenance may be increased by such good meanes as your godly wisdomes shall judg convenient.

Soe shall we be all bounde, and in all duty for ever obleiged to pray for the happinesse of this Honorable House.

Edmund Nott.	John Bull.
Richard Morris.	Thomas Terrie.
John Baylie.	John Greene.
John Cheesman.	Simon Spratt.
John Effeild.	Gilbeart Dodd.

[Endorsed by Sr Edward Dering—"2 Feb. 0.   Braborn pro."]

XXXI.

PETITION to the House of Commons to compel the Impropriator to provide better for their Cure, from the Inhabitants of ORE.

To the honourable the Lower House of Commons in this Parliament.

The humble Peticion of the Inhabitants of the Parish of OWRE neere Ffaversham, in Kent, whose names are underwritten, concerning the Cure of theire souls.

Shewing,

That in regard of the smal allowance for serving the Cure of the

1610-1.
16 Car. I.

sayd Parish, we have not had (for these twenty yeares) any Minister settled among us, save onely one, whose stipend was but 8*l*. by the yeare, to mainteine himselfe, with his wife and children: and thereuppon, chusing rather to steale meate for himselfe and his, then to beg or starve, was arraigned and condemned of felony; to the scandal of our Religion, and reproch of the ministry in the reformed Church of this land.

And that now Sr Robert Honywood the Patron or Parson of this, and many other such like Impropriations, to the number of 14, or more, receiving 30*l*. at least per annum, of the Farmar under him, for the tythe of our parish, and alowing but 12*l*., we cannot have any constant Minister; but such as, serving some other place, substitutes a layman for the ordinary service of the Cure, reading divine service in our church: and, when the cheif Curate himselfe, or any other for him, comes to preach and performe any other duties of the ministry, it is either before or after they have dispatched some other churche more then a mile distant from ours: So that, to our great greife, we cannot enjoy that settled meanes of saving knowledg, and that comfortable ministry of God's word and worship, which we doe earnestly long for; and therefore

Wee your poore Petitioners most humbly beseech you of this honourable assembly in Parliament, amongst other matters of the like nature, tending to the honour of God, to receive this greivous greivance of our soules into your pious consideration and religious care; where we leave it for redresse; beseeching the onely wise God so to blesse, guide, and direct you all, in these, and all other your consultations, that his name may have more glory, and Church and Common weale may better prosper and flourish thereby.

So prayeth

Rafe × Person, his mark.	Thomas Daman.
Moises × Gipson, his mark.	Richard × Price, his marke.
James × Harris, his mark.	Richard Price the younger.
Abraham × Luson, his mark.	Nicholas Clatting.
Thomas × Blaiton, his mark.	Samuel Luson.

1640-1.
16 Car. I.

John Larance.

Andru × Win, his mark.

Thomas × Hil, his mark.

Wiliam × Daman, his mark.

Godfre Slade.

Samell Thomas.

Mathew × Dickeson, his marke.

[Endorsed,—"The Petition of the Parishioners of the Parish of Owre in Kent,"—and by Sʳ Edward Dering " 1640, Febr. Petition Ore *v.* Sʳ Rob. Honywood."]

XXXII.

Petition to Sʳ EDWARD DERING, as Commissioner of the House of Commons, for preferment, or encrease of income to Mʳ STREATINGE, their Curate, from the Parishioners of IVYCHURCH.

3 February.

To the Right Worshipfull Sʳ Edward Deeringe, one of the Knights of the Sheere, elected for the County of Kent.

The humble supplication and petition of the Inhabitants and Parishioners of the Parishe of IVYECHURCHE, in the Libertie of Romney Marshe.

Whereas we are crediblely given to understande of the greate love and care the honourable house of Parliament hath of poore Ministers and Curates, either for the providinge of competent livings for them that are well qualified and have none, by takinge from them that have too many; or by an augmentation of theire meanes which is too small and meane, by reason of the covetousnes of those under whome they serve. As allso, that for redresse heerein, wee are to repaire to your Worshipe, to whome (as wee understande) the care heereof, for our Countye, is committed. These therefore, in all humble and submissive manner, are to beseeche you and entreate you, that you would be pleased to take into your consideration the poore estate of our poore Curate, John Streatinge, Mʳ of Artes, of Lincolne Colledge, in the Universitie of Oxforde, who hath served as a poore Curate heere in Kent, this sixe and twentie yeares, whereof, in our parishe of

Ivyechurche, for the space of these seaventeene yeares, or there- 1640-1.
16 Car. I.
abouts: all which time, he hath demeaned and carried himselfe well,
civilly, orderly, soberly, and honestly, amongst us, and preached the
word of God amongst us faithfully and painefully; and, in his
ministeriall function carried himselfe conformable to the orders of the
Churche; yea, wee so well approve of him, and have found him so
well qualified, that, if he gaine no better preferment, wee could wishe
(if wishes might prevaile and doe him gode) that wee may enjoy him
longer, with a further and more liberall augmentation of his meanes
amongst us: wee holdinge it an unreasonable and unconscionable
thinge, that the livinge of Ivyechurche, being worth, as it is farmed
out, above two hundred pounds a yeare, the poore Curate should
have but thirtie pounds a yeare, he takinge all the paines; and the
doctor, under whome he serves, seldome comminge and preachinge
amongst us; no, not havinge bin once amongst us for the space of
these fower or five yeares. To which request of ours, if you shall
condescende and assiste us heerein (as we doubt not but you will)
wee shall rest,

Your humble, ever thankefull, and

much bounden to, suppliants

Thomas Glover.	Peter Thurbarne.	
Michel Johnson ⎱ × his marke. ⎰	William Tailor × his marke. ⎱ Thomas × Owens ⎰ his marke.	Church- wardens.
Robert Thurbarne.		
John Bedell.	George Cruchman ⎱ his × marke. ⎰	Sidemen.
John Melloway ⎱ × his marke. ⎰	Guye × Furner his marke.	

[Endorsed by Sr Edward Dering,—" 1640, 3 Feb. Peticion. Snargate *(sic)*:
pro Streating."]

1641.
17 Car. I.

XXXIII.

Letter to Sr EDWARD DERING pressing a favourable reply to the preceding Petition.   From JOHN STREATINGE, Curate of Ivychurch.

Right Worshipfull.

5 July.

The Inhabitants of the Parishe of Ivyechurche, in the Libertie of Romney Marshe, at the beginninge of Parliament did present you with a petition on my behaulfe, delivered in by my selfe to your worship, the effecte whereof was this.   That, in consideration I had served allmost fower apprenticeshippes as a Curate; firste, under Doctor Warner in the parisshe of Bisshopsboorne, in the County of Kent, 8 yeares; then, in Ivychurche, under that worthy man Mr. John Sandforde, prebendary of Canterbury; and now under Doctor Jackeson there, for the space of these 18 yeares; yet, never could get any preferment under them (though I have had many good words and faire promises from them); you would be pleased (among the number of the rest of poore schollers) to be either a meanes to helpe me to some small benefice or other ; or else, that I may have an augmentation of meanes allowed me in the Cure of Ivyechurche, which I now serve ; the Livinge beinge worth allmost three hundred pounds a yeare, and I receivinge thereout only thirtie pounds a yeare, though I live in the Marshe, an unhealthfull place, and among rude and ill-nurtured people, for the most parte ; which, if your worship shall be a meanes to effecte for me and them, and theire sakes, I shall rest much obliged to you, and stand bound to pray, so long as I shall live, for the prosperous and flourishinge estate of you and yours heere, with the addition of eternall blisse and happines to your selfe and them heereafter.

Your worship's humble suppliant,
JOHN STREATINGE.

Ivyechurche, this 5 day of July, 1641.

[Superscription.]

" To the right worshipfull Sr Edward Dering,
at his lodginge in Westminster—these."

XXXIV.

1640-1.
16 Car. I.

3 February.

PETITION to the House of Commons, complaining of frauds and exaction in the Lessee of the Tythes. From the Land Occupiers of PROM-HILL and MIDLEY.

To the honnorable house of Commons now assembled in Parliament.

The humble Petition and Information of the Parishioners or land occupiers of the parishes of PROMHILL and MIDLEY, in the County of Kent,

Humblie sheweth,

That the said two parishes of Promhill and Medley aforesaid, lieing together, and adjoyning to the sea side, and as wee conceive by reason of some inundacion of the sea or danger therof, or for other causes, is and hath beene depopulate, and utterly voyde of dwellers, inhabitants, and Churches, or houses, except where 2 or 3 sheepherds abide, that goe to other parishes to Church, by so long time as is beyond the knowledge of any living to the contrary : and yet, notwithstanding, the vicaridge and personage tythes have beene there continually substracted and taken in a reasonable and conscionable manner, untill of late yeares, that the said vicaridges have beene lett to farme unto one Antony Norton, of Rie, in the county of Sussex, who hath very unconscionably racked and improved the said tithes, to the great advancement of his estate, abusing some of the said land occupiers that were illiterate, by setting downe in their acquittances greater summes of money then he had received for a yeares tythes, and the next yeare demanding so much as he had put in the said acquittance; or, if he meant to vex them therupon for more tythes in the Bishop's Courts, then they should be forced to shew the false acquittances, and see therby to condemne themselves, and to prove for him that he demanded of them but as they had paid before ; and for that wee (or some of us), your peticioners, have refused to be so dealt withall, or willingly to paie such extreme and unusuall tithes beyond reason and equity, therefore have wee been vexed and

molested in a very injurious manner by the said Norton in the
Bishop's Courts, to our great trouble and charge, without finding any
redresse or succour in our just causes, by reason of the said Norton's
correspondencie and favour with the said Courts, which he hath
obteined by the great benefitt the officers of the said Courts have received by the number of troubles and suits daily by him commenced
and pursued ; of which said vicaridges and parish of Promhill the said
Norton holdeth by grant or lease from the heires of Sr John Wyles,
late of Canterbury, amounteth to about 120l. per annum; the other,
of Midley, by the grant or demise of Mr. Henry Duke (supposed to
bee now or late dwelling in London), and amounteth to about 120l.
per annum; which two vicaridges or livings, being without cure of
soules, and amounting to such values in the tithes, wee thought good
to informe this honourable house of, being incouraged thereunto by
the declaration lately sent abroad and published, to such purpose ;
and also, for that wee have and daily doe undergoe the exactions in
payments, and vexations by troubles imposed and commenced against
us, or some of us, by the said Norton, of which we praie and desire
to be delivered ; and therefore have made this relacion and informacion to this honourable house.

Humbly praying to bee delivered from the grievous exactions and
oppressions of the abovesaid Anthony Norton, and that wee your
Peticioners may paie such reasonable tithes as they have lately paid,
before the said Norton hired the said vicaridges, soe that wee may
live in peace, and not unjustlie be vexed any more in the said
Bishop's Courts.

And your Petitioners shall ever praie (as they are nevertheles
bound) for God's blessing upon all your pious actions, and to send
them all good successe, and happy ends.

Peter Maplisden.	Sackvile Johnson.
Thomas Bate.	Thomas Smith.
John Bate.	James Robine.
Daniell Browne.	Thomas Higenson.

Thomas Reder.

The marke × of Henry Poten.

Richard Bate.

John Drewe.

Edward Athie.

John × Kingsford, his marke.

James × Jagger, his marke.

Thomas × Norres, his marke.

John Remnant × his marke.

Robert Radford.

1640-1.
16 Car. I.

[Endorsed by S* Edward Dering, " 1640, 3 Febr. Petition, Promhill [and] Midley *v.* Norton."]

XXXV.

LETTER to S* EDWARD DERING, promising immediate appearance, if summoned by the House of Commons, from M* SWINOCKE, Incumbent of MERSHAM.*

SIR,

February.

I humbly desire you to pardon my boldenes in saluting you thus at a distance: did not necessity urge, modesty would have curb'd thys my designe. My petition to your worship is only, that, if you have me questioned in your honourable house, and that a bill bee admitted against me, you will bee pleased to undertake for my appearance; and upon the least intimation from your meanest servant, I shall obey your summons. My fault is only having two livings, and, if that be censured unfit by your honourable house, I shall willingly sacrifice my privat respects to the publicke good; and, in the interim, as I have beene, so, by God's helpe, I will be carefull of the Cure. This I am sure, as there is never a living in the Marsh, so, few of that bignes in the kingdom, better served; for I allow Mr. Baker, a godly honest man, 20*l.* per annum for serving the Cure,

---

* The Letter is dated " Marsham," which I interpret " Mersham ;" if so, this was his second living, and I have called him Incumbent thereof accordingly: his other living was Old Remney.—*v.* No. 36, p. 73, charge 4, where he is proved to have been Rector of Mersham.

and preaching in the forenoone, and 10*l.* per annum, and the church duties, for a lecture in the afternoone. Their Communion Table has beene never removed, nor any innovations even so much as moved to them; and, for my parte, I never so much as cited one of them to any Courte, and am yet to learne the price of a processe. I end as I began, with my humble desier of your pardon; and, if you please to grant mee this lawfull favour, you shall for ever oblige

Your worship's to be commanded,

JO: SWINOKE.

Marsham, this 1 of Feb. 1640.

[Superscription.]

"To the right worshipfull Sr Edward Dering, Knight and Baronet, these present."

[Endorsed by Sr Edward Dering—" 1640, 6 Feb. Mr Swinocke."]

---

6 February.

XXXVI.

PETITION to the House of Commons against Mr LIDHAM their Vicar, from the parishioners of LEYSDOWN in SHEPEY.

To the Right Honourable the Knights, Citizens, and Burgesses of the Commons House of Parliament.

The humble Peticion of the Inhabitants of the parish of LAYS-DOWNE, in the ISLE of SHEIPPYE, in the County of Kent,

Most humbly sheweth,

That for the space of 20 yeares last past, the Petitioners have beene, and yet are, very much vexed, molested, and troubled, both in their consciences, persons, and estats, with the undue practices of Mr. John Lidham, minister of the said parish, as by the particulers hereunder written may to your honours appeare.

1. That he keepeth noe due time for divine service, in the morning or evening of the Lord's day.

2. That he preacheth not above once in 5 or 6 weekes, but readeth

a homilie on the Lord's day, in the forenoone; and constantly goeth
to the Communion Table, there to reade the Tenn Comaundements,
the Epistle and Gosple, with other certaine prayers.

3. He liveth very contentiously amongst us, in citing poore men,
and others, into the Ecclesiasticall Court, for slight and triviall things,
and in conclusion writts letters to the officers there, that, paying
their flees, they should discharg them, who have done accordingly.
And hath publiquely threaten(ed) divers of the Petitioners to sue
them in the High Comission Court.

4. Hee exacteth Tythes for working horses, and hath threatened
the Petitioners, that he will helpe the Commissaries Court to 6 or 7ʰ
a yeare, out of his parrish, by citing his neighbours to the said
Court.

5. Hee extorteth Tithe ffish of poore men, which have taken them
a mile thence, upon the sea sands with netts and hookes.

6. Hee hath taken a lease of Mr. Backer of Lambeth, of the ffishing of a ffleete, which said ffishing belongs to Christchurch in Canterbury, and keepeth netts to take them.

7. Hee hath publiquely reported in the said parish, that, if hee
were angry with any of his neighbours, hee will choose him Churchwardens, because he will be revenged on them.

8. Hee doth make a common practice, every winter, to ffother his
beasts and cattle in the churchyard, under the very walles of the
said Church, which is a great annoyance to the Church.

9. That hee hath in lease fowre severall parcells of land in the
said parish, amounting to 91 acres, or thereabouts, besides Glibe
Land belonginge to the Vicarage, in his owne hands, for which he
will not pay any taxe to the Church or poore, until hee be thereunto
compeld by suite or trouble.

10. He hath taken the Oath made in the last Convocacion 1640,
concerning the new Cannons, and affirmes them to be lawfull and
alowable in the Church of England.

11. Hee hath cited one William Norman, Churchwarden of the
said parish, into the Ecclesiasticall Court, because he refused to raile

in the Communion Table, and put him to much trouble and expence therein.

And soe it is, may it please your honors, the said Mr. Lidham's Ecclesiasticall meanes is worth about 70l. per annum, besides other lands and meanes worth at least 20l. per annum.

The Petitioners being thus vext, molested, and troubled by the said Mr. Lidham, it being a dishonor to God, his word, and Gospell, and soe greate greife to the Petitioners, they most humbly prayeth your honors will bee pleased he may be removed thence, if it shall seeme in right to your honors soe to doe, or to give other releife therein as to your honors shall seeme most meete.

For which they shall ever pray, &c.

Joseph Napleton.
William Norman.

[Endorsed by Sr Edward Dering,—"1640, 6 Febr. Petition, Leysdown in Shepey v. Lidham. Se. pet."]

XXXVII.

PETITION to the House of Commons against their minister, Mr RICHARD TRAY, from the Parishioners of LIDSING and BREDHURST.

To the honourable the Knights, Burgesses, and Commons now assembled in the high Court of Parliament.

The humble Peticion of the Inhabitants of LIDGING and BRED-HURST, in the Countie of Kent,

Sheweth,

1. That Mr Richard Tray, who now liveth at Boxley, in the County of Kent, is Rector and Viccar of St. Maryes, in the Hundred of Hoo, in the said Countie, which, by estimacion, is worth 140l. per annum ; and is not there resident.

2. He is both Parson and Viccar of Lidging aforesaid, and receiveth all the proffitts belonging to the said Parsonage and Viccar-

idge, which, by estimacion, are thought to be worth 40*l.* per annum : and is there also a non resident ; and, neither he, nor any other Curate for him, hath administered the Sacrament of the Lord's Supper there by the space of three yeares last past and upwards.

3. He the said Mr. Tray taketh noe care of the Soules of the Parishioners of Lidging aforesaid, nor hath sett any Curatt over them in his stedd ; whereby, the said Parishioners (at some tymes) neither have had Sermon or divine Service, by the space of twentie weeks together, but are constrayned to repaire to remote parishes.

4. The said Mr Tray is thought to have a temporall estate in monies and lands, to the value of ccl*li* per annum, besides the two livings aforesaid. And yet through Covetousness taketh uppon him the Curateshipp of Bredherst, in the said Countie of Kent, (where he is not resident,) and hireth the tythes thereof of Mr John Swynocke, who is Rector of Mersham, in the said Countie of Kent, the profitts of which Curateshipp are thought to be worth xl*li* per annum, over and above the rent which he payeth unto the said Mr Swynocke.

5. He hath been very contentious with the Parishioners of Bredhurst aforesaid, vexing them with ecclesiasticall suits, and causing many of them to be excommunicated for small and frivolous matters, and compelling them to make submission to him.

6. He is a stirrer up of Suits, and hath given his neighbours money, to sweare in causes which did not concerne himself.

7. He is given to fighting, and did strike one heeretofore the Parish Clerke of Bredherst, in the Church of Lidging ; and is a common Rayler, and a Reviler of his neighbours.

8. The said Mr Tray, being sent for by one of his neighbours in the tyme of his sicknes, when he was like to dye, and the said sicke person being troubled in mynd, did imparte some things unto the said Mr Tray which lay uppon his conscience : and the said sicke person afterwards recoveringe of his said sickness, the said Mr Tray did revile him and obbreath him in the open markett at

Maidston, for the very things which the said partie had revealed to him in his sicknes.

Wherefore we doe most humbly recommend these our grievances to this most honourable house; begging to be relieved, and to have these things redressed in such sorte as to your grave and godly wisdome shall seeme best.

Signatures.

Edward Alchorn, gent., Churchwarden of Bredhurst.*

William Kemsley.

Moses Long, late Churchwarden of Lidging.

Zachariah Johnsonne.

Edward Carter.

George Kinge, his marke ×.

John Drew, his marke ×.

The marke of John Paine ×.

[Endorsed by Sir Edward Dering, "1640, 8 Febr. Petition. Lidsing et Bredhurst v. Tray."]

XXXVIII.

LETTER from Mr RICHARD TRAY to Mr THOMAS GODFREY, with inclosures, exculpatory of the charges brought against him by the parishioners of LIDSING and BREDHURST, to be presented to the House.

NOBLE FFREIND,

I have heere sent you my parliamentary business, only in coppies, keepeing the originall, which, if it be required, I will bring or send upp with all speede. My humble suit to you is, that you would be pleased (for my purgation) to shewe these, or the substance of them, to my honorable and only frend the Lord of Lincolne, to Sir Edward Hales, Sir Humfrey Tufton, the Knigtes of the Sheere, and

---

* Written more opposite " Alchorn " than " Kemsley," but the ink and writing would fix it as belonging rather to " William Kemsley."

1641.
17 Car. I.

Capten Lee, all my very good freindes, humbly desiring, that, forasmuch as that honorable Court allowes noe charges, that Sr Edward Deering would be pleased to keepe the petition from the house, or that uppon the reading and tendring the same to the house, my noble freindes, upon the reasons heere presented, would bee pleased to cast it out, as idle and frivulous, as (if it be true at least) the petition of Goutherst,* under 1000 handes, against their newe minister Mr Wilcock, and divers others, have beene. I am ould, and have lived in the ministery nowe almost 40 yeeres, and would be unwilling in my old age to come uppon the stage, and soe much I pray (if you think fit) acquaint these my frends. And soe, with best respects to yourselfe, and all under your roofe remembred, I committ you all to God's blessing, and rest,

Yours ready to doe you service,

RI: TRAY.

Bredhurst, this 4th of April, 1641.

[Superscription.]
" To my much honoured and approoved friend Mr Thomas Godfrey, at Mr Harrison's house in Knightriders street, these present."

XXXIX.

The inclosures in Mr RICHARD TRAY'S letter, being his defence to the charges brought against him by the Parishioners of LIDSING and BREDHURST.

Whereas Mr. Alchorne and his confederates doe complaine of mee to the most honourable Court of Parliament for many misdemeanures ; for soe many of them (as I can heere of) I answere as followeth :—

---

* Vide No. xxvi. pp. 144, 145, *supra.*—Yet this Mr. Wilcock met with rough treatment afterwards at the hands of the Parliamentarians. See Introduction to Twysden on the Government of England (Camden Society), p. lxxxi.

1. *Ob.*—Hee chargeth mee, that there hath not beene in Lidging Chappell for three yeeres last past, neither baptisme, nor the Lord's supper administered.

An.—Ffor Baptisme, there was never any administered in the memory of man :—and, as for the Lordes supper, I alledge for my defence the order of his Grace of Canterbury ordering the same. Shew the order.

2. *Ob.*—Hee chargeth mee that I should strike one Johnson in the Chappell, in Sermon time.

An.—Ffor my defence heerein, I urge the Certificate of Ro. Penniall, Thommas Hammon, Ed. Frid, and others. Shewe the certificate.

3. *Ob.*—Hee chargeth mee, for disclosing and upbraiding one Mathew Hudsford with certaine sinnes privately confessed to mee long agoe.

An.—Ffor cleering mee heereof, I urge the testimony of Mr. Barrell and Mr. Godden, arbitrators, and of Mathew Hudsford him selfe, and others.

4. *Ob.*—Hee chargeth mee for giving money to procure men to goe to London, and sweare in a suit that concerned mee not.

An.—To this I answere, that my sonne Richard beinge sued by Mr Alchorne, in the arches, for woords, and being gone to Cambridge, at the very time that his Proctor caulled for my sonnes witnesses, I was inforced, in his absence, to let the said witnesses have money to beare their charges.

5. *Ob.*—Hee chargeth mee, for vexing my parishioners with unjust suits and excommunicationes.

An.—To this I answere, that I never sued any man in Bredherst nor Lidging in 35 yeeres ; but only one James Pecknam, and that uppon just cause, as I can make appeere. And, as for excommunicationes, I remember not any, in all that time, but one excommunicated in Bredherst, and that for just cause, as I can shew : and never but one, in all that time, in Lidsing, except Alchorne, or his crue, or by him procured.

And for my cariage in my Cures, and the Value of them, the certificates under all my parishioners' hands will fully convince Mr Alchorne of manifest falsehoods.

Besides, five of the eight whose names are to the petition have and doe under their handes disclaime the same ; and, for the other three, Mr Alchorne and his boye are two, and Johnson above named the third.

Shew their revocation.

If hee charge mee with haveing of 3 Cures, and living uppon none of them, I answere, it is most false; for I live in Bredherst, and that by dispensation of his Grace of Canterbury, uppon good cause graunted mee, as I can shew.

1611.
17 Car. I.

Ri: Tray, sen.

(A Coppy.)

APRIL THE 10th, 1634.

To the most Reverend Father in God, THE LORD ARCHBISHOPP OF CANTERBURY, his Grace, Primate and Metropolitan of England, &c.

1634.
10 Car. I.

The humble Peticion of the Inhabitants of BREDHERST and LIDGING, in the County of Kent, Peculiars to your Grace.

Humbly shewing,

That, whereas your Grace's Petitioners have, time out of mind, resorted, by turnes, to either Chappell of the said Parishes, for the heering of God's woord; and the Parishioners of Lidging to Bredherst Chappell only, for the administration of the Sacraments, and buriall of their dead, where are decent and necessary ornaments provided for the same, at the joynt costs of both the said parishes, the said Parish of Lidging consisting of seven small families.

Oct. 20, 1635.
Upon the Certificate underwritten, I doe heerby give consent, provided that noe inconvenience arise to either of the said Chappells thereby. Oct. 20, 1635.   W. CANT.

Wee most humbly beseech your Grace to bee graciously pleased to confirme the said Custom, soe long as the said Chappells are served by one Minister, as nowe they are. And your Grace's humble Petitioners shall daily pray to God for the continuance of your Grace's happiness one earth, and felicity in heaven.

1635.
11 Car. I.

Wi. Kemsley.	Ri. Willard.
Ro. Stonard.	Wi. Cooper.
James Pecknam.	John Larrance.
John Cooper.	Georg Sutton.
George Page.	Ri. Longley.
William Michell.	Henry Dudson,
George Loan.	*Lidging.*
Thomas Mills.	
Nicholas Forsberry.	
Ri. Weston,	
of Bredhurst.	

1641.
17 Car. I.

23 April, 1635.

I see noe inconvenience, and heereby doo give approbation for the continuing of the Custom, as is desired, till Sr Nathaniel Brent returne, provided that the reparations of Lidging Chappell now in hand bee not hindered heerby.

T. RIVES.

July 9, 1635.
I am of the same opinion.
NA. BRENT.

[Endorsed—"A Coppy of his Grace's uniting the Chappells."]

(A Coppy.)

My defence aboute the blow given Johnson.

I, Ro. Penniall, well remember, that the morning before Mr Henry Grimstone preached at Lidging Chappell, Zachary Johnson of Boxley came into my house, (being a victualling house,) and was soe much in drink, that I the said Robert asked him where hee had beene;—"thou hast," said I, "beene a tipling somwhere all night;" but hee caulled for beere, and said, "I must goe home;" "nay," said I, "you will heere Mr Grimstone preach first at Lidging Chappell:"—"yes, by God," said he, "that I will:" and soe went to Chappell, being more fit, as I thought, to goe to bed, than to God's house.

1640-1.

In witness whereof, I have heereunto set my hand,
this 21st of March, 1640.

ROBERT PENNIALL.

I, Thomas Hamon, can and will testify, that the said Zachary Johnson acknowledged in my heering, that it was that Sunday that Mr Grimstone preached at Chappell, that Mr Tray should gogg or strike him; and said that hee had beene at Stephen Willerd's (an unlicensed alehouse in Bredherst) a drinkeing all the Satterday night before the said Sunday that Mr Grimstone preached at Lidging Chappell in the morning.

1640-1.

It witnes whereof, I have heereunto set my hand,
this 21st March, 1640.

THOMAS HAMMAN.

I, Edward Frid, of Gillingham, being then present in the Chauncell at Lidging, sawe the said Zachary Johnson leaning against James Packnam, and slept, that hee snored againe. Whereupon Mr Tray, sitting just against him, back to back, heereing the noise, turned about and gogged him with his

1641.
17 Car. I.

1640-1.

hand to awake him, and did not strike him, as the said Johnson falsely reports; and heereto I will depose, if neede require.

In witnes whereof, I have heereunto set my hand, this 7th of March, 1640.

The marke of ED. FRID, THE YOUNGER.

The same Johnson did soe snork in his sleepe, at the same time, that I heard him in the boddy of the Church.

March 20th, 1641.   By me, WILL. KEMSLEY.

1640-1.

I, John Kemsley, doe remember the very same with Edw. Frid, and will testify it, if neede require.   March this 21st, 1640.

JOHN KEMSLEY.

1640-1.

I, George King, will testify the very same.   March 28th, 1641.

GEORGE KING, his + marke.

1641.

(A Copy.)

We, Robert Barrell, Clerke, and William Godden, Gent., being arbitrators for the reconcilinge of the differences betwixt Richard Tray, the elder, Clerke, and Mathew Hutsford, yeoman, a little before St. Michaell last past; concernynge one of which differences, viz. that the said Richard Tray did call the said Mathewe Hutsford knave, openly in the streate of Maidstone, in Kent; for which, amongest the rest of the severall complaints on both sides, wee did then reconsile them, to both theire contents. Nowe, for as much as wee doe since understand by the said Richard Traye, that one Edward Alchorn, Gent., under colour of that particuler difference abovenamed, hath given forth diverse reports in severall places; and, to furnishe his malicious Peticion, hath framed a complainte thereof unto the honourable Court of Parliament, suggesting as yf the said word "knave" had been grounded uppon some sinues privatly revealed by Mathewe Hutsford to Mr Tray, by waie of confession, in extremitie of the said Hutsford's sicknes aboute twelve yeares before; which faulte, in this kind, is nowe pretended by Mr Alchorne against Mr Traye; But wee did not soe conceave it uppon the heareinge and examinacion of all differences then betwixt the said Richard Tray and Mathewe Hutsford; but meerely as a word of passion in the present heate betweene them.   In testimonie whereof, wee have heereunto subscribed, this five and twentith day of February, anno domini 1640.

1640-1.

ROBERT BARRELL, Clearke.
WILLIAM GODDEN.

5 Marcii, 1640.

1640.
17 Car. I. I the above named Mathewe Hutsforde have heereunto also sett my marke, testifyinge the same   MATHEWE HUTSFORD, his + mark.

John Grinnel, ⎫ witnesses, testifying the same.
John Weekes, ⎭

John Roiston, of Lidging, labourer, beeing spoken to by Mr Alchorne, about Sunday the 7th of February, 1640, to set his hand to his petition against Mr Tray, to be preferred to the most honourable Court of Parliament, the said John Roiston denied him; then hee in anger forbad him comming uppon his tennants ground, and tould him that if he came any more to fetch any water at his tennants pond, hee would breake his pailes uppon his head, and would pull his house downe uppon him; and that, if hee lived, hee would bee revenged of him.

1640-1.

In witnes of the truth whereof, I, John Roiston, have, this 21st day of February, 1640, set my hand, beeing ready to affirme it by oath, when I shalbe thereunto called.   JOHN ROISTON.

Alsoe, the said John Roiston will affirme, that hee asking George King of Lidging why hee did set his hand to Mr Alchorne's petition against Mr Tray, having given his hand to Mr Traye's certificat about a weeke before; the said George King answered, that Mr. Alchorne came unto him where hee was at worke in Shawsted* Swan, and was very darresh with him, to set his hand to the said Petition, which hee refusing twice or thrice, to provoak him to set his hand to the said petition, hee tould him hee had John Cecill's, John Hudsford's, and other men's handes of the parish to it, with which false report hee got his hand, for which he is very sorry, and thinkes hee was bewitcht, and that if ever the devill had power over him, he had power over him then; for hee did not know what hee had set his hand to, as he confest to Michaell Wollett likewise.

1640-1.

Dated this 26th day of February, 1640.
                         Witnesses heereunto, MICHAEL WOOLLETT.

I, George King, doe confesse all this to bee true, and therefore doe wholy disclaime and disavow what I have subscribed unto, being confident that all or the most part of the said petition is false and untrue.

In witnes whereof, I have heereunto subscribed, this first day of March,
1640-1.   1640.   GEORGE + KINGE.

+ ? "Swar" or "Swaw;" in either case a misrendering, probably, of the word "Shaw," i.e. a plot of underwood.

(A Coppy.)

1641.
17 Car. 1.

Wee, the Parishioners of St Maries, whose names are heere subscribed, doe testify and declare by these presents, that our much respected Parson, Mr. Richard Tray, Master of Arts, is a man of good sufficiency and note for his preaching, wherein hee is and alwaies hath beene laborious ; and is a man of honest, sober, and discreete cariage, free from scandall or any just exception in his life and conversation ; whoe, by reason of his age, and constitution of body, cannot reside amongst us (as hee desireth) without apparent danger of his health (as hee is certified under the handes of learned Physicians), our parish beeing scituated in a marshy place, joyning to the river of Thames: but such speciall care hath he of our soules, that he hath given us power to make choice of our Curat ourselves, and alloweth him 20*l.* a yeere, and the Church duties, for the same, whoe preacheth diligently every Sunday : and besides, either comes himself, or sendeth his sonne (a Master of Arts, and well approoved of) to preach unto us every month, allowing for the same 20*l.* a yeere more, and his diett ; besides, hee every yeere liberally releeveth our poore : Soe that these things, with tenthes, subsidies, and other charges deducted, there accrewes to him not much above 40*l.* a yeere. Hee hath noe other spirituall preferment that wee ever heard of, but only liveth at a place caulled Bredherst, as a Curat, and that, by the dispensacion of his Grace of Canterbury that now is.

In witnes of the truth of all which premises wee have heerunto set our handes.

Thomas Hobs, Gent.	James Holoway.
Ri: Greenegrasse, Churchwarden.	Ralfe Hobs.
John Rugg.	Thomas Ffuller.
· John Gill.	Christopher Potterell.
John Loane.	Jacob Antoninus.
Edward Webb.	John Rootes.
Richard Aburne.	John Raines.
Robert Bond.	William Kilby.
George Parker.	Robert Lownes.
Georg Hubbard.	George Trumper.
Edward Elmsall.	Anthony Cuccow.
William Stubber.	

1641.
17 Car. I.

(A Coppy.)

14th January, 1640.

Wee, the Parishioners of Bredherst, consisting of 15 families, and of Lidging, consisting of 8 small families, whose names are heere subscribed, who, with our predecessors, have beyond memory participated by turnes both in Service and Sacraments, and approved of by his Grace of Canterbury that now is, and by his two Commissaries, Sr Nathaniell Brent, and Mr Doctor Rives, on the joint petition of the Parishioners of both Parishes, doe testifie and declare, by these presents, that our minister, Mr Richard Tray, Master of Arts, whoe hath served us these 35 yeeres and upwards, at both our Chapells, by turnes, as aforesaid, is a man of integrity of lyfe and conversation, free from scandall or any just exception, and of good sufficiency and industry in the worke of the ministery, duly preaching every Sunday in the forenoone, and cathechising all the Summer in the afternoone; one that often releeveth the poore, a due observer and maintainer, to his utmost power, the discipline established for the peace and unity of the Church of England: whoe, for his paines amongst us, hath not formerly made above 20 markes a yeere of Lidging; but now of late, by reason of improving their lands by chealke, it is something increased. And, for Bredherst, he is but a Curat under Mr John Swinnock, Parson of Hollingburne, * whereof Bredherst is reputed a lymme, and paies unto him 15l. a yeere for the Gleab and tieth thereof; whereas, when hee first came to Bredherst (35 yeeres agoe) there was paid to Sr Martin Barnham, for many yeeres, but 13s. 4d. a yeere for the said gleab and tieth, as an acknowledgment of the mother Church of Hollingburn, the cruell rearing whereof (whensoever the said Chapells shalbe divided and served by two ministers) there will certenly follow a great defect in the servcee of God, and that for want of meanes; the profits of Bredherst not beeing woorth 30l. a yeere, albeit the lands bee almost all cholked, which will bee in few years worse, and then it will not be worth above 24l. a yeere at the most, as formerly; soe that then the Curat shall not have above 9^{li} a yeere to serve the Cure, to the unsufferable wrong of posterity.

In witnes of the truth of all which premises, we have heerunto set our handes.

William Kemsley.	Ed. Hills.
Jo. Ponde.	Ni. Forsbery.
Jo. Cooper.	Geo. Lone.

---

* Hollingbourne was only a sinecure Rectory; it had no cure of souls: the Rectors were Patrons of the chapelry of Bredhurst, the incumbents of which were "Perpetual Curates" under the mother church of Hollingbourne.

. . . . Masters, Overseer.
Steven Willerd.
Ja. Pecknam.
Wi. Pecknam.
Ro. Hudsford.
Emmanuell Cooper.
Richard Weston.
Ro. Peniall.
Abraham Harp.

John Loome.
Michael Woollet, Churchwarden.
Jo. Cicell.
Jo. Larrance.
Geo. Sutton
William Natt.
Jo. Roiston.
Jo. Hudsford.
Geo. King.

(A Coppy.)

I, William Kemsley, of Bredherst, yeoman, doe by these presents testify, that Mr Ed. Alchorne did oftentimes solicit me, at Hartlipp alehouse, to set my hand to his petition to be preferred against Mr Tray, our minister, to the high Court of Parliament; but I twice or thrice denying, at length, with much importunity, he got my hand thereunto, beeing much, I confesse, overtaken with drink; but I never heard above 2 or 3 lines thereof; and, for the rest, I doe not know what was therein; I would faine have put him off; but still solicits me thereto, perceiving mee to be much in drink. I am very sorry for soe dooing; for I never knew nor heard but very well of Mr Tray, having beene my minister all my life time. And, therefore, uppon the better consideracion, I doe wholy disclaime and disavow what I have set my hand to, beeing verily perswaded (the palpable and apparant envy and mallice of the said Alchorne against the said Mr Tray, for these many yeeres considered) that all, or the most part, of the said peticion is false and untrue.

In witnes wheereof, I have heereunto subscribed, this first of March, 1640.

By me, WILLIAM KEMSLEY.

This acknowledgment was made by William Kemsley in the presence of
MICHAELL WOOLLET.
MOSES LONG.

(A Coppy.)

I, Moses Long, of Hartlipp, doe heereby confesse, that, uppon the extraordinary importunity of Mr Alchorne, at Hartlip alehouse, I did unadvisedly set my hand to the said Mr Alchorne's petition, to be preferr'd to the Court of Parlia-

1641.
17 Car. I.

ment, against Mr Tray the elder, minister of Bredherst; but what was specified in the said petition I know not; for I confesse I was then much overtaken with drink, or else I would never have set my hand unto it; and I am very sorry I was soe much overtaken as to doe it; for I never knewe nor heard but well of the said Mr Tray, beeing my minister many yeeres; and, therefore, uppon better consideracion, I doe utterly disclaime and disavowe whatsoever I have set my hand unto, being verily perswaded, (the palpable and apparent envy and continuall mallice of the said Mr Alchorne against the said Mr Tray considered,) that all or the most part of the said petition is false and untrue.

1640-1.

In witnes whereof, I have heerunto subscribed, this first day of March, 1640; beeing ready at all times to avouch the premises.

By me, MOSES LONG.

This acknowledgment was made by the said Moses Long in the presence of

WI. KEMSLEY.
MICHAELL WOLLETT.

(A Coppy.)

I, John Drew, of Boxley, upon Mr Alchorne's perswading of mee that he had gotten Mathew Hudsford's hand, and others, to his petition in Parliament against Mr Tray; promising to build me up a house in Rennaulds Wood, and to let mee have a good penny worth in it; and 20 other such like curtesies and perswasiones; hee got mee ignorantly to set my hand thereunto at last; but what there was therein specified I know not at all; and therefore am very sorry for it; for I never knew but well of Mr Tray; and have knowen him these 20 or 30 yeeres. And, therefore, uppon better consideratiENones, I doe utterly disclaime and disavowe the said petition; and am verily perswaded that all therein specified is false and untrue.

1640-1.

In witnes whereof, I have heerunto subscribed, this 21st of March, 1640, and will depose that this, which I have heerunto set my hand, is truth.

JOHN DREW, + his marke.

This acknowledgment was made by John Drew, in the presence of

MICHAELL WOLLET.

(A Coppy.)

I, John Paine, of Bredhurst, uppon the instant and importunate request of Mr Alchorne, hee comming ten times to my house, at least, and inviting mee as often to his house, and there feasting me day and night, and giving mee over much drink, did, at last, get my hand to his petition to be preferrd against Mr Tray to the high Court of Parliament; but what was in the said petition I know not, nor never heard, and, therefore, I am hartily sorry for soe doeing, and doe utterly disclaime and disavowe whatsoever I have set my hand to; being confident that whatsoever is in the said petition specified is false and untrue.

In testimony whereof, I have heereunto subscribed, this seventh day of March, 1640.

1640-1.

The marke + of JOHN PAINE.

This confession was made by John Paine in the presence of

JOHN JEKIN, his father in law.

XL.

PETITION to the House of Commons, to increase the Income of their Minister ELIAS WOOD, from the Parishioners of HINXHILL.

1640-1.
16 Car. I.

To the honorable the house of Commons now assembled in Parliament.

9 February.

The humble Petition of the Parishioners of HINXHILL, in the County of Kent, in the hundred of Longbridge, on the behalfe of our Minister Mr Elias Wood (according to an order agreed upon by this Honorable House, concerning ministers which have not competent livings),

Humbly sheweth,

That our said Minister is a diligent and faithfull Preacher of the Word of God, every Lord's day; orthodox in doctrine, and of godly life and conversation; but his living is a very small parsonage, not above 40*l.* per annum, "communibus annis," and he hath no other meanes for the maintenance of himselfe and his charge of 5 children.

Wherfore wee, the Parishioners aforesaid, humbly pray this honourable Court, that there may be a supply of a competent maintenance for his incouragement, as shall seeme good to your wisedom.

And wee, as bound, shall pray, &c.

William Hales.
Robert Edolphe.
Thomas Andrewe, Churchwarden.
William Brett.
John Criche.
William Rigden.
Roger Smeede.
William Effeld.
Thomas Barke.
Hercules Filpott.

Kenneth Back, Churchwarden.
Henry Morgan.
Nicholas Pierse.
Richard Fflusher.
Reinald Smith.
George Bastock.
Richard King.
Thomas Teeler.
William Harrison.

[Endorsed by Sir Edward Dering—"1640, 9 Febr. Henxhill, pro. Wood."]

XLI.

LIST of specific charges, and the names of the Witnesses, against their Minister Mr SAMUEL SMITH : from the Parishioners of BOUGHTON BLEAN.

9 February.

To prove Mr Samuel Smith's * hanting of alehouses, and playing at tables, and continuing there by night, is Edmon Packingham, and Anthony Edwards.

To prove his drinking of healths and singing of idle catches, is William Abraham, and Ezekiel Maxsted.

To prove that he did speake wordes to this effect : that the kinge

* In the original, it was "his" hanting—and overwritten, in Sr Edward's hand, "Mr Samuel Smith's;" evidencing, that the original petition had been presented to the House by Sr Edward, and that he retained in his own hands the schedule of evidence, marking it with the party's name, for identification.

was not well advised to be drawne away to yeald to the Scotes; and that if he were as the Kinge it should cost him one hundred thousand men's lives rather than to be so drawne away, is Herculas Hilles, and William Hilles.

To prove that the said Mr Smith did say he would warrant the parlamant would com to noe good, is William Hilles.

To prove that the sayd Mr Smith did threten to scite the Church-warden to the Bishop's Court, for not rayling in the Communion Table alter wise; and, to that purpose, as your petitioners beleeve, did chose one Mr William Baker, purposely to rayle in the said alter; and the sayd Baker hath rayled in the sayd table, contrary to the will of the parish: and now we are like to be sued for the charg the sayd Baker was at for the sayd rayling. Sir John Routh, and John Spencer, senior.

To testifi for his bowing toward the table, when he commeth into his desk, and when he goeth out, and at other times, is Hercules Hilles, and Richard Proude.

To testifie he causeth the new maried copple to kneele at the rayle; and that he causeth wemen when they com to be churchd, to weare a white rayle hanging downe theyr backes, is Herculas Hilles, and John Spencer, Ju^r.

To prove that divers of the sayd inhabytantes were scited to the Bishop's Court, for going to heere a sermon at the next parish Church, when the sayd Mr Smith only read service; and, as the Churchwarden did affirme, Mr Smith did urge him to do it. William Huggin and Richard Proude.

To prove that the sayd Mr Smith did say, I scorne to carry the Body and blod of Christ aboute the Church to them which are to receive, and let me know who they be that will not com up to the rayle to receive. Herculas Hilles.

[Endorsed by Sir Edward Dering—"1640, 9 Febr.—proofes—for Boughton Blean."]

1640–1.
16 Car. I.

XLII.

PETITION or Certificate to the House of Commons, enumerating the Vices and malpractises of their Vicar, EDWARD BARBET, from the Parishioners of CHISTLET.

10 February.

The Certificate of the Parishioners of CHISTLET, in the county of Kent, to the honourable House of Commons in Parliament assembled, touchinge the sufficiency in readinge and preachinge and conversation of Edward Barbet, clerke, Vicar of Chistlet aforesaid.

Wee, the Parishioners of Chistlet aforesaid, doe humbly certify, that the said Edward Barbet, livinge heeretofore as a gentleman upon his lands, and havinge by riotous livinge consumed the greatest part of his estate, laye in prison by the space of halfe a yeere and more; and, havinge made composicion with his creditors, betooke himselfe to the ministry, for his better mayntenance and livelyhood, and was presented by the Lord Archbishop of Canterbury to the Vicaridge of Chistlet aforesaid, beinge in his gift.

And, touchinge his readinge of Divine Service, hee reads soe false, and with such ill gesture, and ridiculous behaviour, laughing when some women come into the Church, and soe careles in readinge, that sometimes he reads the Ten Commandments twice over, at morning Prayer, besides many other slips, mistakings, and negligences not fittinge for a minister of God's word.

And touchinge his preachinge, hee is very unable and unfit, in respect hee never studyed Divinity, as may appeare by his weake and unlearned sermons, and yet will not suffer any other minister to preach there, although it bee a funerall sermon, and that the party deceased did desire it.

And touchinge his life and Conversation, it is well knowne, that hee is a common lyer, a notorious swearer, a foule, obscene, and bawdy speaker of Ribaldry, utteringe sometimes such words as are not to be spoken by any modest man, nor to be heard by any

1640-1.
16 Car. I.

Christian cares. And hee is also of an incontinent life; and hath affirmed that marryage was a superficiall ceremony, and that yt was but the mumblinge of a Preist:—contrary to his oath, which is, to maynteine the rights and ceremonies of the Church of England. All which things wil bee prooved by sufficient witnesses, if it bee required.

Steven Hunt.
Paul Barrett.
Robart Austen.
Robert Austen.
Richard Austen.
John Howten.
John × Rath, his mark.
John Mounsteeven, × his mark.
Oliver Hall, × his mark.
Walter Ewell, × his mark.
Robert Cooper, × his mark,
John Mount, × his mark.
Thomas Cook, × his mark.
Richard Chambers, × his mark.
Humphry Churchman, × his mark.
George Knowler.
Beenjamin Jones.
James Harman × his mark.
James Momery, × his mark.

William Knowler, Constable.
John Ratliff.
Richard Whitting.
Richard Dobb, Church-warden.
Thomas × Maxted,
Ffra. × Edwards, } Sidmen.
his marke.
Stephen Rose.
Stephen Gouldfinch, × his marke.
Stephen Kingston.
Thomas Norwood, × his mark.
Thomas Norwood, Junior.
Thomas Colman.
Hendere Hewett.
Edward Halfioy × his mark.
Robart Barbere.
Bartholme Boykin, × his markes.

[Endorsed by Sir Edward Dering—" 1640, 10 Febr. Certificate, Christlet v. Barbet, Sc."]

1640-1.
16 Car. I.

XLIII.

PETITION to the House of Commons, for an increase of Income, from FRANCIS MARSH, Perpetual Curate of GUSTON NEXT DOVOR.

13 February.

To the right honourable the Commons at this present high Court of Parliament assembled.

The humble Petition of FRANCIS MARSH, Master of Arts, and Curat of the parish of GUSTON NEXT DOVOR, in the County of Kent.

Whoe humbly sheweth,

That he, your Petitioner, haveing served as Minister and Curat in the said parish by the space of three yeares last past, hathe, for two of the said yeares, only receaved 9^{li} per annum, and for the third yeare 13^{li}: (foure pounds being added as a pention to him out of the profits of the Parsonage of the said Parish, of long time detayned from his Predecessors); five hundred acres of land, at a place called the Ffrith, and 120 acres of land belonging to Dovor Castle, within the said parish of Guston, not payeing any Tieths to your Petitioner. Soe that he, your Petitioner, uppon the said small meanes cannot maintaine himself, wife, and familie.

The tender consideration of all which said premises your Petitioner humbly referreth to the said right honorable Court for redresse.

And for that honourable favor, he, your Petitioner, will bee ever bound to pray, &c.

Wee whose names are here under written, parishioners of the said parish of Guston, hereby humbly certifie, that all the above written premises are true.

Ed. Prescott.
John Prescott.
John Bird, Churchwarden, his mark ×.
John Gardner.
Henry Gibbon, Sideman, his mark ×.

Edward Howsen, his marke ×.
John Pepper, the elder, his mark ×.
John Pepper.
John Scot.

[Endorsed by Sir Edward Dering—"1640, 13 Feb.   Goceston pro Marsh."]

XLIV.

1640-1.
16 Car. I.

CERTIFICATES of the respective Values signed by the Incumbents of LYDDEN, RIVER, and GUSTON.

15 January.
13 February.

JANUARY 15º, 1640.

I certify by theise presents, that the vicaridge of LYDDEN is not worth above sixteene pounds per annum; and the house belongeing thereunto is not fitt for a clergyman to live in.

As likewise, that the parish of River is not worth above fourteene pounds per annum, with a verry poore house belongeing thereunto; and that my imediate predecessor there dying left his children a great charge to the parish there.

ROBERT POWNOLL, Vicar of Lydden and River.

I testify, that the Archbyshop is impropriator of Guston, which cure I serve, the valuation whereof is but thirteene pounds per annum, with the stipend added from the Parsonage, being 4l. per annum; for the whole meanes is but 13 pounds. Besides, there is no house for the minister. Besides, there are five hundred acres of land pertinent to impropriation that pay nothing to the minister; that there are sixe score acres of land pertinent to my Lord Warden of Dovor Castle, within the precincts of Guston, that pay nothing to the minister.

FRANCIS MARSH, Curat. ibidem.

[Endorsed by Sir Edward Dering, "1640, 13 Febr. Certificate, Lydden, Goceston."]

1640-1
16 Car. I.

16 February.

XLV.

TESTIMONIAL from the Mayor and Jurats of DOVOR, to the good conduct of GEORGE STANCOMBE, Curate of BIRCHINGTON.

Dover Ss.
(L.S.) *

To all Christian people to whom these presents shall come, THOMAS TEDDEMAN, ESQ. Major of the towne and Port of Dovor, in the Countie of Kent, and the Jurats of the same, Justices of the Peace there, and in the Limbs and Precincts thereof, send greeting in our Lord God everlasting.

Forasmuch as we hold it the office of magistrates and the dutie of all other honest persons, to certifie and declare the truth in all matters and thinges doubtfull or suspicious, whereby wrong and injuries may bee avoided, and truth take place and be manifested, especially being thereunto requested.

Know ye therefore, that George Stancombe, Clark, Curat of the parish of Birchington, in the Isle of Thanet, in the said Countie, a Limbe within the Government of this Towne and Port, hath been well knowne to us, for diverse yeares past, and hath, in all that time, civilly, peaceably, and fairely demeaned and deported himselfe towards us, and his neighbours, and thereby gained our and their good esteeme and opinion: so that our testimoniall of his good life and conversation we could not but grant unto him.

In witness whereof, we have caused the scale of office of Maioralty of the said Towne and Port to be putt and scet, the Twelveth day of February, anno domini 1640.

Exa'iat' per me

FRA. RAWORTH,

communem clericum ville et portus Dovorie.

[Endorsed by Sir Edward Dering—"1640, 16 Febr. Certificate. Dovor pro Stancombe."]

---

* The Corporation Seal—St. Martin and the beggar.

XLVI.

PETITION to the House of Commons, that they would annul the recent appointment of their Incumbent, made by the Archbishop, the Patron. From the Parishioners of BIDDENDEN.

To the right honourable the House of Commons, now assembled 16 February. this present Parliament.

The humble peticion of the Churchwardens and others of the parish of BIDDENDEN, in the County of Kent,

In submissive manner sheweth,

That whearas a peticion hath lately bene exhibited to the Hon[ble] assembly by the parishioners of our said parish, declaringe their greavances occasioned by scandalous and offensive Curats placed by the Bishopp of Oxford* (which, amonge other grevances were thought cheifly to occasion the goinge of 13 families out of our said parish), as by the said petition more at large is declared. And whereas sithence, the said Bishopp of Oxford beinge deceased, and the Archbishop of Canterbury haveinge the donation of the Benefice (being above 140l. per annum) hath bestowed the same upon one of his Chaplains, who came and preached one Sunday the 14th of February last, and, after demandinge to be admitted, was denied by the greater parte of the congregation, who doubting now of the authority of the said Bishopp, and very distrustfull of his Chapleine, would nott departe out of the Church, nor graunt him any admittance, untill they were further certifyed from this Honorable assembly.

Whereupon wee humbly desire this Honorable assembly to take the aforesaid Petition into Consideration, and to sett downe some speedy Order in the premisses; if nott (as is most desired) by makinge of our owne choise of a man whose guifts wee have had more experience of, yett for the establishinge of a diligent watchman over soe great a cure, (there beinge above 1,200 Communicants in our said

---

* i.e. John Bancroft, nephew of Archbishop Bancroft.

1640-1.
16 Car. I.

parish) by what way or order in your wisdomes shall be thought meete.

And wee shall continue our prayers for the prosperouse successe of this honorable assembly, in their honorable and just endevours.

JOHN YOUNGE.
AMBROSE DRAYNER. } Churchwardens.

[Endorsed by Sir Edward Dering—" 1640. 16 Feb. Petition, Biddenden *v.* Wilde."]

XLVII.

PETITION to the House of Commons against the Popish Practises of their Rector, Mr JEFFERY AMHERST, from the Parishioners of HORS-MONDEN.

19 February.

To the honorable the Knights, Citizens, and Burgesses of the House of Commons, assembled in Parliament.

The humble Petition of the Inhabitants of the parish of HORS-MONDEN, in the County of Kent.

Sheweth,

That wee have been much burthened and constreyned to the observation and obedience to these subsequent enormities and superstitious observations and ceremonyes of Mr Jeffery Amherst, parson of the said parish, as followeth.

1. Our Communion Table is removed upp unto the wall at the East end of the Chancell, and compassed about with waynscott, and upon the said wall is written these words, WEE HAVE AN ALTAR WHEREOF THEY HAVE NO RIGHT TO EATE WHICH SERVE THE TABERNACLE.

2. He doth goe upp to the said table to read greate parte of the service, and maketh obeysance to the table when as he goeth to it, and also when he retyreth from it.

3. He vehemently urgeth the people to come upp and receive the Sacrament at the said Waynscott about the table, and hath refused for to administer the same unto those whose consciences are weake, and dare not to receive it in that manner, whereby many have beene constrayned not to partake of the Sacrament.

4. He hath caused a poore man of the said Parish for to be presented in the Ecclesiasticall Court of Rochester, for refusing to come upp and receive the Sacrament at the sayd waynscott.

5. He endeavoureth, in his preaching, to mayntaine it to be the true and right manner of administration of the Sacrament, and that such as refuse to receive it in that manner are to be expelled from the congregation, and that theire sinne is as the sinne of Chorah, or such like; and likewise hath a Curate under him that preacheth after that manner.

6. He, in his preaching, doth cast reproachfull names on such as refuse to come upp to receive the Sacrament at the waynscott, as Puritans, and itching Puritans.

7. He continually boweth at the name of Jesus, and presseth his people to observe new gestures in the Church.

8. That the tythes of the said parish doth amount to the yearely value of 250l., or thereabouts; and that he the said Mr Amherst hath the Rectory of the parish of Southease, in the county of Sussex, the tythes wherof amount to the value of 100l. or thereabouts, and is theire non resident.

Wherefore we doe most humbly beseech this honourable assembly to take these our greivances into consideracion, and to doe for us in all things as to theire grave and Godly wisdome shall seme most expedient. And wee, as in duty bound, shall ever pray.

RICHARD DAY.
JOHN OSBORNE.

[Endorsed by Sir Edward Dering, "1640, 19 Febr. Petition, Horsemonden v. Amherst, Pet. Sc."]

XLVIII.

PETITION to the House of Commons, against Dr GIBBON the Rector, for debarring them the use of the Spring of Water on the Glebe Lands.   From the poor Inhabitants of SEVENOAKS.

To the honourable the Knights, Cittizens and Burgesses in this present Parliament assembled.

The humble Petition of the poore Inhabitants of SEAVENOCK, in the county of Kent.

Shewinge,

That the Towne of Seavenock is a place consistinge of many poore Inhabitants, whoe through theire poverty are constrained to drincke water instead of beere ; and that the sayd Towne, standing upon a hill, is watered onely with three publique springs, two whereof are out of the Towne, and the third in the Glebe land of the Rectory of Seavenock, neere unto the Church.

That, tyme out of mynde, the Rectors there have given free liberty to your peticioners, and other formerly poore Inhabitants of Seavenock, to fetch water at the sayd springe, whereby your petitioners were refreshed, and the Rectors there sustained noe damage thereby.

That, about 4 yeres since, Doctor Gibbon, now Rector of the sayd parishe, did with a stronge high stone wall barr your petitioners from fetchinge any water there.

That, thereupon, the Justices of that devision, takeinge it into theire consideration, did order the sayd doctor Gibbon to convay the sayd water by a pipe from the sayd springe to the wall which he had built, that your Petitioners might come thither, and receive the water there.

That, allthough there bee a pipe to convay the water, the pipe is for the most part defectyve, and the sayd doctor can att his pleasure stopp the sayd water; and the said water is often wantinge, by meanes of the sayd wall, whereby your petitioners want that refreshinge that they formerly found by the sayd water, and thereby are constrained to drinck and make use of well water, whereby your petitioners are become more infirme, and subject to infection and sicknes.

Most humbly therefore besecheth your honors, that the sayd doctor Gibbon may answer the premisses, and that your petitioners may have free liberty to come to the sayd well, as they formerly have had.

And your petitioners shall, as in duty bound, pray, &c.

[There are no signatures. It is endorsed by Sir Edward Dering— " 1640, 19 Feb. Sevenok v. Gibbon—Se."]

1640-1.
16 Car. I.

XLIX.

PETITION to the House of Commons, praying that their Vicar, WILLIAM GERVIS, may be removed, for Popish practices, &c. From the Parishioners of STURRY.

To the Honorable House of Commons assembled in this Parliament.

23 February.

The humble Petition of divers Inhabitants of the Parish of STURREY, neere Canterburie, in the County of Kent.

Shewinge,

That, wheras the Inhabitants have just Cause to complaine of William Gervis, Preist of the said parish, as followeth:

1. That he hath a large Crucifix painted, in a frame, hanginge in his parlour; and is famouslie noted for a forward Agent in superstitious and Popish innovations.

2. That he threatned the Churchwardens of the said parish to cite them to the high Commission, if they would not set up the Communion Table Alter wise, and rayle it in; which thereuppon was

CAMD. SOC.   2 B

1640-1.
16 Car. I.

donne accordinglie, to the charge of the said Inhabitants, and perill of Idolatry.

3. That, since the said Table hath beene soe placed, he hath read parte of the divine service in the ministers deske, and parte at the said Alter, to the prejudice of the edification of the assemblie, he havinge a very lowe voice; and his constante practice hath beene, before his second Service, to singe the 43^d psalme; and when they singe, "then will I to the Alter goe," then he presantly came out of his seate, and did goe to the said Alter, and bowed three times in goinge up to it, and in comminge downe.

4. That he hath, divers times, urged the people to receive the Communion kneelinge before the said Rayle and Alter; whereuppon divers received kneelinge there, at Christide, 1639; others refusinge, he begann to reade the thanksgivinge; and then, seeinge a disturbance amongst the people, he left off readinge, and ministered to them kneelinge elsewhere. And, uppon Thursday before Easter last, he refused againe to give the Sacrament to those that would not come to the rayle, sayinge, if he came to them, he should tread on theire cloathes, and spill the wine &c., and then said, "If there be any heere which have not as yet received the Sacrament, it is for that they have not given their names over night, nor paid their offerings; but yet, if they will come and kneele at the railes, I will administer to them;" and so, pausinge awhile, and seeinge they would not come before the Alter, he furiouslie thrust open the doores of the said Rayle, and came out, sayinge, "I will administer to you, but you shall be sure to be cited to the courte," and so, in greate passion, he gave the holy Sacrament to them, and, presently after, caused them to be cited to the Bishoppes Courte. And, uppon Easter day last, after he had given the Sacrament to those which kneeled before the said Alter, he began to reade the thanksgivinge, and, on a sudden left readinge, and went and administered to some of those which did not come up to the said rayle; but, beinge in greate passion, when he gave the bread, he sayd the wordes which are appointed to be said when the wine is given; and so in greate hast made an end, and

1641.
16 Car. I.

went out of the Church in a rage, refusinge to give the Sacrament to twelve or thirteene persons then present, and kneelinge, ready to receive it.

5. That the booke of new Cannons beinge newly come forth, he presantlie published them to the said Parishioners in the Church, and did speake much in Commendacions of them, with expressions of greate joy and triumph.

6. That, upon Palme Sunday last, Margarett, wife of Thomas Cullin, beinge come about two miles to be churched, in a very rainy day, and beinge present at Church before the said William Gervis had begun his second Service, the said William Gervis refused to church her, and therupon she was constrained to returne home againe, beinge very sicke and weake, for that she was constrained to be led by two women.

7. That one James Hornsey, occupyinge land in the said parish, to the value of about 200l. per annum, who came once to the said parish Church to the makinge of a Cesse, and once to be witnesse at Baptisme, and, afterwardes, comminge to the said Church in a very rainy day, his owne Churche beinge further from his dwellinge, the said William Gervis did cause the said Hornsey to be cited to the Bishopps Courte therefore.

8. That the said William Gervis (beinge at odds with Richard Bellamy) did cite Anne the wife of the said Richard to the said Courte, only because she did misse standinge up at the Creede, although she was necessitated therunto, beinge very greate with child.

9. That the said William Gervis hath beene a longe time very contentious towards the said Parishioners, to theire greate trouble and charge.

10. That the said William Gervis, beinge a meane Preacher, is a grosse non Resident, holdinge two livings, with Cure of Soules, farr distant one from the other, he beinge Vicar of Sturry aforesaid, and Parson of Snave in Romney Marsh.

The most humble and hartie petition of the said Inhabitants is,

1641.
16 Car. I.
that the Premisses may be taken into the consideration of this honorable house; that the said William Gervis may be removed from them.   And your petitioners shall (as in duty they are bound) ever pray, &c.

Henry Harryson.	Edward Young.
James Blayland.	James Hoarnse, × by his
James Allen.	marke.
Michaell Terry.	Thomas Pennel, × by his
Richard Bellamy.	mark.
Thomas Janing.	Roger × May, his marke.
Thomas Coroke.	Vincent Bilingherst, his marke.
Peter Ambrose.	John × Stauk, his mark.
Thomas Idenden.	Thomas Arnoll, his × marke.
Henry Robarts.	John Gare, × by his marke.
Roger Canton, by his	Robert Daad, × by his
marke ×.	marke.

[Endorsed by Sir Edward Dering, " 1640, 23 Feb.   Petition.   Sturry *v.* Gervais.—pet. Sc."]

L.

PETITION to the House of Commons for a better Income to the Minister, and for the Union by Act of Parliament of the two Parishes.   From the Parishioners of SUTTON NEXT DOVOR and LITTLE MONGEHAM.

27 February.
To the honorable the Knights, Citizens, and Burgesses of the Commons house of Parliament.

The humble Petition of the Parishioners of the parish of SUTTON JUXTA DOVOR, in the County of Kent.

In all humble manner shew,

That, whereas the parish Church of Litle Mongham hath bene

long utterly ruined, and the parishioners there assigned, by the most Reverend Father in God George, late Archbishop of Canterbury, upon their owne humble petition, to heare the word, and receive the Sacraments, at Sutton, which they have accordingly done, for twenty five yeeres and upwards; and whereas the Rectory of Sutton, which is worthe 50 or 60 lib. per annum, is impropriated to the Archbishoprickc of Canterbury, and the lease to expire within lesse then a yeere; and, whereas, we have now an able, honest, orthodox, and painfull preacher, who payes rent for the house he dwels in, and is allowed for his maintenance but ten lib. per annum, out of the rectory of Sutton, and fourtie shillings per annum, *durante beneplacito,* by the rector of Litle Mongham, which rectory is worth 40 lib. per annum.

Forasmuch therefore as there are not twenty housholds in Sutton aforsaid, and not above ten housholds in the said Litle Mongham, Sutton Church ffiting to receive them all, being not above 100 Communicantes in both, and the distance being but a litle mile,

They humbly pray that a better allowance may be provided for a setled Minister; and that both Parishes may be united by Act of Parliament. And your peticioners shall pray, &c.

William Brett.	William Stokes, senior.
Tobyas Brett.	Thomas Willson.
Thomas Brett.	Jeremy Wilkes.
John Smith.	Thomas Wright.
William Hasselby.	Christopher Burton.
Nicholas Hodgman.	Thomas Corke.
Jeremy Heyward.	Henery Willson.
John Phillpott.	William Stokes, junior.
Edward Seale.	Henry Cocke.
Tho. Ffoch, jun.	Henry Stoles.

[Endorsed by Sir Edward Dering, " 1640, 27 Febr. Sutton juxta Dover."]

LI.

CERTIFICATES of the respective values and condition, &c. of the parishes of WYE, CRUNDAL, MOLASH, and LYMINGE.

6 March.

The Towne of
Wye.

Kent.

The parsonage of the Towne and parish of WYE is impropriat unto the Bishopp of Canterbury; and is worth per annum 200*l.* by estimation. The minister is Doctor Richman, who is a painefull preacher, and of good life, and hath a Stipen of 50*l.* per annum, from the parsonages of Newington, Brensett, Bocton Allofe, and the Vicaridg of Wye. And there are three Tytheries which pay nothing to the minister, vid₅., Townes Barne, Longeporte, and Craphill tythery.

Crundoll.

a

b

The parsonage of CRUNDOLL, in the hundred of Wye, is of the value of 100*l.* per annum, by estimation; Steven Thomas is Rector there; hee preacheth usually but once in 14 dayes; hee useth to bowe at the name of Jesus. In his preachinge, hee often inveyeth against Puritans, sayinge that it will not bee well untill they be out of the land; and, for the proof of his doctrins, hee citeth the booke of Common Prayer.

Witnesses, GEORGE FFINCH.
PETER MARSH.   *a.*

THOMAS BRISSENDEN.
JOHN HUKINS.   *b.*

Molash.

The parsonage of MOLASH, in the hundred of Filburow, is impropriated unto Mr Thomas Diges; and is worth 60*l.* per annum. The Vicaridg is Dr Jackson's, worth per annum 20*l.* and is served by Mr Keth, a poore Curate, that cannot preach, a common alehouse haunter, and a drunkard; who, upon a Lord's day, came into the Church, and could not read service, by reason of his drunkenes at that time, to the great dishonor of God, and the greife of all good people there.

1640-1.
16 Car. I.

Witnesses, RICHARD AMIS.
ROBERT SMYTH, } of Molash.
with many more.

Lyminge.

The parsonage is impropriate to Mr John Roberts, and is worth 200*l.* per annum, by estimation. Mr Michell Barnes is Vicar, and hath 30*l.* per annum from the Parson, and his Vicaridge is worth 30*l.* per annum, by estimation. Hee hath 2 Chappells, Parlsford* and Stanford. His ordinary preachinge hath formerly been once in 3 weekes, but now hee preacheth once in 14 dayes. Hee did urge the Churchwardens to rayle in the Communion Table, and to sett it upp to the east end of the Chancell; and, the Churchwardens not willinge to remove or rayle in the Table, the sayd Mr Barnes caused the Churchwardens to be scitted to the Ecclesiasticall Court twise; and, in the end, they were injoyned by the said Court to rayle in the Table, and sett it upp. Hee hath, in his preachinge, and otherwise, urged and caused the people to come upp to the Rayles to receave. Hee is a common frequenter of alehouses. On the 1st of Feb. 1640, there was a meetinge at Henry Boulding's house, who is Clark of the Parish, by divers of the Parishioners, where hee the said Mr Barnes did speak to the justifyinge of the Papistes havinge of Images, and sayd they worshipped not the Images, but had them in remembrance of Saints, sayinge, they were in a righter way then wee. And, beinge asked by Richard Cozins of the same parish, why Shadrak, Mesach, and Abednigo would not worshipp the King's Image, hee answered, that it was a ffable.

Churchwardens. { WILLIAM HOGBIN.
RICHARD COSSINS.

Witnesses. { RICHARD COSSINS.
JOHN SPISSER.
and divers others.

[Endorsed by Sr Edward Dering, "1640, 6 March. Certificate—Wy, Crondall, Moldash, Liminge."]

* *i.e.* Padlesworth, commonly called Palsworth and Palsford : Stanford and Padlesworth are chapelries attached to Lyminge.

1640-1.
16 Car. I.

LII.

PETITION to the House of Commons against their Vicar Mr EDWARD
ASHBERNHAM, from the Parishioners of TUNBRIDGE.

8 March.

To the honorable the Knights, Cittizens, and Burgesses of the
Commons Howse, assembled in Parliament.

The humble peticion of divers of the Parishioners of the Parish of
TUNBRIDGE, in the County of Kent, in the behalfe of themselves,
and others of the said Parish,

Humbly sheweth,

That the said Towne of Tunbridg is a greate market towne, and
very populous, having about 2,000 Communicants living in the said
Parish, and that Mr Edward Ashbernham, (who is now Vicar of the
said parish, and hath pluralitie of benefices,) is one that seldome
preacheth himselfe in the said parish; but is rather an enemy unto
sound preaching; having often refused to permit godly ministers to
preach in his pulpit, although he hath bene thereunto much requested, and neither he himselfe, nor any other, either preacheth or
catechiseth there on the Lord's dayes, in the afternoone; and he hath
threatned his parishioners for goeing to other Churches to heare sermons, when there was neither sermons nor Catechising in theire
owne Church.

That hee is likewise a great Innovator, having introduced into the
worship of God many Innovations, as namely,—turned the Communion table altarwise, rayled it in, made Cherubims of carved worke
over it, and the picture of a dove over the ffont; that he commonly
boweth himselfe unto the altar, and at the name JESUS, and enjoynes
his parishioners to come up to the railes to receive the Sacrament of
the Lord's supper; by meanes of which innovations divers of the best
minded families in the said parish have removed theire dwellings into
other parishes, and some gone out of the kingdome.

That he keepes a Curate under him named Mr Childrens, who is

also a greate Innovator, every way conforming himselfe to all the formalities and Innovations before named.

That the said Mr Ashbernham is a man of a prophane life and conversation, being so farre from restrayning others from using sports on the Lord's dayes, that hee himselfe will stand at his dore, and see yong people at theire sports, and laugh at them; being also a common frequenter of Tavernes and Alehouses, and a drinker of healths.

All which your peticioners humbly present to this honorable assembly, most humbly beseeching you to take the premisses into your favourable consideracions; together with the miserable condition of soe many poore soules in the said parish, who live in darknesse and ignorance, destitute of the saving meanes of grace; and, in Commiseration thereof, to take such order therein for theire releife as to your grave wisedomes shall seeme meete.

And your peticioners, as bound, will ever pray, &c.

WILLIAM DRYVER.
JOSEPH × MERCER.

[Endorsed by Sir Edward Dering, "1640, 8 March. Petition. Tunbridge v. Ashbornham."]

LIII.

LETTER to Sir EDWARD DERING, begging to press their petition for the restoration of their Vicar, Mr. BRIGHAM, who had been illegally ejected by the Archbishop. From the Parishioners of ASH.

RIGHT WORSHIPFULL,

By that large testimony you have given, wee are confident of your constant affaction to works of piety and Justis. It is the common opinion, that care longe, his grace will be past grace; his unworthy dealling with our parrish hath wroght the decay of Religion amongst us, which cannott be repayred but by much care and toyle, by hewinge stones out of a Rocke. Wee humbly thanke you for your lovinge respect to our petition, and reddines to further it. Wee know you are imployed about high and waighthy matters of greatest consequence; our humble sute in the behalfe of the rest of our parishinors is, to intreat your remembrance of our affayres. Mr Brigham sayth, and we belive it to be true, that hee is damnifyed above one hundred powndes by being unjustly put from Ashe; and his humble desire is, that hee may be relived from him that displaced him; and we know that the Vicaridge house in Ashe is very smale and rotten, and the tythes of the three parsonages in Ashe (wee are perswaded uppon better consideration) are worth, att the least, six hundred pownds per annum. Our sute in our petition is, and wee humbly desire, that Mr Brigham may be restablished in Ashe, hee beinge illegally displaced, a suffitient meanes provided, and the Vicarage house new bilt, and the Pigion house there repaired for him, and made fittinge for a Reverent minester to reside in, and to live with comforte amongst us: the good you shall doe for our perplexed parish herein will multiply God's blessings one your selfe and familye here, and enlarge your Crowne in heaven.

Your worshipp's servants and poore Petitioners, ever to be commanded.

Ffrom Ashe, the 16th of March, 1640.

[No signatures. The superscription is "To the right worshipfull Sr Edward Deeringe Kt and Barronett, att his Lodginge these be presented," and endorsed by Sr Edward—" 1640, 17 March—parish of Ash."]

--- --- ---

LIV.

1641.
17 Car. I.

PETITION to the House of Commons for providing them with a regular Minister. From the Parishioners of HUCKING.

To the honorable the Knights, Citizens, and Burgesses, assembled in the high Court of Parliament.

March.

The humble Certificate and Peticion of the Inhabitants of HUCKINGE, in the Countie of Kent, shewing these theire ensewing greivanes.

1. That the said Parish of Huckinge is impropriate to the Deane and Chapter of Christ Church Canterbury, and the Parsonage tithes thereof are worth lx^{li} by the yeare, by estimacion.

2. That, although the said parish doth consiste of eight score Soules, or thereabouts, yet have wee had noe setled minister amongst us by the space of thirtie yeares last past.

3. That, by the space of the said thirtie yeares last past, wee have had preaching but once in a moneth, at the most, except it hath beene uppon some extraordinary occasion; whereby wee, our children, and servants remayne much untaught in our duties to God and men.

4. That, many tymes, wee have not had Common Prayer and divine service read amongst us for the space of a fortnight or three weekes together.

5. That, for the present, now, for many years last past, wee have had noe minister resident amongst us, who might direct or comfort us in the tyme of sicknes.

And the ground and reason of all these our greivances, wee conceive to be, for that there is not any meanes allowed that might, any wise, answere the Labour of an honest and paynefull Minister amongst us: The usuall allowance for the service of the Cure of the said Parish having usually beene but x^{li} a yeare at the most.

Wherefore, wee doe most humbly and heartily beseech this honorable assembly, (even for God's sake,) to commiserate our condicions, and to make such a godly provision for us, for the tymes to come, that we, and our children after us, may have cause to prayse God for you, with all our soules.

John Allene ✕.	Edward Renells ✕.
Thomas Ffigge ✕.	Edward Hearst ✕.
Robert Packmane ✕.	William Robisone ✕.
Robert Readeare ✕.	Thomas Ashbee ✕.
John Dow ✕.	John Hooker ✕.
Alexander Piinkeman ✕.	James Knowlles ✕.
Stephen Gollding ✕.	

[Endorsed by Sir Edward Dering—" 1641, Mar. Petition. Huckinge v. Canterbury."]

LV.

PETITION to the House of Commons against the Vices and Neglect of their Rector, ROBERT CARTER. From the Parishioners of STOUR-MOUTH.

To the honorable house of Commons nowe assembled in Parliament.

The humble Petition of the Parishioners of the parish of STUR-MOUTH, in the County of Kent.

Shewinge,

That Mr Robert Carter, Master of Arts, nowe Parson and Vicar of Sturmouth aforesaid, which livinge is of the yeerely value of 140*l.*, or thereabouts, is a man zealously observant of all Innovations, as boweinge and cringinge to the Communion Table, a man very troblesome and contentious, a common haunter of tavernes and alehouses, and a great gamster, stayeinge there, drinkinge and gameinge, sometimes three, and sometimes fower whole daies and nights togeather.

And, for maynteyninge these his lewd courses, and recoveringe his

1641.
17 Car. I.

losses susteined by gaminge, hee exacteth excessively in his tithes; for whereas there is a custome in the said parish, time out of mind, that noe marsh or pasture land there should paie above xij*d.* per acre for tithes; yet hee sued your petitioners, to compell them to paie more; and, although the same was remooved by prohibition into the King's Bench, and the Custome there prooved, yet hee nowe sues five of your Petitioners for the same matter againe, and threatneth to have all his tithes in kind, and to enforce your peticioners to bringe his tith of milke into the Church Porch. And because hee cannott find causes enough to vexe your Peticioners, hee endeavoureth to make some; ffor, when his parsonage Tithes have been justly set out, accordinge to the Statute, hee refuseth to fetch them away, and letts them stand still till they bee spoiled, and then threatneth to sue your peticioners for them.

In his preachinge, hee is soe obscure that fewe or none can gaine any savinge knowledge by him. About seaven months since, upon a Sunday, when hee had appointed a Communion, in the midst of his Sermon hee brake out, and told your peticioners that they might goe all to the Devill, if they would, for hee would take noe more care of them. And not longe after, preachinge a Sermon of love, before he came out of the Pulpit hee threatend to sue all your petitioners for wages for a Clerke, whome (without consent of the Parish) hee had put in (the old Clerke livinge), and accordingly cited many to the Ecclesiasticall Court, who (upon theire apparance) were bid to paie their fees, and bee gone; they had nothinge to saie to them.

And hee beeinge lately suspended by the Ecclesiasticall Court, for not churchinge 4 women that refused to come up to the raile; and a minister beeinge appointed to serve in his stead, by the Churchwarden, hee locked up the Church doore, and kept your peticioners without any service at all.

Moreover, hee hath shewed great dislike to this honorable assembly, saieinge, that, if the Kinge wanted money, hee might sell his shippinge.

Your Peticioners therefore humbly praie, that this honorable

1611.
17 Car. I.

house wilbee pleased to call the said Mr Carter before them, to answer the premisses. And, forasmuch as the livinge of Sturmouth is able to recompence the paines of an able minister (such an one as Mr Huntly was, who beeinge late Minister here, was, for a small matter, displaced by the Archdeacon of Canterbury), that you wilbee pleased to restore the said Mr Huntly to his said livinge againe, or some other godly minded man, for the comfort of your petitioners soules. And to set downe some Order for the Confirmacion of the said Custome of Tithes of Marshland. And that your petitioners may be satisfied all their costs and charges which they have spent by reason of his vexacious suites.

All which, your peticioners leave to the consideracion of this honourable assembly.

Thomas Proude.	James ✗ Word, his mark.
William Joodg.	Roger ✗ Penny, his mark.
Thomas Hogben.	Andrew ✗ Legham, his mark.
Thomas Huffam.	Gregory Wheatnall, ✗ his mark.
Roger Wyborne.	John ✗ Legham, his mark.
Thomas Wilkinson.	Petter ✗ Mose, his mark.
John ✗ Hills, his mark.	Thomas ✗ Saweyer, his mark.
Henry ✗ Measday, his mark.	Henry ✗ Gladis, his mark.
John ✗ Baker, his mark.	Phillop ✗ Wallop, his mark.
John ✗ Maye, his mark.	Richard ✗ Norwood, his mark.

[Endorsed by Sir Edward Dering, "1641, 31 March. Petition, Stourmouth r. Carter, &c. mag."]

LVI.

LETTER to Sir EDWARD DERING, recalling their petition against their Incumbent Mr. E. NICOLS, and their Curate Mr. Jo. FREEMAN. From the Parishioners of SNARGATE.

RIGHT HONORABLE SIR,

7 April.

Wee, the parishioners and inhabitants of the parish of SNARGATE remember our dutye and service unto you. Where as of late, by the instigation of a malignant humour, being to precipite in preferringe certaine articles against our Curate, and committed to your worship's vew by the handes of Mr John Streating, who delivered them unto your worship, being at London. These are to certifie your worship, that our intent was not, by any meanes, to disgrace him, or, in any wayes, to disparage his sufficiency in not being able to discharge the Cure of soules committed to his charge; for we confesse him to be both very able, sufficient, and painefull, in dispensing the word of God; but onely he seemed to carry himselfe something too lofty, and to be hasty towards us, which thing we perswade ourselves will be much amended. We, therefore, shall humbly desire your worship, to proceede noe farther in preferring these articles against Mr Ffreeman; for we are now all willing to keepe him to be our Curate, and to be the best meanes (both by our good words, and in subscribing our hands) to doe the best we can for him, to helpe him to better meanes, for the better maintainance of him, his wife, and children; for we all confesse his deserts are well knowne to us, and to the whole country round about us, that he deserves far greater meanes then is now alowed him; for which we doe not onely cease from preferring our sute against him, but, withall, humbly intreate your worship to be his prolocutor (for some competent salary) to that honorable house of Parliament, when occasion shall be offered; for which we shall pray for the blisse of you and yours whilst we remaine parishioners of Snargate; and ever wish the happie pro-ceedings of our Curate, Mr John Ffreeman; and soe prayeth every parishioner of Snargate whose hands and names are heere subscribed.

1641.
17 Car. I.

James Ffin, by his marke.	Robert Morris, by his marke.
Robert Norton ×.	Richard Ffreebody.
Thomas Brogle, by his marke×.	John × Cousen, his marke.
George Broughton.	William Rayner.
The marke × of John Tourner.	Thomas Elles, × his marke.
The marke × of George Crutch-man.	The marke of Gabriel Melken.
	George × Pierce, by his marke.

Donne and confirmed in the presence of

Thomas Brette, Bailif of Romney Marshe.
Christopher Brice, Justice of the Peace.
Thomar Hoarde, Curatus de Snave.
Nicholas Gouldhill.
March 28, 1641.

And further, we, the above named parishioners of Snargate, doe humbly desire your worship to deliver all those articles that we preferred against our Curat Mr Freeman to himselfe, when he shall demand them. And likewise allsoe that which wee petitioned against M^r Ed. Nicols, having nothing against him concerning his life and conversacion, but onely for some abatement in our tithe, which sute we cease allsoe, wishing him all happinesse in Christ Jesus.

[Superscription.]
"To the right honorable Sir Edward Deeringe, one of the elected knights of the Sheire for the County of Kent, and now of the Kinge's Majesties honorable high Court of Parliament at Westminster, now assembled, be these with speede delivered.—Hast—Hast." And endorsed by Sir Edward, "1641, 7 Apr.—Certificate—Snargate."]

LVII.

LETTER to Sir EDWARD DERING, inclosing the preceding one, and asking for the return of the Articles of Complaint against their Incumbent and Curate. From the Parishioners of SNARGATE.

RIGHT HONORABLE SIR,*

We the parishioners of Snargate humbly desire your honor to deliver all such articles as weare committed to your hands by Mr John Streating, that weare preferred against M^r Ed. Nicols for some

---

* Evidently this and LVI. were one inclosed in the other—one missive.

abatement in our tiths; and likewise, all those articles that weare preferred against M^r Jo. Ffreeman our Curat; that this messenger, Christopher Caterman, may bringe them to the parish againe, for our sute is ceased: and all is well, both for our tiths, and likewise for our Curate; and we are in love and charity, as heere may appeare by our hands subscribed in this letter inclosed.

1641.
17 Car. I.

[Superscription.]
"To the right honorable Sir Edward Deering, Knight and Baronett, at his Lodging at Sir Henry Gibbs his house in in St Martin's lane, neere Charing Crosse. Or at the signe of the Sheeres neere the Abbie gate at Westminster neere London, be these delivered with speed and saftie."

[And endorsed by Sr Edward, "1641, 7 Apr. Snargate."]

LVIII.

PETITION to the House of Commons, representing the pitiful salary paid to their Curate by the lessee of the Parsonage. From the Parishioners of WHITSTABLE.

To the honorable house of Commons nowe assembled in Parliament.

13 April.

The humble peticion of the Inhabitants of the Parish of WHITSTAPLE, in the County of Kent.

Humbly shewinge,

That, whereas the Rectory of Whitstaple was antiently impropriated to the Archbishops of Canterbury, and noe Vicar endowed to serve the Cure there; but the Archbishops for the tyme beeinge have maynteyned a Curat to serve the Cure, and have allowed him what they thought fit. And although Sr Maurice Abbot Kt. (who hath the lease of the said Rectory from the Lord Archbishop of Canterbury) hath letten the same for 160l. per annum; yet, he will allowe but 10l. per annum towards the mayntenence of a minister to

CAMD. SOC. 2 D

serve the Cure; soe as your petitioners are all together destitute of a minister, because soe small an allowance will not maynteine him, unlesse your peticioners should allowe him somewhat out of their purses, as heeretofore they have beene inforced to doe, to their great losse and prejudice, most of the parishioners there beeinge meane men.

Your peticioners therefore humbly praye that you wilbee pleased to take the premisses into your consideracion, and to set downe such order therein as in your wisdomes shall seeme best. And your peticioners shall always praye, &c.

Ralf × Rayner's marke. ⎱ Church- Grigorye Kempe. ⎰ wardens.	Robert Leucock × his mark.
	Thomas Inice.
William × Graythron's mark.	John Stilling.
Weter × Henman's mark.	John Steevens.
John × Vigas.	Reynold Henman.
William × Ffurner's mark.	John Hewson.
Edward Graythron's × mark.	Edward Hayard.
Edward × Wheatnall's mark.	John Simpsonne.
Thomas × Holloway's mark.	

[Endorsed by Sʳ Edward Dering—" 1641, 13 Apr. Whitstaple."]

LIX.

PETITION to the House of Commons against the Perpetual Curate, ROBERT BARRELL. From the Parishioners of MAIDSTONE.

To the honorable the house of Commons assembled in Parliament.

The humble peticion of the Inhabitants of the king's towne and parish of MAIDSTONE, in the countie of Kent.

Sheweth,

That whereas our towne and parish is verie greate and populous, consisting of or about six thousand inhabitants, and the tithes thereof amounting to the yearlie value of 400*l.*, at the least, and having but one parish Church for so greate a people to repaire unto: the Archbishop of Canterbury, being our parson, and receiving all our tithes and profitts, hath taken no further care for us, but to continue over us one Robert Barrell his Curat there, who is thus quallified:

1. Hee is verie carelesse and negligent in his place, himselfe sometymes not preaching amongst us above once in a month or 5 weekes, except it bee a funerall sermon, wherein he aymeth more at his owne gayne then our good: and, when he preacheth, he very often strikes at sincerity and forwardnesse in profession, under the names of faction, schisme, and singularity.

2. When the said Mr. Barrell is absent, or will not preach himselfe, he setts up in his place (to frequently) such as by their inabillitie cause rather dirision to the people then matter of edificacion; and, although wee have offered to choose an able man, and to maynetayne hym at our owne charge, who might take paynes to instruct us in the afternoones on Sabbath daies (necessarie occasions hindering servants and others in the forenoones), yet he refuseth; by reason wherof much ignorance, lewdnes, and disobedience doth raigne amongst us. And noe wonder why he is thus negligent, [and] averse, himselfe haveing said hee hath not the cure of our soules.

3. Hee is not onlie negligent hymselfe to preach; but hath alsoe rebuked a painefull neighbouring mynyster for preaching twice on the Sabbath dayes, telling hym, that he had power to crush halfe a douzen such as he and Mr Wilson were; and that the said mynyster did much disgrace the clergie by preaching twice on the Sabbath daies; and that preaching in the afternoone was but prating and babling.

4. Hee hath sett himselfe, with all violence, to molest and prosecute in the Ecclesiasticall Courts such as, being well affected to the Word preached, have gone from their owne parish to heare a sermon on the Sabbath daie, in the afternoone, though he refuse to preach himselfe, whereby he hath much sadded their hearts, and wasted their estates.

5. By his owne confession, he hath brought Innovacions into our church, causing the Communion Table to be sett up to the wall, at the east end of the chancel, and there to be railed in; hymselfe hath given adoracion to the said table, and vehemently urgeth the people to come upp to the raile (if they will partake of the Sacrament); and hath broken out into such rage and passion against such as have forborne to come to receive the Communion at the said raile, that many, whose Consciences are weake and tender, have refrained to come to the Sacrament, and others he hath scited to the Ecclesiasticall Court at Canterbury, for not coming.

6. Hee hath the Rectorie of Boughton Malherbe, in the countie aforesaid, and is not there resident, but leaveth his people to an hireling.

7. Hee is verie covetous and contentious, exacting of us more and greater tithes, and other duties, than have beene formerlie paid, or are due, and citeth, sueth, and vexeth those that will not pay hym his demands, whereby many are inforced to paie hym what he will have, to avoide charge and trouble. And the better to inable himselfe in these his vexatious suits, he hath gott a lease of the Archbishop of parte of the Vicaridge tithes.

8. Hee is a common taverne haunter, to the great offence of some, the evill example of others, and greate scandall of the mynystry. He is of a haughtie and proude carriage, discountenancing magistracie, verie envious, and of a conversacion altogether unsutible to his function.

9. Hee hath had many Curats under hym, most of them being pott companions, of a verie scandalous and of an evill life, one of them leaving a Bastard child behind hym in our towne, and others of them gamsters; many of them coussining and defrauding poore tradesmen, by getting their goods into their hands, and then runnyng away; few of them but idle, unable, unapt to teach.

10. The said Mr Barell himselfe hath beene indicted for grosse and palpable perjury.

Wherefore, wee doe most humbly beseech this honorable assembly, to take into your Consideracion these our greivances ; and to do for us, in all things therein, as to your grave and godly wisdome shall seeme best expedient.   And wee, as in duty bound, shall ever pray, &c.

1611.
17 Car. I.

John Bigg.	Thomas Taylor.
Andr. Broughton.	Samuell Veroll.
Martin Jeffery, Maior.	Robert Usborne.
Thomas Swinnocke.	John Startout.
Ambrose Beale.	Thomas Ffletcher.
Rob. Swinocke.	Ric: Dan.
Caleb Bankes.	Nic: Milles.
Samuell Marshall.	Hen. Wightman.
Robert Withinbrooke.	Tho: Wightman.
George Maplesden.	Tho: Cripps.
Henry English.	Rob: Philips.
Richard Crispe.	Jam: Newenham.
George Hall.	Rob: Marshall.
Thomas Swinock, Junior.	Peter Malin.
John Wale.	Jo: Broke.
Francis Lambe.	Jo: Keley.
John Sutwicke.	Ric: Wassall.
George Maplesden, Junior.	Edw: Peirse.
Thomas Swinock, Junior.	Nic: Seger.
Thomas Besbech.	Mildmay Maplesden.
James Ruse.	Walter Godden.
Thomas Crompe.	Jo: Wilmot.
Thomas Abraham.	Edw: May.
John Harris.	Tho: Walter.
Nicholas Wall.	Ro: Brooke.
Thomas Stollton.	Rob: Bigg.
John Hogben.	

[Endorsed by Sr Edward Dering—"1641, 17 May.   Petition.   Maydston v. Barell."]

LX.

PETITION of WILLIAM GARNONS to the BISHOP OF ROCHES-
TER, requesting his adjudication in the persecutions against him by
RICHARD CHASE, Rector of STONE.

To the right reverend father in God John Lord Bishop of
Rochester.

The humble petition of WILLIAM GARNONS, of St. Buttolphes,
Algate, London, Gent., one of the Attorneyes of his Majesty's Courte
of Common Pleas att Westminster.

Sheweth,

That one Richard Chase, Parson of Stone, in your Lordshipp's
dioces, haveing much afflicted the parishioners there with causelesse
libelling and suites in lawe, att length, by himselfe and his brothers,
singled out one John Ware, a very substantiall Inhabitant there,
and prosecuted him with various libells and actions, in severall
his Majesty's Courtes, spiritual and temporall, giveing out, that they
would not leave him worth a groate; and that the said Mr Chase
would live upon one Parsonage, and spend the other in lawe against
him and his frends. And your Lordship's petitioner, being a stranger,
and comeing, long afterwards, to live in the said parishe, was imployed
for the said Mr Ware, to defend twoe of these suites depending in
the said Courte, and to prosecute one other against Mr Chase, for
not takeing of Tythes duely sett out for him, for which hee libelled;
which, together with the like causes, hath byn severall tymes prooved
against him. And the Petitioner, in Michaelmas and Hillary tearmes
1636, was attorney against him in a prohibition upon an agreement
for tythes, drawne with his owne hand, which hee, together with
many other agreements with the said Ware, had formerly broaken.

---

* It must be 1637, 1638, or 1639, because Bishop Warner succeeded Bishop Bowle in
1637, and Bishop Bowle, uncle of Mr. Chase, is spoken of herein as the late Bishop,
" predecessor to your Lordship."

And Mr Chase, haveing rayled against the reverend Judges, threatened Juryes, and most dispitefully traduced Sergeant Clerke, and generally all such as were any way imployed against him, or his party, especially the peticioner, whoe never wronged them in any kinde, Hee, his father, and brothers, sought, by secreate messages, and indirect meanes, to plant dissencion betwixt the peticioner and his wife, and one Sr Henry Carewe, a very auncient knight, hir uncle, of whome they had both very much deserved many yeeres together, and were assured of a very large Requiteall, had not the said Chases soe abused them, and, at length, soe deluded him, that they tooke the peticioner's house over his head; and, not soe contented, Mr Chase, that yeere followeinge the Prohibicion, would not suffer their tythes to bee taken, doe what they could, by tendringe, giveinge of notice, from tyme to tyme, for the divideing, sett[ing] out, and takeing away the same. And, after Divine service, upon Sunday the xxvjth of March then imediately followeinge, Mr Chase's man, and one of his brotheres, on his behalfe, threatened the peticioner, att the Churche doore, sayeing, that they would give him lawe enough; and, on the morrowe morneing or before, his tythe gatherers conveyed a Bullock of the peticioner's out of his yard to the pound, and divers of his brothers, with his said men servants, lay all that Munday lurkeing about the peticioner's grounds, watching opportunity, and hurrying his cattle, sheepe, and young lambes (some not a weeke ould) to the pound, and forced him to fetch severall Replevins: and, shortly after, brought divers triviall, yet intricate, suites in law against him, in his brother Mathew Chase's name (a person of smale value), and now dares not proceed therein: and, in Michaelmas tearme then alsoe followeing, three of his brothers, and divers other lewd persons, perceiveinge that your peticioner and his wife, and some of his servaunts, were heere in London, committed a fowle and barbarous Ryott att Stone Castle, then the peticioner's dwelling howse, and dragged one of his maideservaunts out of doores, and, conscaleing their names many dayes, kept the posses-

---

* Stone Castle then belonged to Sir Henry Carew, Knight.

163[7]. sion thereof by force, untill they had eaten up and consumed all the
Beefe, Bread, and a greate parte of other provision there.

And the said Mr Chase, in the Interim, and before the peticioner's
sheepe were shorne that yeere, procured a . . . . . Citation against
him, for Tythe of Calfs, wooll, and lambs, and forced him to above
xx marks charge, in proveing his said Cause, and is now ashamed to
have the same heerd in a publiq and legall way; and the petitioner,
before Michaelmas was 12 months, haveinge examyned and made
good proofe of his parte by 14 wittnesses, and procured publicacion,
and done what in him lay to hasten an end thereof, his Councell
found that his Proctor, in alledging a Custome of a penny a Calfe
weaned or sould with the Cowe, had, among other things, left out
the tender of the mony accordinglie, both which were well prooved;
by this and the like meanes, in favoure of Mr Chase, (as the peticioner
beleeveth,) and of the long sicknesse of the peticioner, which continued in greate extremity from July untill Christmas last, and
sithence, the peticioner was delayed of his Tryall; and the Peticioner,
last Sommer, acquainted his said brother, that, in respect hee had
heerd that Doctor Wood was sometymes a sojourner with Mr Chase,
in his house, and hee and his children allyed to him by marriage;
and that, for theis and the like reasons, Mr Chase had often threatened
the parishioners of Stone with him, that hee intended to peticion your
Lordshipp to heere the said Cause yourselfe, and had provided a
peticion to that purpose.

Nowe, soe it is, may it please your Lordshipp, that the peticioner
daylie expecteing to heere from his Proctor (as hee formerly had
donn) that the said Cause was reddy for heereing, Mr Chase, in the
meane tyme, takeing advantage of the peticioner's sicknesse, procured
the Peticioner's Proctor to bee present att a clandestine heereinge
thereof heere in London, in a chamber, as hee is informed, without
the Register, and without the Peticioner's or his Counsell's knowledge;
untill a Courte had passed in the Countrey, and centence concluded
against the Peticioner, and hee condempned in the whole tythes and
costs of suite.   And, for as much as the said Cause was soe heerd

upon some advantagious point in lawe left open, as aforesaid, for M^r 163[7].
Chases benifitt (as the peticioner hath heerd, and doth beleeve) and
not upon the meritts and equity thereof: and, for that there being
but twoe Proctors in that Courte, and their places att the disposicion
of the Judge, your peticioner verily beleeveth, that his Proctor
durst not give him notice of the said heereinge. And, to the end
your Lordshipp's peticioner, after his greate trouble and charge, may
have a faire heereinge, according to the trueth and equity of his
cause; and the rather, for that Mr Chase might have had the same
heerd upon such by-matter before the Peticioner was put to soe
greate charge, hee being onely directed by his Proctor, and not
knoweing any such thing, or the fforme of proceeding there.

Hee humbly prayeth your Lordshipp to heere the same cause yourselfe, and, in a judiciall or arbitrary way, to end and determyne the
same, att your Lordshipp's pleasure, unto which the peticioner shall
humbly submitt himselfe, hopeing Mr Chase will doe the like, hee
being far more morigerous* towards your Lordshipp . . . . . . towards his Uncle, your Lordshipp's predecessor, and more fearefull of
comenceing causeles suites. And that all proceedinges upon the
said surrepticious centence may, in the meane tyme, cease. And
the Peticioner shall ever pray for your Lordshipp, &c.

[In dorso: "Peticion to the Bishopp of Rochester 163*. Chase and
Garnons."]

--- --- --- ---

* "Morigerous," *i.e.* mannerly, dutifull. The word "than" is probably omitted after
"Lordshipp." The Uncle was Bishop Bowle.

1611.
17 Car. I.

LXI.

PETITION to the House of Commons against their Rector, Mr RICHARD
CHASE.   From the Parishioners of STONE.

23 May.

To the Right Honourable the Knights and Burgesses of the
House of Commons.

The humble Peticion of the Inhabitants of the parishe of STONE,
within the county of Kente,

Most humbly sheweth unto this honourable assembly, that your
Peticioners have many yeares groaned under the insolent oppressions
and by continuall vexations of their Parson Mr RICHARD CHASE,
whoe hath not only starved our soules for want of spirituall foode,
but, by his vexatious suits, as much as in him lay, hath endeavoured
to take away our corporall foode, and soe utterly extirpate our selves
and families.   Nor had wee ever any hope of any the least releife,
hee haveinge invested himselfe in the Bishopp's favour, as well as his
service, which his Lordshipp could not but well knowe was on
purpose to have more power by his Lordshipp's countenance to
oppresse, beinge well enformed of his former contentious life, which
made his owne Uncle * both upprayd him for his ingratitude, and
hate him for his contention, beinge our former diocesan, and hee
that gave him two † such great liveings.

But nowe God hath made this blessed Parliament not only a
helper of our miseries, but our preservers in our just complaints,
wee most humbly offer theis articles unto this honourable assembly.

Humbly beseechinge, that, seeinge Mr Chase is soe well provided
of another liveinge, with a faire house, and in an excellent ayre,
where hee setteth his whole delight; and that hee makes noe other
use of ours, beinge unhealthy, (as himselfe, brothers, or both, gave
out,) but to vex his parishioners with dayly and unnecessary suites,
and only add fuell to his contentious spiritt; and that hee himselfe
confesseth; the other beinge sufficient to maintayne him.

* *i.e.* Bowle, Bishop of Rochester.
† *i.e.* his other living, Chislehurst.

You would be pleased to lett your poore peticioners enjoye soe much favor as once to have a learned minister dwellinge and resident amongst us; beinge noe contemptable liveinge, but worth 200*l.* per per annum, and may satisfye a learned preacher, for which your Peticioners shall ever pray to God for his protection of you and your grave consultations.

WILLIAM GARNONS.
JOHN WARE.

[In dorso by Sᵣ Edward Dering—" 1641, 23 May. Petition. Stone *v.* Chase."]
['There is another copy of this petition with " Sᵣ An. Welldon " on the dorse, and in that the name is written " Chasey."]

LXII.

ARTICLES presented to the House of Commons against their Rector, Mᵣ RICHARD CHASE, by the Parishioners of STONE.

Articles presented to the high Court of Parlament, by the humble Petitioners of the Parish of STONE, in Kent, agaynst theyr Parson, Mᵣ RICHARD CHASYE.

That Mᵣ Chasye was noe soner instituted and inducted then he began to shew his Contentious spiritt, as well by vexatius suts agaynst his petitioners, as by picking quarrells agaynst the Curat, a very honest man, and one that took soe much paynes in instructing his flock, that wee love him noe less then he us, that Mᵣ Chasye did, by denying payment of his Stipent, and other ill usage, soe weery him, that he left us. Nay, although his uncle, our then diocesson, and one had wholy preferd hym, commanded payment; yet, untill the Archbishop had threatned suspension, he would not pay any.

That since, wee never had other then such Curate that did not prech more syllily then seldom : and, now, since our Church hath bynn burnt, wee have had neyther prayers nor any other function, ner thes two yers : and he would have dismist his Curat assone as the Church was burnt, which had bynn all one to us, wee having noe

1640-1.
16 Car. I.

usc of him; but nowe, of late, wee have none resident in our parish to bury our deed. Soe that as Mr Chasye leves our soules cure to the neighbaring ministers, soe our bodyes to lye as noysom Carrion, unless the Dead will bury ther dead.

That, upon the burning of our Church, we resorted to the Bishop of Rochester, his lord and master, to desyre som place to serve God in for the present; but, as wee were not sufferred admittance to his Lordshipp, soe had this messag sent: "His Lordshipp had taken order with the Parson;" and the Parson gave this answer to the Curat in our presence telling him a place was found convenient, consecrated, or used formerly for the service of God, That he should not dare to offitiat there, or in any place, without his order, which order since he hath not given, beeing full two yeres. Nowe, wee humbly appeale to this honourable assembly, whether 200*l.* per annum doth not deserve prayers in two yeres once to be sayd in our Parrish.

That, although a Carpenter offerred to make the church servisable for many ages for 140*l.*, of which twenty would be for the Chancell, the stone roofe beeing untouched by the fyer, yet this neyther could be obtayned; and, although it cost now 180*l.*, yett are wee never the nerer to serve God in it then before. Soe that it take of very much from our benevolence.

That, very lately, wee all addressed ourselves by an humble petition, to complayne that our Church was no forwarder, and desired his Lordshipp's assistance; but Mr Chasye's power was so great with his Lordshipp, that wee obtayned neyther Justice nor Civill usage from his Lordshipp, only telling us wee did it out of Splene; and, for a farwell, had this most skornfull answere from Mr Chasye: "What have you now gotten by your Complaynt?" Soe that all our hope and help now only reste in this honourable assembly.

That Mr Chasye, both in profession and practise, hates the name of peace; therfore doth make us very conversant with the lawe, although never instructs us, by himself or any other, in the Gospel of peace.

1640-1.
16 Car. I.

And this apperes by an Arbitracion, in which his parishioner's arbitrator yelded to more then was Reason, bycause his parishioner had not tythed aright. And, when all was yelded, Mr Chasye, in playne termes, tould the arbitrator, that it was not that he desyred; but to make him spend mony for the charg of a Dynner. And, for a full satisfaction of his contention, wee desyre noe other then that the Ecclesiasticall Court, the Bishop's Temporall Court, and the Nisi Prius be examined for the multitude of Suts agaynst your Peticioners commenced, betwixt him and his brothers, all of them having dependence of his purse and plesure.

To every of thes articles, all in generall, or some of us in particuler, whose names are subscribed, will take our Oath.

John Ware.	John Lake.
Thomas Elyott.	The marke of Midm. ✕ Draper.
Richard Lake.	The marke of Myles ✕ Alkinson.
The marke of Thomas ✕ Howord.	The marke of Thomas Lambe ✕.
William Everest.	The marke of Thomas ✕ Symons.
Will. Ffrankwell.	William Garnons.
Richard Gooddenn.	John Nottinghame.
The marke of Thomas ✕ Paltock.	The marke of John Evans ✕.
Martyn Holmden.	The marke of James Lorkin ✕.
	The marke of ✕ Richard Masteres.

[In dorso—" Stone—Articles against Mr Chase and the Bishopp in Parliament, 1640, 16 Ca."]

LXIII.

TWELVE ARTICLES presented to the House of Commons against their Rector, Mr RICHARD CHASE, by the Parishioners of STONE.

Articles presented to the high Courte of Parliamente by the humble Peticion of the Inhabitants of the Parishe of STONE, in

Kente, against their Parson, Mr RICHARD CHASE, Clarke, Chaplayne to the Bishopp of Rochester, their diocesian there.

1. That Mr Chase, immediately after his institution and Induction, began with diverse vexatious suites and libells, and pickinge of quarrells by himselfe and his brothers (his agents therein) against the parishioners, to infringe their auncient customes of tythinge there used; and haveing the then diocesian his uncle and patron, and Dr Wood, the Chancellor there, his kinsman, pursued the same with greate violence. And hee and his brothers, whoe only depend upon his purse and pleasure, gave out in speeches, that they would live upon one parsonage, and spend the other in lawe against the said Inhabitants, and forced them to the expence of ccc lib. or upwards, in lawe, besides other losses and dammages by them sustayned therby.

2. That, by pickeinge Quarrells against the then Curate there, whome the parishioners affected for his industrie in instructeinge of them, Mr Chase indeavoured to weary him out, by denyeinge his stipend and other ill usage, and beinge, by his said uncle, the late Bishopp, (whoe only preferred him,) commaunded to pay the same, yett would not doe it, untill hee was by the Archbishopp under payne of suspencion; soe that the Curate beinge putt to more charge and trouble then his salary was worth, was inforced to leave the parishe; and sithence, wee have had noe able preacher there, nor upon a Sabathe daye, before the Church was burnt, neither service nor sermon, morneinge nor eveninge, nor any minister to bury the dead, there beinge a corps to bee buried that day.

3. That hee suffers the parsonage house and buildings to become ruinous, and without hospitality, ever since his beinge Parson there; and, for 4 or 5 yeares togeather, before the Church was burnt, suffered the arched Roofe of the Chauncell, for want of sufficient Cover, to become broaken and decayed, and above 200 or 300 foote of the windowes to remayne unglazed; soe that wee were often inforced to forsake our pewes for shelter from wynde and weather; nor could the Communion Table bee kept drye in tyme of rayne; in soe much, that, sometymes, it rayned upon the wyne and bread of Consecracion,

at the tyme of receiveinge of the Sacramente.   And, albeit, the said 1640-1. 16 Car. I. Channcell received little damage by the late fire, haveinge very little combustible matter in it, yett Mr Chase hath caused a very greate parte of the Breife mony, to bee uncessantly wasted and bestowed upon the same, soe that the Church is like to remayne unfynished.

4. That, as Mr Chase, before the burninge of our Churche, would not provide or suffer any able minister in our parishe, nor came him-selfe above once or twice in a twealve month, and then only to reccon for tythes, or pick quarrells, to goe to lawe, or aboute pay-mente of his assessments for the poore, which hee seldome payed without troubleinge the Justices of Peace therwith; or, to preach a funerall sermon for money: Soe, as soone as the fyre hapned, hee indeavoured to discharge his curate; and wee haveinge peticioned the nowe Bishopp, his Master, that wee might have prayers read in our parishe, hee soe farre opposed the same, as that wee have had none thes twoe yeares, and upwardes, and nowe noe minister to bury the dead.

5. That hee is very insolent, prowd, and haughtie, in all his accions, and hath gotten into the nowe Bishopp's favour, and to bee his Chapleyne, of purpose to countenance his brableinge suites, and hath bragged of it; soe that, upon our peticion, wee could obteyne neither admission to his Lordshipp, nor redresse of our wrongs; and hee and his brothers have brought soe many brableinge suites att lawe, and libells against us, they ordinarily becomeinge the one wittnesse for the other of them, and, beinge many, have soe persecuted us, that wee dare not see one another's tythes sett out, beinge often therunto required, for feare of revengefull suites, they haveinge given out, that they would live upon one parsonage, and spend the other in lawe against us.

6. That, as Mr Chase and his brothers, in their usuall walkeinge togeather, doe consult howe to bringe suites and accions against us, soe, when they please, they will not suffer their tythes to bee taken, albeit duely sett forth and tendred; but yett libell for the same, and

sometymes twice or more for one and the same thinge; and have brought severall accions att lawe, for one and the same trespasse, makeinge only some coulorable distinction in pointe of tyme, or the like, and have procured Doctor Wood, their kinsman, to hould Courts, of purpose to expedite their litigious suites and libells, where M⟨r⟩ Chase has had more libells then all the ministers in the dioces besides; and, upon a late arbitracion with one of us, upon some small mistake in tytheinge, haveinge obteyned his will, hee said, 'twas not the tythe hee desired, but to putt the partie to the charge of a dinner. His usuall sayeinge is " his will is his will, and hee will have his will." And howe hee and his brothers have indeavoured to attayne the same, appeareth by the multitudinous suites in the said Courts of Rochester, and in the greate Courts at Westminster.

7. That hee and his brothers doe ordinarily endeavour to seeke causes of suites against us, and, to that end, doe keepe insufficient fences towards the streets, lanes, and neighbours grounds, of purpose to take our cattle in their grounds; soe that wee dare scarce drive our cattell by the wayes, or suffer them in our owne grounds, without a keeper beinge by them; and their servaunts often privily conveyed into their grounds; and soe accions of trespasse brought against us, or to the pound, and wee forced to replevyn our cattle. And, after many provocacions, findeing one of the parishioners unwillinge to goe to lawe, they layed their dung upon his dunghill, and, afterwards, carried away all togeather, of purpose to provoke him to suite of lawe.

8. That M⟨r⟩ Chase and his brothers doe commonly use rayleing speeches against the Common Lawe, and Judges, Jurors, and wittnesses, when their brableinge suites passe against them, as commonly they doe, threatninge them with the Starr Chamber, and otherwise; soe that jurors and wittnesses beinge summoned, often tymes dare not appeare, or doe their duety, for feare, they beinge soe wilfully proane to revengefull suites of lawe, and other mischievous courses. And they commonly goeinge 3, 4, or more togeather in company, to demaund or take tythes, the neighbours of smaler retinewe are forced

to lett them tythe and take what they please, and chopp and chaunge their tythes as they will themselves. And yett, of aboute xx severall accions tryed att lawe, they never had one scarce fairely passe for them, albeit some of themselves alwayes become wittnesses on their owne parte.

1640-1.
16 Car. I.

9. That the said Chases, since their comeinge into our parishe, have committed severall riotts, forcible entries, and detayners, and other fowle and barbarous misdemeanors, and have byn indicted and fyned for some of them. And they have threatned some of the most substantiall inhabitants not to leave them worth a groate; others, that they should not keepe as much as a henn in the parishe; and bound over another to the assizes, and there maliciously indeavoured to indict him for his owne sheepe, falsely supposeinge it to bee stolen from them.

10. That Mr Chase, haveinge twoe acres of Gleabe Land, in the upper side of a feild of 6 acres, in Stone, called Parsons Banck, which tyme out of minde had layne togeather undivided or distinguished by bounds, and hee and his predecessors had therfore alwayes taken rent for the same twoe acres of the tennant for the tyme beinge, according as the residue of the feild was letten, Mr Chase upon a soddayne displeasure against the tennant refused the rent, and, instead of entringe into his owne two acres, entred into, plowed up, and sowed the whole feild with corne, and detayned the same two yeares togeather; and, albeit the tenante of the greater and best parte of the said feild payed a deare rent for the same, dureinge the said 2 yeares tyme, to his landlord, and was soe deprived of the injoyment therof, yett Mr Chase brought twoe or three severall accons of trespasse against him, for vexacion; whereas one might have served for tryall of his tytle, yf the same had byn denyed him, as in trueth it was not. And the same afterward comeinge to bee divided by a Jury, the said Mr Chase and his brothers opposed the same, and soe threatned the Jury as that the same yett remaynes undivided.

11. That Mr Chase was a very busy parson in the late convocacion house, and a diligent observer of the late Papisticall Church Cerimo-

nyes introduced; and, beinge chapleyn to the said bishopp, and allyed to Dr Wood his chauncellor, whoe was alsoe sometymes a sojourner in Mr Chase his house, soe farre prevayled, that most parte of us were inforced through feare, att intollerable rates, to compound with him for our tythes,—by the greate, in mony, for feare of oppression and wronge, beinge voyde of all hope of favour or justice in the said bishopp's courts, or of any meanes to avoyde his brothers' testimonyes, beinge commonly his witnesses in all his brableinge suites.

12. That Mr Chase and his brothers brought most of their suites att lawe, in the name of one Mathewe Chase, without distinction of senior or junior, they haveinge Mathewe Chase their father, and Mathewe Chase their brother, then liveinge with them ; soe that, when their causes past against them, as commonly they did, the defendants knewe not against which Mathewe to demaund costs, and soe often lost the same, they, after tryall and verdict for the defendant, sometymes pretendinge the same to be the suite of Mathew th'elder, and other tymes of Mathew the younger, att their pleasure, to defraude the defendant of costs.

[Endorsed—" 12 articles against Mr Chase et al.—1640, p' parishioners de Stone."]

[There are no signatures.]

— — — —— — —

LXIV.

PETITION to the House of Commons, from WILLIAM GARNONS, late of Stone, detailing the persecutions of RICHARD CHASE, Rector of STONE.

To the honourable assembly of Knights, Citizens, and Burgesses of the Commons house of Parliament.

The humble peticion of WILLIAM GARNONS, late of STONE, in Kente.

1641.
17 Car. I.

Most humbly sheweth the severall wrongs, oppressions, and persecutions hee hath suffered by Doctor Wood, Chauncellor to the Bishopp of Rochester; Richard Chase, Clerke, his kinsman, Chapleine to the said Bishopp; Mathewe Chase, John Chase, Thomas Chase, and William Chase, brothers of the said Richard Chase ; and by the said Bishopp, and one Henry Scudder, Clerke, and others, by the said Chase's procuremente.

1. That the said Richard Chase, beinge by the late Bishopp Bowles, his uncle, preferred unto two of the best Benefices within the said Dioces of Rochester, viz. Chiselhurst, where the said Chase himselfe liveth, and Stone, where the Petitioner lived, both worth above 400*l.* per annum; hee, and his said brothers (his agents), immediately upon his induction into Stone, indeavoured, by various accons, suites, and libells against the Petitioner, and other Inhabitants of Stone, to infringe their auncient Customes of Tytheinge there used, and gave out in speeches, that hee would live upon one parsonage and spend the other in lawe against them.

2. That, upon the Sabboth day, beinge the 26th of March, 1637, the said Mr Chase sent one Zacceus Weare, and the said Mathewe his brother, both his servaunts, to demaund tythes of the Peticioner, well knowinge that there neither was nor could bee, as then, any tythes at all due unto him from the peticioner : which said Zacceus and Mathewe att the Church doore, presently after divine service that day, openly threatned the peticioner, on the said Mr Chase's behalfe, sayeinge, amongst other things, that they would give the peticioner lawe enough; and, on the morrow morneinge, before daylight, the said Mr Chase's servaunts privily conveyed a younge heyfer of the peticioners, out of a stronge palled yard, from his dwellinge house to the pound; and, in a replevyn therof, a verdict was afterwards found for the peticioner against one of Mr Chase's servaunts, who, beinge poore, never payed the damages.

3. That, on the morrowe after the peticioner was so threatned, beinge Munday the 27th of that March, the said Mathewe, Thomas, and William Chase, Zacceus Weare, and John Harbert (all ser-

vaunts to the said Richard Chase), lay all day lurkinge in and about the peticioner's grounds, and severall tymes hurried his cowes, some reddy to calve, cattle, sheepe, and young Lambes, some not a weeke ould, to the pound, and forced him to fetch severall replevyns that day; and. to deprive him of damages, in one of the replevyns, kept the said Weare out of the jurisdiction of Rochester Courte, where the same depended, untill all proces were out, soe that the peticioner could not procced therin, and is therby deprived of those costs and dammages alsoe.

4. That the peticioner attendinge the Tryall of one of the said replevyns att Rochester, where he was a stranger, the said Chases and their father beinge there present, caused the peticioner to bee twice arrested, in the face of the Court, att the suite of the said Mathewe Chase (being a person of small worth), upon twoe acčons of trespas "pedibus ambulando," for supposed goeinge by an auncient pathway leadinge to the peticioner's dwellinge howse in Stone, which the said Chases had then freshly plowed upp, to sowe with Corne ; and the peticioner haveinge justified the goeinge in the said pathwayes, by plea, and made good proofe that the same were then freshly plowed upp by the said Chases, and not newe trodden againe, and brought the said Causes to a tryall in one day, a verdict past for the peticioner in the morneinge in the one of them, which the said Thomas Chase perceivinge, beinge sworne a witnesse therein for his brother, and sayeinge what he could for him, the other beinge upon the same yssue touchinge the said pathwayes, the said Thomas, in the afternoone, deposed that the said pathwayes were newe trodden and visible, which beinge disproved by diverse severall and credible witnesses, hee said, in evidence to the Jury, that hee did see the peticioner lyeinge alonge in the feild, twoe rodds out of the said pathwayes, reedinge upon a booke, or some papers, about twoe dayes after the said replevyns ; and soe a verdict was given against the peticioner in the said second trespas ; which 2 supposed trespasses did, upon evidence att the tryalls therof, appeare to bee but one, and donne at one and the same tyme, and only for vexacion divided into

twoe distinct tymes and accōns.   And the said Thomas a common wittnesse for his said brothers Richard and Mathewe, in all their brableinge suites.

5. That for avoydeinge such vexacious suites, and for that the said Chases had given out that the peticioner should not keepe soe much as a henn in the said parishe, hee was inforced, from the said 27th of March that yeare, to keepe upp and fodder his cowes and cattle in his yards, untill hee could procure chapmen to buy them, and then to sell them away, some with calves by their sides, and others reddy to calve, and lett out his pastures, all at greate losse, and shortly after to forsake his dwellinge there, by reason of theis and diverse other oppressions which hee suffered by the said Chases, and others by their procurement, as heerafter is menčoned.

6. That, before the peticioner could sell away his said cowes hee had twoe calves fallen, which were afterwards sold away by the cowes sides, wherby two pence for the fall of the said twoe calves soe sold became due by custome of the said parishe, for tythes therof, to Mʳ Chase; as alsoe one lambe, and about twoe fleeces of wooll in kinde, that yeare; but the peticioner, in Mʳ Chase's absence (hee not comeinge within the said parishe scarce once in a twelve month ordinarily), could not procure any of his servaunts or tythgathers (sic) to receive or take away the same, or to see the same divided or sett out, albeit hee oftentymes gave them notice therof, and desired them to doe the same; nor would any of the Inhabitants, by themselves, or their servaunts, see the same donn. beinge often therunto requested, some of them alleadgeinge that they durst not, the said Chase and his brothers were soel itigious, others sayeinge they would rather ride 40 myles with the peticioner another way : and one of the said tythgatherers confest hee durst not receive them, or see them divided; and att harvest followinge, the peticioner was enforced to borrowe and hire laborers and others, from tyme to tyme, from theire workes in other parishes, of purpose only to see his tythes of corne and hey sett out, none of the parishe dareinge to doe it, for feare of revengefull suites.   But, in May that yeare,

before the peticioner's sheepe were shorne, the peticioner was cited before Dr Wood, into the consistory of Rochester, for tythes of the said calves, wool and lambe, and there proceeded against with greate violence.

7. That the Peticioner was enforced to retayne a proctor in the said courte, whoe depended on Doctor Wood (there beinge but two, and one of them his menyal servant), whoe, in favor of Mr Chase, in draweinge upp the peticioners allegation concerneinge the said custome of a penny a calfe sould by the cowes side, omitted to alleadge a tender of the said 2^d for the said twoe calves, accordinge to the said custome. And the peticioner desireinge Doctor Wood that the same might bee amended, he therupon threatned the petitioner to question him in the high Commission Courte, for moveinge him therunto; and the peticioner was enforced to bringe his wittnesses, 14^{en} in number, first to Rochester, to bee sworne, and then to London, to bee examined by one whoe had byn Doctor Wood's man, and had lived with him in Mr Chase's house; nor could the peticioner bee admitted to have his wittnesses examined by any other, nor to minister interrogatoryes unto them, of the points materiall on his parte to bee proved.

8. That the Peticioner, nevertheless, by 14 substantiall wittnesses, made good proofe of the premisses, and of the said custome of a tythe penny for a calfe sould by the cowes side, and of the tender of the said two pence for the said twoe calves accordinglie, and of the tender of the said tythe lambe and wooll in kinde, and retayned his Councell, and att greate charge prepared the said cause reddy for heereinge in the said consistory of Rochester; but the petitioner, by meanes of these and other troubles occasioned by the said Chases, fell into great extremity of sicknesse, wherof Mr Chase takeinge advantage, privily, unknowne to the peticioner, or any for him, procured Dr Wood, in his chamber att Doctors Commons, to give order for a sentence against the peticioner, which was donne accordingly, and the petitioner condempned in the whole tythes of calfe, lambe, and wooll in kinde, and costs of suite to 10l. in the whole, to his extreame

1641.
17 Car. I.

losse and damage, and to the disherison of him, and others the said parishioners, of their said auncient and lawfull customes: which 10*l.* the petitioner shortly after, upon payne of excommunicacion, was cited to pay, and did pay, "ob metu excommunicacionis," and then alsoe payd 3*s.* 4*d.* to M*r* Chase's proctor, to enter an act in the courte for the peticioner's discharge, and that hee had payed the same "ob metu excommunicacionis;" but the said Doctor, and M*r* Chase, have therupon caused a submission unto the said unjust and surrepticious centence to bee there entred.

9. That the Peticioner, soe soone as hee was able to goe abroade and had notice of the said centence, preferred the peticion annexed to the nowe Bishopp of Rochester, amongst other things, humbly desireinge a judiciall heereinge of the said cause in his consistory, and, for his lordshipp's satisfaction of the greate wronges don the peticioner, delivered him the perfect coppyes of his said wittnesses, under the Register's hand: but his Lordshipp, takeinge upon him to rebuke his said chaplyn, gave the peticioner some hope of redresse, untill the tyme of appeale was past, and then utterly discerted the said cause, and would never restore the said peticion, nor, untill Hillary Tearme last, the coppye of his witnesses, nor admitt the peticioner to his presence to demaund the same, but detayned the same twoe whole yeares and upwards, and yett suffered his Chapleyne to proceed and take out proces upon the said centence, as aforesaid.

10. That M*r* Chase, by himselfe, his father, and brothers, shortly after, laboured S*r* Henry Carewe Knight, in his extreame age, against the petitioner and his wife (S*r* Henryes Neese), of whom they had deserved great reward, and, by letters and false tales soe farre prevailed, that some of them, unknowne to the petitioner, privily tooke their dwellinge house over their heads. And the xiiij*th* of October the same yeare, before the petitioner's tyme expired, or their tearme commenced, in his absence, they and their servaunts, to the nomber of eight or nyne, brake into his said dwellinge house called Stone Castle, and by force dragged out his maid servaunt by head and shoulders, turned out his mastiffs, and, concealinge their names,

with gunns, holbards, and other weapons, in forceble manner kept the possession by the space of a fortnight, untill the comeinge of the Justices of Peace, and, in the meane tyme, ransacked the said howse, spent and consumed all his provision of victuall, wood, powltry, and other goods and necessaryes, and imbezilled others, together with diverse bookes, papers, and bills of accompt, and refused to deliver unto the peticioner and his wife comeinge home from London, the meate provided for their dinners that day, or his saddle, to ride to the Justices, or his deske with bookes and papers lyeinge open : and, albeit five of them were indicted, and afterwards fyned in the Kinges Bench, for the said ryott and forceible entry, and that, in a replevyn of part of the said goods which were repleviable, the petitioner had 30*l.* damages given by verdict, yett, for a greate parte therof, not repleviable, or omitted for want of accesse into the said howse, or imbezilled, as bookes, papers, and the like, hee is still without remedy, without the assistance of this honourable assembly.   Besides, the said Chases, by removeinge the said last-mencioned cause from courte to courte, through five or six courts of law and equity, att Westminster and elsewhere, have forced the peticioner to more trouble and expence in lawe, and otherwise, then treble the said 30*l.* damage amounts unto.

11. That, for avoideinge the said Chases perceutinge courses, the petitioner, about the tyme aforesaid, gave 40*l.* fyne for a lease of a house in Horton Kirby, in Kent, about 4 miles distant from Stone Castle, for his owne dwellinge amongst his wives freinds ; but the said Chases, in further pursuit of their malice against him, and to drive him out of that country (as they had threatened), when as hee should have removed his goods and dwellinge thether, secretly advised and stirred upp one John Davis, the petitioner's undertenaunte therof, and one Henry Scudder, Clerke, and others, to detayne the possession against him, whoe, in the name of one Thomas Scudder, of whome the petitioner had taken the same, and, without his privity, by the like advice commenced a suite in Chauncery against him, supposeinge the same to be a mortgage, which beinge disproved, as

well by the lease itselfe, as by many wittnesses examined on the peticioner's behalfe, and the cause in Hillary Tearme 15° Car. R. comeinge to heereinge, they, under hand, made such meanes, that the master of the Rolls and Baron Trevor, whoe was procured to sitt there that day, threatened the peticioner to give costs against him, in case the deposicions of his wittnesses were redd att the heeringe. And, after the order of decree drawne upp by the Register, the said master of the rolls, with his owne hands incerted and added severall matters not charged in the bill, nor proved nor questioned att the heeringe; wherby the Peticioner hath byn ever since deprived of his said dwellinge, and alsoe of the said 10*l.*, besides 30*l.* att least spent in that suite.

By reason of these and many other oppressions, wrongs and persecutions, under which the peticioner hath suffered by the said Chases, and other the persons above named, and by their procurement, especially since the said 26th of March, 1637, hee, his wife, children, and family have byn forced to forsake their said country and dwellinge at Stone,—are deprived of their said howse taken for their dwellinge at Horton, and the 40*l.* fyne given for the Lease therof, to sell away their goods and howsehold stuffe, lett out their grounds att losse, and neglect his owne and other men's private affaires, forced unjustly to pay divers greate somes of money, to loose other somes, and a great part of his goods, to his extreame losse, and damage of 300*l.* att least, besides great and continuall charge in journeyeings, and otherwise, and the losse of 50*l.*, longe since promised as a guifte unto the peticioner's wife by the said Sr Henry Carewe (hir Uncle) att his death, and above 100*l.* more due and deserved by her and the peticioner, for often sojourneinge and entertaynment of him, his freinds, and servaunts, from tyme to tyme, and many yeares ymployment of the greatest part of their tymes and labours, in and about his affaires and businesses, as by almost a hundred severall letters written unto them, and otherwise, may appeare, (hee, by the meanes aforesaid, dyeinge in displeasure with them,) whereby the peticioner, his wife, children, and family, are brought to great want and sicknesse; and hee disabled to seeke redresse, his said adversaryes beinge wilfully prone to litigious and endles suites.   The said Mr Chase haveinge a parsonage spare,* of about 200*l.* per annum, over and besides all charges, to spend in lawe; wherby the Peticioner, his wife, and children, and family, are almost utterly undon and ruyned, whoe formerly lived in good creditt and esteeme.   Wherewith the Peticioner being greived,

Most humbly prayeth this most honourable assembly to examyne the severall matters aforesaid, and the peticioner's sufferings therin, that hee may bee righted and repayred in his estate, and restored to what hee hath byn forced to expend, deposite, and pay, or have lost as aforesaid, and restored to his said howse att Horton, by the said unjust order or decree taken from him, and to his costs and damages thereby sustayned, and hee settled in peace against the like vexations in tyme to come.   The way how to doe it hee presumes not to prescribe you, but humbly leave it to your grave wisdomes.   And pray God to blesse all your councells and consultacions.

WM. GARNONS.

[Endorsed—" Garnons' petition to the Parliament, 17 R. Ca. 1641."   It is in duplicate.]

LXV.

PETITION to the House of Commons, against their Curate, THOMAS VAHAN, from the Inhabitants of Chatham.

To the Right Honourable the Knights, Citizens, and Burgesses of the House of Commons, assembled in Parliament.

The humble petition of the inhabitants of the parish of CHATHAM, neere Rochester,

Sheweth,

1. That Thomas Vahan, Preist, (for so hee saith he is,) and with

* Spare—*i.e.* kept in reserve.

much greife wee utter it, is a man superstitiously affected in urging and pressing of ceremonies in his pulpit, teaching not only making them things indifferent, but pressing them to be things of necessity to bind the consciences of his hearers under a bitter curse.

1641.
17 Car. 1.

2. Hee hath laboured, these two yeares and more, to sett the Communion Table altar wise, rayled about, giving his reasons out of the pulpitt, for the decensie of it, complaining how hee is abased in administering the Sacrament, going from pew to pew, as one that dealeth almes, or a doale to the people.

3. By provoking the people in his publique teaching to bow knee at the name of Jesus, binding the consciences of his hearers unto a necessitie of that act, under a curse, that their bowells might dropp out that did not observe it.

4. The soundness of his teaching may easily be gathered by what is expressed, who is much wearied in the paines of his ministrie, as he hath in the pulpit often delivered seldome preaching was that hee looked for, by an order (as he saith) from authoritie, but blessed be God for that miraculous worke in preventing of it; hee being urged by the Apostle's words, that his dutie did consist in preaching, and to bee instant in season and out of season, " In season," he saith, is, to preach upon Sundaies in the forenoones, and, " out of season," in the afternoones.

5. Hee hath long continued, in the pulpit, to utter his bitter exe-cracions against the Scottish nation, and hath often done it since the High Court of Parliament assembled; viz., calling them daring Rebells, whose faith is faction, whose truth is treason, whose religion is nothing but rebellion, that seeke to invade this kingdom. " Lett them bee as a wheele, O God, and as the stubble before the wind, and lett the Angell of the Lord scatter them, lett them bee as Oreb and Seb, like Zeba and Zalmunna;"—"lett them be scattered in Jacob, and dispersed in Israel;" "putt a hoock into their nostrills, and turne them back by the waie they came."

6. Hee is a man much dignifying himselfe, and velyfying of others who are orthodox and sound, with the name of Puritanicall

1641.
17 Car. I.
Ministers, the whole kingdome fairing the worse (as he said) for such.

7. Hee is a turbulent man, full of differences and controversies with his parishioners.

8. Hee is very negligent in visiting the sick, and catechizing the youth of the parish.

9. Hee never praid for blesseing upon the former Parliament, nor yett for this, till of late.

10. Hee hath delivered in pulpitt, that the scripture is noe scripture without the authoritie of the fathers.

Wee need say no more; but are bold to close up all in our humble petition, that this honourable house would please to be so favourable a helpe as that wee may be supplied with a man orthodoxall, sound, and profitable, painefull in his ministry, and peaceable in his conversation; that God by him may be honoured, and wee edified. And, as duty binds, we shall ever pray.

Thomas Vahan hath bin Curate of Chatham about five yeares; Doctor Balcancko,* then Deane of Rochester, with the Prebends, placed him there, who gave him a lease during life. Its a limbe of the Cathedrall, from whence if something were added more, to make up a competencie for an able man, were a good worke, which wee leave to the grave consideracions of this honourable and high court of parliament. But for the present maintenance, as it now is, we conceive it not worth above 60 or 70 pounds per annum.

Jo. Short.	James Benns.
James Marsh.	Miles Broughton.
T. Goddard.	Richard Holborne.
Cha. Bowles.	Joseph Pett.
Laurance Fisher.	Thomas Day.
John Watearman.	John Wright, × his mark.
Guy × Jones, his mark.	Nath. Apslyn.
John Vinkell.	Thos. Williams.

* i.e. Dr. Balcanquall.

Morgan Griffin, ⨯ his mark. John Lesher.   1640-1.
Laurance Haiton.   F. Reginalds.   16 Car. I.
George Woode.   Wm. Lawrence.

[Endorsed by Sir Edward Dering, " 1641, 7 Junii. Petition. Chetham
v. Vaghan."]

LXVI.

PETITION to the House of Commons against their Vicar, DOCTOR
PEAKE, from the Inhabitants of TENTERDEN.

To the Right Honourable the Knights, Citizens, and Burgesses 10 July.
of the Commons House of Parliament.

The humble petition of the Inhabitants of the towne and parishe
of TENTERDEN, in the County of Kent,

Sheweth,

That, whereas the said towne and parishe, beeing an auncient
corporacion, and a very populous place, which heeretofore flourished
under the teachinge of godlie and paynefull ministers, who, for these
forty yeeres last past, and upwards, have beene, for the most part,
resident amongst them, and provided for them sermons on Sondayes,
both forenoone and afternoone, to their great comfort.

But now of late, Mr Doctor Peake, one of the prebends of Canterbury, and parson of Acris in Kent, being presented to the Vicaridge
of Tenterden, which is of the yeerely value of two hundred pounds,
or neere therabouts, by the Deane and Chapter of Christ Church,
Canterbury, therof Patron, who are also proprietors of the Rectorie
impropriate of Tenterden aforesaid, beeing of the yeerelie value of
one hundred pounds, and upwards; hee the said Mr Doctor Peake
hath not beene resident, nor will reside himselfe upon the said
vicaridge, nor provide your petitioners a Curat that will preach, or
catechise, on Sondaies, in the afternoone. But hee hath given an

expresse charge to a late Curat of his not to preach on Sondayes in the afternoone, as the said Curat hath reported; nor will the said Mr Doctor Peake, although hee have better then five hundred pounds per annum, spiritual livings, allowe a Curat competent mayntenance for the serving of the said cure; neither will hee suffer your petitioners, (though they have made it their suite to him) to provide and mayntaine, at their owne charges, a conformable minister, to preach on Sondaies in the afternoone.

Neither hath hee, at this present, nor hath hee hadd since the beginning of January last, any Curat at all resident amongst them, but sometimes one, sometimes another, such as could or cann bee gott at the cheapest rate, viz. for a noble, or seaven shillings and eight pence a day, at the utmost, are procured to supply the cure on Sondayes.

And beesides, the said Mr Doctor Peake hath so much neglected his charge, that, at the generall Fast enjoined to bee kept thorough out the whole kingdome, in July last, the duties beefitting so holy and religious a work were, to their great greife, very slightly performed, neither his Curat nor himselfe beeing at all present that day to doe the service; insomuch as, hadd it not beene for a schoolemaster of the parishe newlie entred into the ministry, whoe preached one sermon little more than halfe an houre, the place hadd not beene at all supplied; and as it was supplied, the exercises of the Fast not beeing continued a competent and convenient time, as hath beene heretofore used, a good part of the day was, by the ruder sorte, spent in the ale-houses, to the great dishonour of Almighty God.

And, moreover, he exacteth of the inhabitants of the said parishe many undue and unaccustomed fees, as namelie, twelve pence for ringing of the great bell at a buriall, a fee never heard of there till now late. And whereas the ancient and accustomed fee to the Vicar there for a marriage hath beene but eighteene pence, hee doth now exact, somtimes two shyllings, and sometimes fower shillings, for evrie couple married.

Neither will hee suffer his owne Curat, nor any other comfortable

1641.
17 Car. I.

minister, to preech at any buriall, unlesse hee (though absent, and resident about twenty miles of) may bee paid tenn shillings a sermon if his Curat preach, and twentie shillings a sermon if a stranger preach, for the hire of his pulpit.

And further also, hee exacteth of poore servants more then their accustomed offerings at Easter; and hath threatned, unlesse they will give him his demaunds, to sue them in the Ecclesiasticall Court for the tithes of their wages, beeing a tithe never paid, nor scarce ever heard of, in the said parishe.

And hee, also, at Easter Communions, in the yeere 1640, did disgracefully put backe some poore servants of the said parishe from receiving of the holy Sacrament, beeing there ready with the rest of the congregation to receive the same, meerelie because they would not pay him twelve pence a peece for their offerings, although they hadd beefore tendred him their accustomed offeringes, or more. And, beesides, hee threatned many more, that, unlesse they would pay him twelve pence a peece for their offerings, it should cost them twelve shilling a peece before hee hadd donn with them; or used words to that effect.

And hee also caused tenn poore servants, or laborers, of the said parishe, to be unjustly cited into the Ecclesiasticall Court at Canterbury, beeing about twenty miles distant from Tenterden, meerely for vexacion, upon pretence that they did not pay him their accustomed offerings at Easter in the yeere 1640, nor did receive the holy Sacrament then; whereas they did all of them then receive the Sacrament at his owne hands, and hadd beefore paid, or tendered him, their accustomed offerings, or more; and, accordinglie, they did all of them so depose in the said Ecclesiasticall Court; excepting two only, who, upon his said citation, fled the parishe: and therupon they were all of them dismissed the said Court. But, though the judge thereof did publikelie manifest his great dislike of such oppression, yet hee neither did, nor could, as was then said, allowe them any costs or charges, though, in truth, it cost, or stood them in, about fifteene or sixteene shillings a peece.

By reason of all which doeings of the said Mr Doctor Peake, diverse of the said parishe have and are like to remove their dwellings from thence, which beeing of late tould him, hee, not at all moved therwith, hath given out speeches, that, though the houses there stood emptie, yet hee is sure he shall finde the lands there, or to that effect.

All which your petitioners have thought fitting to represent to this honourable assemblie, humblie intreating that you would bee pleased to take the same into your pious and grave consideracions; and to give your Peticioners such relief therin as in your great wisedomes you shall thinke meete. And your petitioners shall ever pray, &c.

Tho. Shorte.
John Witherden.
Freeg . . . Stace.
John Reade.
Samuell Curtis.
William Plummer.
Thomas Huckstepp.
Jo. Baker.
Ric: Reete.
Ric: Scriwen.
Nich. Enyot.
Lewes Clements.
Daniel Hopper the elder.
Richard Masters.
Job Cushman.
Mych Reete.
Richard Lucas.
Clement Widon.
Richard Highestedd.
John Fuller.
Jo Smith.
Jo. Hamper.

Simeon Dartnell.
William Gillebald.
Richard Seath.
Sa: Shorte.
Jo. Austen.
Thos. Selherst.
Samuell Wiellcock.
Thomas Bedingfield.
Samuell Finch.
Tho. Iden.
John Finch.
Tho. Taylor.
Wm. Stretton.
Tho. Brett.
George Haffenden.
Robert Wolball.
Thos. Haffenden.
Richd. Haffenden.
Henry Gyrdler.
Thos. Baytup.
Wm. Playfer.
Luke Younge.

1641.
17 Car. I.

George Humphrey,

Aminadab Henly.

Daniell Duncke.

Thos. Houlting.

James Duncke.

John Scotchford.

Thomas Tilden.

William Stretton, Junior.

John Waters.

Thomas Iggulden.

Richard Elfiche.

John Sander.

Peter Phillpot.

John Hooke.

Nath. Posier.

Robert Ashenden.

Peter Shorte.

George Tilden.

Thos. Butler.

Thos. Simons.

John Crouch.

James Wide.

Daniel Baytop.

Abraham Caffinch.

Anthony Weller.

Edward Boys.

Edward Caffinch.

Stephen Neate.

John Becar.

Ried. Swanten.

Danl. Hopper.

John Gyrdler.

Robt. Willes.

Saml. Bedar.

John Wood.

Thos. Eldredge.

[Endorsed by Sʳ Edward Dering, "1641, 10 July—Petition—Tenterden
v. Dʳ Peake.]

LXVII.

PETITION to the House of Commons, for increase of Income, &c. to the
Perpetual Curate. From the Inhabitants of FOLKSTONE.

To the Honourable assemblie of the House of Commons.

The humble Petition of the Parishoners of the Towne of FOLKE- 16 July.
STON, in the Countie of Kent,

Sheweth,

That wheras Folkeston being a maior towne, and a large parish
extending itselfe two miles into the shire, the parsonage wherof, being
an impropriation, and belonging to the Sea of Canterburie, the Lords
of Canterburie still leasing out the same, and reserving to themselves
80*l.* per annum, and a renewing fine everie fourth yeare, the tennant

wherof now is Mr Arnald Brames, who hath yett to come eleven yeares in itt, and letteth out the same for 300*l.* by the yeare; and yett the Lord of Canterburie doth allow his Curate at Folkeston but the bare stipend of 20*l.* per annum, without having a house to live in, or any other helpe whatsoever.

Now your Petitioners doe humblie pray, that you would be pleased to grant such a competent allowance for the maintenance of the Minister of Folkeston, as in your wisdomes and pious care shalbe thought requisite; and, wheras the Curate of Folkeston that now is, is a sicklie aged man, and faileth much in his voice and sight wherby he is not soe able to performe his ministeriall dutie as he himselfe would, and the parish requireth, your Petitioners doe further pray, that they may have a yonger and a more pregnant man, for the performing of holy and divine service, and yett the old minister now being may have some exhibition to keepe him during his life, and afterward the same to revert to the minister of Folkestone againe.

And your Petitioners shalbe bound in all dutie and thankfulnes to pray for your prosperous succes and happines.

Basil Dixwell.	Henry Tiddyman.
Marke Dixwell.	Henry Rolfe.
John Dixwell.	Benjamin Master, Major.
William Reade.	Henry Kennett, Juratt.
William Jenkin.	Thomas Inmith, Juratt.
Thomas Denn.	Thomas Stiles, Juratt.
Richard Francklin.	Robart Culverden, Jurat.
Stephen Hobdaye.	

[Endorsed by Sr Edward Dering,—" 1641, 16 July—Petition—Folkeston."]

LXVIII.

1641.
17 Car. I.

PETITION to the House of Commons against their Vicar Mr JOHN DENN. From the Parishioners of DARTFORD.

To the Right Honorable the House of Commons at this present Parliament assembled.

4 October.

The humble peticon of divers of the parishioners of the parish of DARTFORD, in the Countie of Kent,

Humbly sheweth these their severall agreeveances following, viz.

That their Parsonage is an Impropriacion; the Bishopp of Roches-ter, being the Impropriator therof, receiveth twentie five pounds per annum of Edward Dearcey, Esquire, and hee receiveth of Marke Fielder, the farmer therof, one hundred and thirtie pounds per annum: our vicaredge is also worth an hundred pounds per annum.

That our minister, John Denn by name, is a man of an offensive life and conversation, a common taverne haunter, excessively given to drinking of wine, in so much that hee many times reeleth in the streete, and cannot goe upright.

That hee hath laboured much, by perswasion, for the use of cere-monies, and for the standing up at gloria pater, and, on the Commu-nion day, he allwayes preacheth in the surplesse, and in his tippett or whood.

That hee preacheth but once a weeke, namely, on the Lord's day in the forenoone, they haveing a great congregation depending upon his Cure; and, because the parishioners doe desire two sermons a day, hee not preaching himselfe, nor suffering any other to preach in the afternoone, saith, that there is none worse then those that doe desire so much preaching, and they that doe preach so much.

That hee hath raised the price of his duties to a farr greater rate then formerly they have been; for wheras formerlie, for mariage, his predecessor tooke but eighteene pence, hee taketh three shillings; and for a sermon at a buriall, his predecessor never tooke above ten shillings, but hee will have no lesse then twentie shillings, and hee hath raised his tithes of marsh land, six pence in every acre.

Upon a tyme, hee being requested to visite a sick man, who thought to have some comfort from him, for his soules health; hee was so much in drink, that hee was not able to pray, nor to performe any other good dutie towards him, but, asking the sick man what comfort hee would have of him, hee told him that hee should not die this fitt, but hee would give him some black cherrie water.

Thomas Rogers, Esquier, beeing a justice of the peace there, on a tyme, intreated him to let an honest minister preach in his pulpitt; but hee would not suffer him, nor give any way there unto.

That hee is of such a proud hautie spiritt, that there is no honest man able to live by him; as for our cheife men, hee accounts them no fitt objects for his wrath, hee is of such a high spiritt.

May it please, therefore, this honorable assemblie, to take these severall complaints into your godlie and serious considerations, and, for redresse thereof, to doe heerin as to your great wisedomes and godly dispositions shall seeme most meete.

ROBERT WATTS.
BARNARD ELLIS.

[Endorsed by Sir Edward Dering—"1641, 4 Oct.—Petition.—Dertford v. Mr Den."]

LXIX.

PETITION to the House of Commons against their Vicar, THOMAS HIGGINSON, from the parishioners of ROLVENDEN.

The parishioners of ROLVENDEN, in the countie of Kent, unto the honorable House of Commons, humbly sheweth,

That THOMAS HIGGINSON, Vicar of Rolvenden, beinge for many years Vicar of the sayde parish, hath beene a very negligent preacher of the word, and scandulous in his life, whereby ignorance and

* There is no date. I supply it by conjecture.

prophanenes hath much abounded, to the scandall of the ministry, and great greife of all those that are well affected, as will be proved by those who have subscribed these articles with their handes.

1. Uppon a certayne time, he haveinge given warninge for a Sacrament, certayne of the parish comminge to be catechised, and to pay their offringes the Saturday night before the Sacrament, divers of them were fayne to goe to the alehouse, where he was drinkinge, and some of them he caused to stay there so longe with him, that they were togither distempered with drinke.   JO: CROTENDEN.

2. He hath beene a very often frequenter of houses of ill resorte, and much given to cursinge and swearinge and excesse in drinkinge.
RICHARD SHEAFE.

3. He hath not only frepuented common alehouses, and houses of ill resorte; but he hath often done it on Saturday nights, till eyght or tenne o'clocke at night.   EDWARD CLEFTON.

4. He was, at a buriall, so far in beere, or wine, that he was not able to read the buriall.   ALCES × CLEFTON.

5. He lay, within five miles of his owne house, four dayes tiplinge and drinkinge in an alehouse, and spent ther, halfe the vallue of his horse.   RICHARD RABSON.

6. When he was catechisinge children, he did use cursinge speeches, in the middest of the congregation, to the ill example of others.
ARTOR ROBERDES.

7. When one asked his advice, whether he, beinge in want of wood, might not take of his neighbours, he said "Yea, rather then sit a cold;" and sayde further, "Lett men fetch out of the wood (it beinge his neighbour's wood) till he forbade them."
Witness to this, WILLIAM DAY, who is since dead.
Witnesse that he said it, ROBERT GIBBON.
JAMES × CHITTENDEN.

8. He, at the buriall of Mr Gee, did kneele at the grave, while the buriall was read.   JO: HANSONN.

9. He did not preach but once in eighteen monthes togither, and, many times, three weikes togither, not so much as the church dores open, and in one full month, viz., from the 17° of January to the 21° of February, not so much as prayers read.

RI: SHEAFE.

10.   He, on the Saboth day, would not come to church, nor bury the dead, and yett, rod the same day ten miles from his owne house.

RI: SHEAFE.

11. Uppon settinge up of the aulter, he oposed the parish all that he might, and would have the same sett up in the most superstitious way he could, and sayde it should be sett accordinge to the Cathedral Churches, and so he caused it to be done, as neere as he could.

RI: SHEAFE.

12. A certeine time, the Churchwardens takeinge out the Communion Table from the aulter rayle, causeinge it to be sett in the most convenient place in the chancell, where it formerly stood, he standeth up in the church, on a Lordes day, in the middlest of the congregation, and speaks to the Churchwardens, reproveinge them for removeinge the table from within the rayles, sayinge, if they removed it, he would cause them to answer it in another place, and further sayde, he would not adminester the Sacrament any where, if the table were taken out; also, he could afford to send the people away without administration of the Sacrament at that time.

GEORGE DAY.

Wherefore, we humbly beseech this honourable assembly, to take it into their grave consideration, that so he may be ordered accord-

1641.
17 Car. I.

inge to your wisdome; and your petitioners shall ever desire your prosperity and welfare.

Ri: Sheafe.	Giles Cadwell ✕ his marke.
Alexander Weller.	Daniel ✕ Baythopp, his marke.
William Davy.	James ✕ Ch .. den, by his marke.
Richard Gibbon.	John ✕ Willson, by his marke.
Steaven Ghyrdler.	Robert Clifton.
George Gyrdler.	George Preston, ✕ his marke.

[Endorsed by Sir Edward Dering, "Petition.—Rolvenden v. Higginson p. Rich. Sheafe et Rob. Gibbon."]

1641.
17 Car. I.*

LXX.

PETITION to the House of Lords, to increase the Income of their Vicar, from the Parishioners of WALTHAM.

To the most Honorable House of Lords, assembled in Parliament, or such as it may concerne.

The most humble suite of us the parishioners and officers of the parishe of WALTHAM, in the countye of Kent,

Presenteth,

That our parsonage by lease held from the Sea of Canterbury is att the least of an hundred and twenty pounds annuall value; our vicarage poore, and not worth above thirtie and five pounds yearely, or there about; our moderne Vicar Mr David Neishe, a man of exemplar life and conversation, and a most diligent preacher; for whome wee humbly begg that there might bee some competent addition of necessarye maintenance; and, not knowing how this may bee effected (as wee most heartely desire), wee humbly implore the aide and assistance of this most honorable and highe Court of Parliament.

* No date. I have assigned it conjecturally.

1641.
17 Car. I.

And this granted, wee shall ever bee bound to pray for your happie success in your greate proceedings, and shall ever remaine,

Your most humbly obliged Servants,

George ✗ White.

Henry Maxted.

The marke ✗ of John Boulden.

William Gregorie.

Walter Clarke.

Robert White, Churchwarden.

The marke of ✗ John Gregorie, Churchwarden.

William Hayward.

Ben Peere.

John Nayler.

George Gorham.

Clement Court.

The marke of Thomas Uffington. ✗.

Stephen Court.

Edmund Hogben.

INDEX.